Lieutenant-Commander T. J. Cain, R.N. (Retd)

H.M.S. *Electra*

As told to A. V. Sellwood

Futura Publications Limited
A Futura Book

A Futura Book

First published in Great Britain in 1959
by Frederick Muller Ltd

Hutchinson Library Services Edition 1971
First Futura Publications edition 1976
Copyright © Lt.-Com. T. J. Cain 1959

ISBN 0 8600 7330 0
Printed in Great Britain by
Hazell Watson & Viney Ltd
Aylesbury, Bucks

Futura Publications Limited
110 Warner Road
Camberwell, London SE5

Preface to an Epitaph

"H.M.S. *Electra* attacked through the smoke, and was seen no more. . ."

From the first communiqué of the disastrous
Battle of the Java Sea, February 1942.

"May on the bridge, with Harry close beside him . . . Number One with the gun armament, and me with the tubes . . . 173 of us, officers and men together, we came to the barrier of the smoke, and then passed through it, emerging near-blinded into a dazzling and alien world.

"All our friends had vanished. We were naked to our enemies. We were Beyond the Smoke!"

Lieutenant Commander Cain,
Electra's senior survivor.

▼

Contents

I

"What! No Morning Tea?"

EXCEPT for the noise of the rain, roaring into the greasy waters of the Clyde with the turbulence of the sea cascading from a trawler's scuppers, the scene was silent. The men were fed up and far from home; they were, in addition, exceedingly cold and wet.

At the time of their arrival on the pier a musically inclined A.B. had proclaimed on a mouth organ that they were going to hang out the washing on the Siegfried Line: but gradually he had switched to other themes, growing ever less boastful as the weather worsened until, after a dirge-like rendering of "Good Night, Children, Everywhere", even his stout heart—or wind supply—had faltered. There was no more music.

It was now at least an hour since the player had piped down, but the grief of his former audience was not attributable to their loss of harmonic entertainment. For even the memories of the girls they'd left behind them were being steadily displaced by more immediate poignancies.

Little rivulets of rainwater, creeping furtively beneath the collar bands that flaunted (allegedly) Nelson's Three Great Victories, dropped coldly on to the manly but wilting flesh beneath the snow-white vests. Mouths bearing the bitter-sweet aftermath of countless cups of tea, long since consumed, and the acrid inheritance of too many cigarettes, most mercifully duty-free, no longer gave vent even to the tired men's cusses. Their heads had come out of the clouds—and their hearts were in the square toes of their boots, thus keeping company with their feet which, sore from long standing in the crowded corridors of the blackened train, were now so numb that they didn't even shuffle. It was Too Bloody Bad—it was Greenock at its worst.

*   *   *

From the experience derived from a numberless succession of unsung departures and wan-dawn goodbyes generations of morose mariners have come to recognise, though not to relish, certain peculiarities of the Clydeside Climate.

It is not sufficient to say that it is always raining at Greenock, for it is "always raining" at Manchester and Wigan: nor would it be doing the place full justice to suggest that the violence of the rain at Greenock is unparalleled by the violence of the rain elsewhere, for, to cite but one comparison, it can be little worse than the downpour that falls on the rice-fields of Burma during the peak period of the Monsoon. No, the fact of the matter is that the Greenock Rain owes its truly unique reputation not so much to its extent as to its selectivity, which is considerable. Greenock, as every sailor knows, is always wetter in war-time than in peace-time. And the rainfall of Greenock is always more intense on the quayside—where there is no shelter and the wind is at its fiercest—than in the town itself.

But an even more remarkable attribute of the local climate is the way in which it seems to be engaged in a perpetual conspiracy against H.M. Forces; and in particular the Navy. For though it may be content to confine itself to a harmless drizzle when the Fleet is away and the lads are far from the land, Greenock reserves the nastiest of its manifestations—its Regular Soaks—for the occasions immediately preceding the mariner's farewell; occasions that are euphemistically known in Service circles as The Embarkation of a Draft. And this, as you may have gathered, was one of them . . .

It was early 1940; but however "phoney" the war might be

our distresses were painfully genuine. It was the prelude to the Shining Hour; but here, in the Scots part of the island, the outlook was so dim as to be practically opaque. True that a lustreless dawn was succeeding the hopeless night, but the transition was gradual, and its benefits were dubious. The first wan light crawled but feebly into the sky, with the reluctance of an ancient serving man aroused from bed to sweep up a bottle-party's aftermath. Its approach was red-eyed and peevish, its touch was palsied, and it brought with its pale advance no respite from the weather.

The men, awaiting the long overdue arrival of the duty launch that was to remove them from this inclement shore, and carry them out to the ships that, silent as sleeping dogs upon a hearthrug, were as yet invisible in the murk downstream, stood huddled together in a sort of confused lager of kitbags, small suit-cases, and mysterious brown-paper parcels.

At first they had tried to ward against the weather's violence by tucking their heads into the upturned collars of their greatcoats, thus presenting, with their hair blowing out untidily from their saucer-like caps, a spectacle akin to that of several sparrows—each seeking shelter beneath the shadow of its wing. But as they had all too soon discovered, a precaution so primitive was but of scant avail against the persistent malignancy of the local climate. For although the navy-blue serge of their regulation outer garments could absorb, like blotting paper, a considerable amount of moisture, there comes a time when even blotting paper reaches saturation point. And so had they.

Not that it had seemed so bad a few short days before, when, tiddly and rollicking and accompanied by the girl friend, Jolly Jack had bragged: "Me, I'm a small ship man, myself!" Nor had it seemed so bad when he'd flashed his Navy Woodbines among his poor relations, the conscript and envious pongoes, and had expended with a swagger a month's back pay in a day. Of course it was tough in the Andrew, and no one would claim otherwise. But it was a good life, Ma'am, and a man's life, Ma'am—as he'd explained to the Little Old Lady whose suitcases he'd lifted on to the luggage rack. And I'd never go back to the Shore, Ma'am . . . it's a wonderful thing the Navy!

Wonderful. With the wet patches lengthening over their precious Sunday best—the Number One Rig that so recently had been tended by the loving hands of wives and mums—the motley collection of matelots had their doubts, not for the first time, about the advantages of a seafaring career. They had been waiting for that damn boat for hours already: they might continue to wait for it for hours to come. And if, in the meanwhile, the naval arrangements that had brought them to this godforsaken hole could be criticised on account of the fact that nothing had been laid on, it was also abundantly clear that nothing was going to be turned off.

It continued to rain—I got soaked to the skin!

*   *   *

Shouldn't have joined if we couldn't take a joke . . . and maybe my presence on the pierside was one of the biggest jokes of all.

The son of a Chief Stoker, I could look back—at the start of 1939—on a period of eighteen years' continuous service, in which I had risen from the obscurity of Boy Seaman to the rarified heights of Gunner (T). Furthermore, like many another chap who has come up the so-called "hard way", I had found plenty of fun and excitement in the process. I had been to sea in practically every type of Royal Navy ship, from battle-waggon to submarine, and had travelled the world over, from Calcutta to North Cape. I had had good times, and bad times, and the taxpayer had footed the bill. Yet now—scheduled for home service—I could look back without nostalgia, for there was so much to look forward to. I was happily married, a confirmed family man, and viewed with pleasure the prospect of a "cushy" spell ashore. Here at long last, was a chance to settle down ... then came the War.

Said Belles, when I turned up at the front door with a self-conscious look, and my appointment in my pocket: "All right, Tim, I can see that you're pleased with yourself. Now tell me —what's the ship?"

"Oh, so you've guessed." I felt suddenly guilty about the way in which I'd caught the prevalent enthusiasm, and had hollered for active service. "I'm—er—well, I'm back in destroyers, my dear. They call her the *Electra* ..."

Belles was silent for a moment, thinking of our two small sons. Then with a somewhat weary smile she said: "I'd have thought you would have got more sense by now ... but you're just as mad as the rest of your pals. You chaps will never learn."

Very probably she was right; for my subsequent behaviour was naïve, to say the least.

First, told that I would join *Electra* at Rosyth, I had dashed off there immediately, expecting—with the simplicity of a raw recruit—to find her where they had said she'd be, and being overwhelmed with astonishment to find that she was not. I should, of course, have known much better.

The process of joining one's ship is simple enough in theory, but complicated in practice. A King's Cross train does not turn up at London Bridge, and rarely, if ever, is a coach bound for Birmingham diverted to Torquay. But ships, when engaged in war, are less predictable in their movements, and the vessel that sets out for Plymouth may well end up in Nova Scotia. Your train must stick to the rails: your bus is confined to the roads: but the seaways of the world give scope for far-reaching manoeuvres, and warships move eccentrically, there is no accounting for their whims. All of them are naughty dogs— prone to slip their leashes, and dash off for a lark around the corner. But the worst offender of all is the destroyer; for the destroyer is incorrigibly a wanderer. It goes, or is sent to, the most unlikely places. It makes its departure at the very shortest notice. It is fidgety, and aggressive, and its life is often short . . .

In all it took me fourteen days to find *Electra*, and I travelled a thousand miles to track her down. First I went to Rosyth, and next I went to Scapa, and from Scapa I went on a useless tour of Scottish ports and harbours until, by the time I came to Greenock, my faith in service guidance was about as low as the glass on the Navy Office wall.

Thus when they said that my ship would be "in tomorrow" I answered with a disbelieving shrug, for I'd heard it all before. And when "tomorrow" came and still there was no sign of her I inwardly wrote her off—"sunk without trace", as some Job's comforter had hinted. Nearly two hundred destroyers were now serving beneath the White Ensign, and it must be difficult for the Navy to keep tabs on every one of them. Accidents happened, must be happening all the time, and all I would see of *Electra* would be a pin-up extracted from "Jane's Fighting Ships".

And then on the fourth day the summons came and caught me unprepared. Barefooted, sleepy-eyed, and roused from uneasy slumber, I had listened half dazed to the brusque efficient-sounding voice that came through the telephone in the boarding-house's draughty hall. "Your ship is in," snapped Authority. "And you'd better get down to the pier at once. It's immediate!"

I was in such a hurry to catch that stray destroyer that I didn't even stop for a cup of tea. As Belles—on the mark as usual—had prophesied, "You chaps will never learn."

*   *   *

When the launch—an M.F.V.—eventually came alongside it was with an indescribable show of gallantry and dash, as though rescuing the weary crew on the pier from impossible odds and daring the jaws of death to do so. No apologies were offered for its late arrival, nor indeed—such was the men's depressed, deflated state—were apologies expected. True that its skipper piled insult on to injury by giving them a provocative "Hey, step lively there!" but bus conductors say worse things on occasion, and they have no gold stripe upon their sleeves to give their edicts an increased authority. No, mumbled the draft, there was no use complaining. This was the Andrew, and the way the Andrew did it. In the meanwhile they began to forget their present petty miseries and became concerned instead about the future.

For as the light lengthened and the launch chugged fussily through the greasy water its passengers were able to pick out of the retreating murk the lean shapes of the ships to which they were assigned, the ships which, for an unspecified time to come, were to be their only shelter and their contracted liability and were to carry the White Ensign, with varying degrees of fortune, to every quarter of the globe and against every adversity of war. For months, or maybe years, these rakish hulls were to be the repositories of each individual's fears and frustrations, high hopes and stubborn loyalties, and whether they would serve as homes or sepulchres would depend on the luck of the draw—which no one could foresee.

The men in the M.F.V. were seldom introspective and yet, as their gaze roved questingly along the grey line of the escorts, it is probable that every member of the draft felt something of the drama of the moment and—however unimaginative—was impressed by its personal implications. For much of the time their ships would have many points in common. They would be hopelessly overcrowded and tumultuously noisy; they would echo the sound of laughter and of curses, the clamour of the klaxons, and shudder beneath the whip-crack of the guns. Their skins would peel beneath the blaze of the sun, or the splintering touch of the ice: their bones would cry out for

mercy—but not get it—from the hammering of the ocean.
And yet, such similarities notwithstanding, the line that would
divide their respective destinies would be sharp-defined,
irrevocable—the difference between life and death.

The launch swung into midstream, and they felt the pull of
the tide. The wild west wind from the yet unseen Atlantic
roared unexpectedly around their ears, deafening them to the
gurgle of the turning screws. And then, as the pier behind them
dwindled to a distant smudge beneath the gaunt gantries that
fringed the riverside, the men abandoned their momentary
reveries, and turned to practical matters. Their noses sniffed the
salt, and their faces sensed the spray—but their stomachs were
ruddy well empty. The Navy owed them a breakfast.

*   *   *

Completed in 1934, and a product of Hawthorn Leslie's
yard on Tyneside, H.M.S. *Electra* was typical of her time. She
was much smaller than the Tribals—and half the size of the
Darings of today—but her lines were trim and pencil-slim, and,
with her thrusting bows and lean funnels, she looked eager,
aggressive, and extraordinarily graceful.

Like most British ships of the 'tween-war period she was
somewhat undergunned, when compared with her foreign
rivals. Against the six five-inch guns of the Japanese, and the
five five-inch of the latest German destroyers, *Electra* could
oppose only four four-sevens. But her endurance was good and
she was an excellent sea-boat. She carried eight torpedo tubes,
my special responsibility.

There were nine of the E class in all, and their construction
had given work to thousands, sorely hit by the run-down in
Britain's naval strength and the effects of the trade depression
on the merchant service. Yet few of those who saw *Electra*
building could have sensed the full significance of the occasion.
For while the ship's birth was due to a belated realisation of the

dire effects on the Navy of the treaties of London and Washington, she was to reflect in her too-brief life the tragedy of two decades; a decade of retribution following a decade of neglect. Cradled during the aftermath of the Manchurian Incident she was to get her guns as the Nazis marched to power. Fledged and off on trials as Mussolini prated of Mare Nostrum, she was to reach maturity during the Spanish Civil War.

Yet though such events may have failed to cast their shadow before them when the champagne bottle cracked across *Electra*'s bows and she slid gaily down the slipway and into the embrace of the River Tyne, there were doubtless a few reflections among the more thoughtful of the onlookers regarding the period that had preceded the decision to commence her building.

Before the arrival of the E class the Royal Navy had been forced to make-do with less than thirty new destroyers in more than fifteen years. Furthermore, over the same period, hundreds of older destroyers had been sold or scrapped. Not until the years of reality, when we were to be so humbly grateful to the Americans for lending us forty of their own "antiques", were the disastrous consequences of this policy to be felt in full; but, even in the early 'thirties, there were misgivings regarding its wisdom. *Electra*—all things considered—had come none too soon.

*   *   *

Hopelessly overworked, monstrously overstrained, and back from a brutal buffeting in the North Atlantic, *Electra*—as the M.F.V. approached her—betrayed the extent of her industry and zeal only by the crusted salt, impossible to hide, that stained her stacks. I liked her as soon as I saw her.

It was daylight when we came alongside. All hands had been piped to breakfast, and the upper deck was deserted save for the coxswain, four seamen and a pink-cheeked and hearty product of the R.N.R. who—having got the all-important mail inboard—greeted me cheerfully, and with a minimum of words.

"So you're Guns relief? Well, I'm jolly pleased to meet you. Now let's go below, and get some grub."

We were off to the wardroom within the very next minute.

"You don't believe in wasting time?" I hazarded, travelling at the double to the hatch, and almost tumbling down the ladder.

"We travel on wheels," Charles bawled; then, turning sharply into the narrow passageway, we came into major collision with somebody making knots in the opposite direction.

A mighty, quite unprintable, oath was hurled along the deck by the newcomer, and Charles stepped in quickly, with a courteous introduction, "Lieutenant Commander Lee, allow me to present the new Gunner."

A pause, and a pair of very bright eyes regarded me from beneath a disordered thatch of hair. Then a huge black beard wagged enquiringly over my head, and a hand as large as a ham imposed its relentless grip. "Then welcome to the family, Guns. We're ruddy glad to have you."

"Thank you, Sir," I replied, in the dazed belief that this must be the Captain.

The grip tightened. Two more of my fingers went for a burton; what was meant to be a friendly tap registered between my shoulder blades, and nearly folded me up.

"Chief to you, Guns, or just only plain Tom Lee. But only Sir when we ruddy well have to. Do you get it?"

I got it. And he was called away.

"A tough bird, that!"

Charles laughed. "Our Engineer, and an England Rugby finalist. Enormously strong—but full of good nature."

I was still nursing my bruised paw when we met the First Lieutenant.

Few destroyer officers can be said to glitter, not after ten days of convoy work in foul weather—and certainly not before breakfast. But Lieutenant Jenner-Fust R.N. was a remarkable exception, he *always* glittered. "It is," he once told us, "an idiosyncrasy of mine."

At the time of my arrival he was the sole occupant of the wardroom, and somewhat daunting. For whereas the Greenock weather had wrought havoc with my appearance, Number One, despite his recent hardships, would have been a credit to a Whale Island parade. His uniform was immaculate, and beautifully tailored. His hair was sleek, and his cheeks were smooth. His tie looked as if it had just come out of the shop; and the glow of the wardroom's small electric fire was reflected in the tips of his shining shoes. By contrast I felt like a tramp.

"Hallo, Guns, I'm here to do the honours." The voice was friendly, despite the glitter.

"Shocking weather you've been experiencing ashore," he added sympathetically, "or so we gather from the mail . . ."

I answered, somewhat lamely, that maybe we'd have a good summer, then realised, from Charles's guffaw, that Number One had a quaint sense of the ridiculous, and liked to watch his victims take his conversational gambits deadpan . . .

Names don't mean much on a destroyer; you take the title appropriate to the job. Guns, Doc, Subby, or Number One, the introductions are informal, and quickly over with. But a destroyer's wardroom has a revealing atmosphere, and it is surprising how much can be guessed at from the nature of the grin, the pressure of the handshake, the trend of the conversation. *Electra* was a "happy ship", and I sensed it in the first few minutes; as we yarned over breakfast I felt that I had known my new messmates for years.

Only once was I a little confused, at the laugh that went up when I tentatively enquired if I should have reported to the Captain before sitting down to eat.

"But won't it look odd that I haven't shown myself?"

"Now steady, Guns," said Charles, "you won't get far on THAT tack! But surely you know our Sammy Buss?"

I replied with some restraint that I had never met Lieutenant Commander Buss, but had heard of him.

Number One's tone was sugar-sweet. "The Captain," he said, "has just enjoyed a few hours' sleep, the first real sleep he has had for ten extraordinarily dreary days. Just now he will be wallowing in a bath, and later he will be reading his mail. So it would be best if you await his summons. That pleasure should come at about half past ten of the clock."

"Sammy's had his breakfast by now," murmured Charles. "But if you don't wait until he calls for you he'll gobble you up for elevenses."

Sammy Buss, I recalled with some unease, was known throughout the service as "a bit of a character".

*   *   *

When the Lower Deck says that a man is a "character" it is bestowing the highest tribute it can ever offer, a tribute that establishes not only the recipient's own fame but also, by association, that of his ship as well. The pre-war Navy literally bristled with characters.

From Bill Bateman (A.B.) and Froggy French (Telegraphist) to Joe Beckett (Lieutenant Commander) and John Kelly (Admiral), their every idiosyncrasy was noted and reported. And every story descriptive of their originality or eccentricity was retailed with maximum exaggeration to an admiring audience—an audience of one hundred thousand men, scattered in ships and shore stations from Pompey to Hongkong.

Thus, when I confessed to having heard of Sammy, I had been guilty of an understatement. For Sammy was quite a legend. He was tough they said, and rough they said, and his language could blister and burn. He was tempestuous, temperamental, and ruthless on the rampage. But he was also a first-rate seaman, a fellow who knew the sea and all its vagaries, a chap who carried somewhere in his dome an index of every rivet in his ship and every problem of her company. A born leader, he was a fair one too. Come up in front of Sammy, and you'd get your whack; be it leave or punishment, he never did things by halves, although you had to watch out for squalls!

In time I, too, was to regard Sammy with the affection accorded him by the men he led, the affection that he so well deserved yet would have eschewed with an incredulous oath or two had it been shown. In time I, too, was to understand his whims and foibles, and accept them as inevitable by-products of that vast stamina which he strained to the utmost in his almost zestful devotion to duty, and his continuous pursuit of action. In time . . . but I must confess that on the day I joined the ship I would cheerfully have thrown my Captain over the side; were it not for Naval Discipline, were it not for the fact that he was so much bigger than me.

2

The Happy Ship

"BRAND New, I suppose?"

The black brows came together, forming a shaggy V over a face the colour of Tudor brick.

"Yes, Sir."

A growl, and then disconcertingly, "Now isn't that just my ruddy luck!"

I felt that no answer was called for.

"Now Mr. McDonald here," said Sammy, "is the best Gunner I have ever had, so there's me being fool enough to send him through for Lieutenant . . . and now I've lost him and they've sent me *you*. But I can still be fool enough to do the same for you, if you're good enough, Mr. Cain. But you've got to be good, understand?"

"Yes, Sir."

Another scowl, and the Captain's eyes, angry, rather small but penetratingly bright, bored into me. "Because if you're not good, Mr. Cain . . . if you're idle or unwilling, or just congenitally weak-witted, *then I'll break you*. Is that clear?"

I said that it was clear.

"Very well, then, and just one last word of warning. Never think that you can flannel me, so never attempt to try and flannel me! I have served twenty-five years on destroyers, most of the time as First Lieutenant or Captain. So don't try anything on, for I know all the ruddy tricks. Never try to flannel your Captain. Is that understood?"

"Yes, Sir."

A Pause . . . "Well? What are you standing there for?" he roared. "I've said all I've got to say, and there's plenty of work to do. So you'd better get on with it!"

I reeled out of the cabin, feeling that I'd just taken a bashing from a side-on sea.

"Is he always like that?" I asked, dismayed.

McDonald laughed. "Oh, you'll soon get used to Sammy. He's a wonderful chap, knows the job from A to Z . . . knows his men, too."

Then, catching my expression, he laughed again. "But cheer up, old man, he's always angry at first! You wait—you'll find that you'll be devoted to him in the end."

I reflected that it seemed unlikely.

*   *   *

It is often said that the temper of a ship is dependent, in the ultimate, on the character of her Captain. But although there is considerable truth in the argument it would be foolish to attempt to carry it to extremes. For to presuppose that a ship—in order to be "happy"—must have a Captain who is a sort of cross between Mr. Chips and a first-class nannie would be to flout the experience derived from history, especially destroyer history.

There are many happy ships in the Royal Navy, but few of the men who command them are addicted to scattering sunbeams. And neither are Captains R.N.—or even Commanders and Lieutenant Commanders R.N.—of standard type, much though the landsman may imagine them to be so. Not one of them is exactly like the other, except that each must be handled with some degree of care. Just as, in gardening, the finest roses may possess the sharpest thorns, the Royal Navy, too, has its prickly but precious products—Sammy Buss was one of them.

A few minutes after my first interview with Sammy *Electra* got under way for Glasgow and a boiler clean, and our next meeting was at lunch.

Displaying their warped sense of humour, my new mess-mates had arranged for me to sit next to the Captain, and I did not relish the arrangement. For Sammy's opening gambit was: "And just how long have you been sitting on your backside—enjoying the peace of the Shore?"

I meekly replied: "Eighteen months, Sir."

Which just about did it.

For he threw down his knife and fork, buried his head in his hands, and then exclaimed in a sort of groan: "Eighteen months he says . . . eighteen blessed months ashore. Good God. I wanted a *sailor* . . . and now they've sent me yet another sea-sick landlubber to puke down my voice-pipe!"

All was quiet. Out of the corner of my eye I caught the sly grins of Jenner-Fust and Charles, and inwardly cursing them explained in all innocence, that I had served on many ships, including destroyers and submarines, and had never yet been sea-sick.

"But how interesting . . . how very, very interesting! Now pray tell me, sir, to what do you attribute your amazing immunity from sea-sickness?"

My tormentor, all polite attention, turned on a fascinated smile. And, suddenly nettled, I retorted savagely: "Because I was born with gyroscopic guts of course—and they're ruddy well slung on gimbals!"

No sooner were the words out than I regretted them; then strange choking noises came from Sammy and I realised, with relief, that he was laughing. "You'll do, Guns! You'll do, by God. Spoken like a little gentleman, a man after my own heart.

"And you've not to worry," he added. "We're going to get along together, you and I."

And Sammy was right; we did.

*   *   *

As the days went by, and *Electra* pushed her way through the bullying Atlantic as escort to a convoy, I took stock of my companions.

The ship's officers were predominantly "regular", and most of the men were Royal Fleet Reservists, veterans of periods of seven or twelve years' service who had been recalled when the fleet mobilised. We had also a group of Pensioners who, having served in the "Great War", were engagingly cynical about the prospects of the existing conflict being as "little" as some of the optimists ashore asserted.

"Just wait," they used to say with relish, jerking gnarled thumbs towards the east. "Just wait! 'E's saving it up, that's what 'e's doing, Saving It Up."

As indeed "he" was.

On the other hand the ship could not take too much credit for clairvoyance, for already she had been given a slight preview of the Shape of Things to Come. And, although unshakeably confident regarding ultimate victory, the company could judge from experience just how unpleasant the Shape could be.

For the West in general the so-called "phoney war" was to last for seven months, but for *Electra* it had endured for only a few hours—the interval between Chamberlain's speech, announcing the commencement of hostilities, and the sinking of the liner *Athenia*.

*　　　*　　　*

It was the first blow of the war, the first time in over twenty years that the dirt-brown of fuel oil had spilled over Atlantic waters.

The U-30 had struck without warning, torpedoing a ship crammed with one thousand passengers, practically all of them civilian, and many of them children, and *Electra*, putting her tail down, had travelled at full speed to the scene of the attack, two hundred miles off the coast of Ireland.

Athenia was still afloat, but sinking slowly, when Sammy found her. Surrounded by wreckage and the inevitable oil slick, she lay at a drunken angle, with the falls of the lowered boats trailing in the water, and giving her an untidy, bedraggled, appearance, accentuating her air of helplessness. Some of her boats were still inboard, the shock of the explosion having torn them from their davits, but the majority lay around the ship, although staying sufficiently clear to dodge the suction that would follow her sinking.

Two other destroyers arriving, Sammy set one of them to circle the scene, and ward against fresh attack, while the other got her boats away to join *Electra*'s in searching among the wreckage. Next he began to cope with the liner's boats, coming alongside with hundreds of survivors, all of whom had to be housed and clothed and fed.

An influx of civilians—many of them in their night clothes— was something not catered for in Ship's Standing Orders, but everything seemed to fall into place, smoothly and quickly. The sick and the wounded were given the officers' cabins, the lower mess decks were turned over to the women and children, the upper mess decks were thronged by men . . . So effectively was the operation conducted that, after the first twenty minutes, the small destroyer had received so many guests that she was almost bursting at the seams: but Sammy was still not satisfied. There might be more survivors, trapped in the ship herself, and he wanted to make sure.

There was only one way of doing this, and gallantly did the crew of the whaler do it. They brought their boat right along-side the sinking liner, and *Athenia* sailors swarmed up the falls. They scrambled over the slanting deck, and searched deep into the bowels of the ship; subjecting her to a meticulous check as the water eddied around them, and the hull slid ever lower. They searched hard, they risked their lives, and they found just one.

One hundred and twelve people died with the *Athenia*.

But *Electra* and the other rescue ships saved over a thousand more.

*   *   *

War at sea has been defined as "long periods of intense boredom, with short periods of intense fright". The description is a fair one, although in 1939 and the early 'forties a sense of frustration accompanied the boredom; for there never seemed to be enough ships or planes to do the many jobs demanded, and our role—although not exciting, and by no means frightening—was a very exacting one. Thus, in maintaining *Electra*'s reputation as a "happy" ship, much depended upon the petty officers. They didn't let her down.

My own immediate team was headed by Ted Mash, Torpedo Gunner's Mate. A stocky, broad-shouldered Londoner, "Tiger" was a rugged, dependable type of fellow, shrewd, good-humoured, and very well liked by the tube's crew, despite his intimidating nickname. For Mash was a "tiger" only in respect of his courage, and the way in which his strength was allied to speed in movement. Ably seconding him in his labours was another robust character, Big Bill Brayley, and both of these tried P.O.'s were veritable towers of strength. Possessing all of a cockney's wit and stamina they were merciless to slackers: but, knowing their own jobs inside out, they were always ready to help the new boys, and their good-humoured philosophy made light of difficulties. Which was just as well. For we were always being confronted by difficulties, especially those which were created by our old enemy, the Sea.

*   *   *

Number One turns over the watch to me: " . . . westward is the Commodore, *Exmouth* is the escort's senior boy, and we're keeping station on *Inglefield*, bearing red four-two."

The convoy has assembled in the Pentland Firth: I try to adjust my eyes to the darkness.

"Course 283," says Number One, "and zigzag Number One Five. Got it?"

I answer Yes.

"Well, keep the weather right, or else I won't relieve you."

The scene is routine, tranquil, as I take up station behind the gyro repeater and watch the compass and the clock. Then, as *Electra* comes on to her new course and Charles takes the reports from the watch, Sammy appears on the bridge.

Drawing in a gusty breath of the night air, he sniffs briskly and suspiciously at the sea and growls: "Looks like being a dirty night. Where's *Inglefield*?"

I point her out; a dark smudge, rocking slightly on the rising swell.

Sammy growls again. "What's her distance supposed to be?"

And, when I tell him, shakes his head. "No, you're outside distance—come in three degrees, and come up one knot."

Oh, Blast the Man, I think, as I make the correction. For how can he *know*? But Sammy has an uncomfortable knack of being right.

Tonight he's in a restless mood; anxious to keep everyone on their toes. He prowls around the bridge, then switches on the asdic repeat. He switches the set off, switches it on and off again, clears his throat noisily, sticks his head over the bridge rail. Then he moves on to the Pelorus,* to glare at the card and snap: "Your light is too bright!"

But when—with uncharitable but unspoken thoughts—I dim the damned light still further the figures on the card can scarcely be seen, and I go thirty seconds adrift with the next leg of the zigzag. Oh Blast! And all because of Sammy . . .

"Port fifteen, steer 283 degrees." Correcting my fault I try to appear unconcerned about it, and next, to my relief, the

* Master gyro repeater.

Captain's head and shoulders disappear, as he sticks his upper half through the canvas screen that protects the inboard end of the chart-table.

About the size of a normal desk top, but covered with glass and painted black to exclude all light, the sheltered table is not a bad spot on a winter's night. But now, with Sammy there, it's more than overcrowded. For the Captain is wearing his trusty British warm, a garment for which he has a strong sentimental attachment, having purchased it—as he so often relates —"when only a snotty". And over it he has draped the biggest "pusser's oilskin" that the ship can supply, until he's the size and shape of a polar bear—and about as unwelcome, from Charles's point of view.

For Charles, an excellent navigator, is inclined to be pedantic about his trade. Regarding charts as objects of art he graces them with the thinnest of lines, the neatest of notations, and he likes to be left alone with them, and hates to see them roughly handled; but Sammy has no such finer feelings, and now, with his huge bulk sprawling over the table, so that the rain runs down his nose and drips directly on to the spot where the "fix" has been recorded, he crushes my poor colleague remorselessly into a corner and asks, rather testily, where the ship is supposed to be.

Charles tries to point, finds he has not got any room, then bleats rather thinly: "Right in the middle of that pool of water, Sir!"

But Sammy is oblivious to sarcasm: "H'mn, bit of a south-westerly set . . .," he soliloquises, "should alter course about twenty-three hundred."

Then, after a minor earthquake has shaken the canvas cover, Charles is left on his own again.

"Where is she now, Guns?"

SHE, of course, being the *Inglefield*.

I point into the darkness.

"But where's my glasses?" demands Sammy. "Where the devil are my glasses? Bah!" (Losing patience.) "Here, give me yours."

And he snatches them from me, almost unshipping my ears, and mumbling: "Lord, how I wish people would leave my glasses alone! Can't keep 'em for a moment!"

A pause, followed explosively by: "Good God, Guns, what in blazes is wrong with your eyesight? These ruddy things are focussed for an elephant!"

I wait resignedly, while the Captain adjusts my property to his satisfaction and conducts a quick, efficient check, followed up by an approving grunt. "Good, that's all right. Now keep in station . . ."

His last words before he clatters off to his little sea cabin are: "The weather is going to be filthy."

And Sammy, as usual, is right.

*   *   *

On the smooth leg of her zigzag course, when the sea was ahead of her, *Electra* rode quite well; contenting herself with an occasional dizzy climb to the crest of the waves, or a fall into space that sent our stomachs into our mouths, and showers of ice-cold spray into our faces. But when she got on to the awkward leg of the zigzag, when the sea was on her starboard bow, each wave slid a vicious punch into her belly, rolling her atrociously and hurling solid sheets of water along the upper deck. The nights were very dark, but the breaking foam glowed with a luminous light, so much so that there were times when we on the bridge—cowering in misery behind the taut-stretched canvas—had the strange illusion that the body of the ship had vanished, and that we were suspended on an island, completely self-contained. The watches seemed to come round with a bewildering rapidity, and, dazed by the noise and the pummelling of the sea, few of us had more than one ambition

... to get down to our cabins, and the smell of old sea-boots and oilskins, then roll like logs into our bunks, and sleep.

But despite the violence of the elements, and despite his supreme fatigue, and despite the fact that any sensible U-boat would remain in the calm depths of the ocean, and not venture even a peep from its periscope at the wild world up top, the Captain, as active as ever, had not got his head down until 1 a.m. and had ordered me to call him at half past two. And this I did, though with some misgivings, for the hobnails understandably could be expected to be rugged.

"Captain, Sir . . ." There was no answer from the voice-pipe. So I called again, but still without result. And then, quite suddenly I was overwhelmed with sympathy for Sammy, thinking of the way he drove himself, and of the effects that his sacrifice must have on even his iron stamina. Absolutely flaked out, that's what he must be! We junior officers con-sidered ourselves hard done by, I reflected, but the Captain's sleeping time had been almost nil. And at last his fatigue had caught up with him.

Then, as I pressed the buzzer, I almost jumped out of my skin. For, high above the gale, a well-known voice boomed out: "For God's sake, Guns, put an end to it, put an end to this bloody bell-ringing . . . *For God's sake stop, I say.*"

Yes, Sammy was right behind me, rested, vigorous, and swathed in his monstrous working gear. In boisterous good humour he said that he had woken a good five minutes before my call; and I believed him when he added: "I can wake any time I like, my boy—any time I decide I'll wake. I WILL myself to wake!"

*   *   *

The bad weather continued for another two days, but, on the morning of the third, it began to moderate. The long

Atlantic rollers, still white-capped, surged past the ship with a menacing hiss, but no longer did they race and roar across the decks. The wind, after whipping the spray inboard with the force of hailstones, began to whimper instead of scream. And then, as the light brightened, the dark shapes to starboard—assuming an individuality which had been lacking in the murk of the preceding mornings, revealed themselves as ships—ships of all sorts, of all sizes, and of every condition of repair. Some were rust-ridden, or white with the salt of the ocean, while others were surprisingly spick and span, as though fresh from the builders' yards. Some looked impatient, as though straining to be off, and others lumbered along like cart-horses, struggling beneath an unbearable load. Yet all of these vessels had at least one thing in common—their funnels were belching smoke, columns of thick black smoke, and the smoke was contributing to a cloud, a cloud which must have been visible to every U-boat west of Ireland.

On my way to the bridge I ran into Number One, coming down from his action station.

"Morning, Guns, what's for breakfast?"

"None for you, I'm afraid, young chef has been seasick in the porridge."

"Really? But I'd never have noticed! But anyway, I've news for *you*. Hobnails, my lad . . . Hobnails, large size!"

As always, Number One was very much on the mark, as I discovered a moment later, when I innocently enquired of Charles: "Where's the Captain?"

There was a roar from behind me.

"Have you gone blind or something? If you can't see me from two feet away, how the hell can you hope to keep station?"

I gave my smartest salute, I could think of no other reply, and *Electra* set off on her task of rounding up the stragglers until, inevitably, she came to Tail End Charlie.

Well astern of the convoy, and with the strong wind blowing the funnel smoke untidily over her bridge and superstructure, Charlie was clean, but very old-fashioned. Now, as she
waddled stubbornly towards us, I was reminded vaguely of
Kipling's "British coaster", and unguardedly said as much.

"Stuff and nonsense!" snapped Sammy, overhearing. "I shall
have my officers *writing* poetry next. The bridge, Mr. Cain,
is no place for nattering about verse! This isn't Bloomsbury . . ."

He turned his attention back to Charlie, and shouted through
the megaphone: "What's wrong with you? Can't you keep up
with the convoy?"

To which a rich Geordie voice replied: "Keep up with the
convoy? With the rotten muck they've given us to burn we
couldn't even keep up with the times!"

On the whole, *Electra* thought this rather funny, but Sammy,
his hobnails worse than ever, was by no means amused and
gave Charlie a comprehensive bawling out until, over the space
between the ships, came the unexpected and rude rejoinder of
"Blow you, Jack, I'm doing the best I can."

It would be quite impossible to do justice in print to the
rumpus that followed, for frayed tempers snapped, and adjec-
tives flew thick and fast—with Charlie putting over a long-
drawn-out description—nine-tenths slanderous—of Sammy's
appearance, ancestry and manners, and Sammy giving at least
as good as he'd got. Once, in this verbal war, which lasted
several minutes, the fascinated ships' companies saw a hint of a
truce when our new chum yelled: "All right—I've got steam
now. See me in Halifax and I'll buy you a ruddy pint!" But our
Captain's reply to the offer was uncompromising. "I'll see you
in Hell," he said, "and I'll buy you a poker". And hostilities
continued.

Then, just before we parted, the master of the merchantman
climbed on to the wing of his bridge, and, waving an arm like a
tree-trunk and disdaining the loud-hailer bellowed: "Goodbye

—and there's no hard feelings. You've done me a power of good."

"Goodbye, and I'm pleased to have met you," Sammy bawled back, "Good luck, and look after yourself."

For the rest of the day *Electra* was a peaceful ship. Her Captain was in high good humour, and the hobnails had temporarily vanished.

*　　*　　*

The weather worsened when we left the convoy, and a howling hail-laden wind and the crash of the sea made it difficult to hear, to see, to think. When I took over Jenner-Fust's bunk in the sick bay—it was impossible to traverse the ship to get to our usual quarters—I found that one of the deadlights was leaking, and that water, inches deep, covered the floor, rolling from side to side with the roll of the ship. But I was too dead-beat to care. At 4 a.m. on staggering back to my watch-station I saw that the ship was enclosed by some of the highest seas I had ever encountered. Then *Electra*, like a traction-engine labouring uphill, drove up a green steep slope of water, staggered on the crest, and fell like a stone into the shadowed valleys below. A sickening crash followed, and she did not recover in time to ride the next wave, which broke on the foc'sle, rolled the ship to starboard, and swept down the port side like a seething torrent.

A horrific moment! Holding on for dear life I seemed to be at an angle of about eighty degrees to the deck, and looking up into a solid wall of water, riding high above the bridge. "My God, we'll go for a burton if this one breaks," I thought; then *Electra* shook herself free.

" . . . the biggest wave I have ever seen," I shouted.

And Sammy roared back: "Can only remember one worse, and THAT was in a typhoon!"

He swayed up to me. "Were you scared?"

"*Scared*? If I'd let go of the compass there was only the signal lamp between me and the Atlantic."

"No good to you . . . you were never any bloody good with *signals*."

The Buffer scrambled on to the bridge. A wiry, hard-bitten product of the old school, and Number One's right-hand man, Watkins was never one to waste words. Now he reported tersely that something had broken loose in the foc'sle. So could he go out and try to secure it please?

With the light growing stronger we peered over the rail just as a roll of the ship brought the rogue sliding across the deck to bring up against the guard rail stanchions, bending them like pins. An ammunition locker! Made of steel, and weighing over a ton, it had been ripped from the deck to which it had been welded as if its fittings were no more than paper. We looked at each other, thoughtfully. The locker was crammed with shells. Then the Buffer said: "I think we can manage it, Sir."

Sammy considered. To secure the runaway would be a dangerous job; to leave it would invite damage to the ship.

"Well, all right. But volunteers only, and make sure they are wearing their lifebelts. You'd better go with them, Guns. Get everything ready and let me know when you go out to the foc'sle."

*　　　*　　　*

Volunteers? No need to look for them; they are already waiting, down in the galley flat. Fred Castle and Job, Meader and French and Palmer . . . all experienced seamen, all knowing what the job entails. Then Sammy, told that we're ready, pulls the ship slightly to port to give us—for precious seconds only—a bit of a lee; and we dash into the wind.

Electra rolls and the locker rolls too. We jump on to the foc'sle, grab desperately a handhold, cower breathless and drenched as the deck beneath us seesaws and the ship thrusts her nose into the foaming sea. But now, as her bows come up, an icy torrent rushes aft, and carries the locker with it. Hurled over and over by the violence of the waters, tossed like a small pebble on the beach when the waves are breaking, it comes at us terrifyingly, with the roar of a runaway train. For a moment I gaze appalled and then, with a terrific crash, it brings up all standing against the foc'sle ladder-head, smashing the rails beside it.

"*Now!*"

But my shout is lost in the din of the gale. And is not in any case required. For all these men, these volunteers, are sailors; each, following his own hunch, knows that it is Now. We move as one, with heaving lines and cordage. We curse, and grit our teeth . . . and the brute is at last "corralled".

Back on the bridge I report in detail, and Sammy says: "Tell 'em from me, Well Done."

I pass the Captain's message, and the Buffer answers dourly: "Let's hope there's an extra tot of rum in it."

But behind his sceptical exterior he is pleased. For praise from Sammy is praise indeed.

*　　　*　　　*

It was to be the proud boast of *Electra* that she never lost a merchant ship entrusted to her keeping.

In laying the foundations of this pleasant distinction which was to earn us the title of "Lucky 'Lectra", Sammy spared nobody—least of all himself. For he made it a point of honour that he, as Captain, should be exposed to the maximum discomfort, and that he should not be content to suffer equally with the men but should always exceed their suffering. Thus it was rare indeed if, in the course of a voyage that might last from seven to ten days, he left the vicinity of the bridge or permitted himself more than three hours' consecutive sleep. Small wonder therefore that the warning of "hobnails on the liver" should be frequent; or that, on receiving it, all hands should "stand from under!"

To the belligerent, tempestuous Sammy, Jenner-Fust, with his nonchalance and polish, provided a perfect foil. Each was dissimilar to the other, except in his skill and devotion to the Service. Yet each was complementary to the other; they made a wonderful team. There was one occasion, however—and one occasion only—when this perfect partnership appeared to be endangered. It happened like this . . .

Electra arriving at Rosyth for a boiler clean, Sammy had been able to grant the troops the rare luxury of three days' leave. The men of the First Watch swarmed ashore within minutes of the ship's docking, and Sammy and most of the other officers followed. But Jenner-Fust, Charles and I, were left in charge of the Second Watch, which was to commence its leave half an hour after the return of the first party, due back at noon on Wednesday. Then along came Gould, to put the cat among the pigeons.

Chief Petty Officer Alfred Gould was a round-faced cherubic-looking character, who displayed at times an almost Pick-wickian benevolence. Like Watkins he was a first-class seaman and was much respected by the company who—with their sailors' flair for seeing beyond appearances—well realised that whereas the Buffer was by no means as stern as he pretended, the Coxswain was by no means "soft". But, like every other worthwhile petty officer, Gould had the interest of the troops at heart. He seldom lost a trick when given a chance to play for their comfort or convenience; and one such chance now offered.

"A special train will be leaving the dockyard station at eleven o'clock tomorrow. It will be taking a large draft down to London, Sir."

Jenner-Fust was wary. "And very nice for the draft. But what's it to do with us?"

"Well, Sir . . ." Gould hesitated. "I was wondering, just *wondering*, if I mightn't be able to fix a place on that train, a place for our chaps I mean?

"So, *if* I could, do you think it would be in order for the Second Watch to leave a bit earlier than planned? If they could leave at 10.30 they'd just have time to catch the train. Do you think you could stretch a point, Sir?"

It was a tricky question for we guessed that Gould was telling us only half the story. He must already have fixed things, otherwise we wouldn't have heard a word. Furthermore, he was quick to emphasise that he and the other P.O.'s would not expect to be included in the party.

Well, what to do? In many respects the request was reasonable enough, but to grant it would entail *Electra* being emptied for a short time of all but officers and petty officers. On the other hand the men deserved a change, and when the only sort of emergency they might be called upon to face would be Fire or Man Overboard it seemed rather hard that they should be robbed of their chance of seeing their homes again. So, after mulling it over, Jimmy gave his consent and the Second Watch left at half past ten, as happy as skylarks.

Came eleven, and the arrival of Sammy. Earlier than expected, he came striding along the dockside with an extra jauntiness in his manner, and immediately I suspected he was up to no good. The suspicion was justified. He came up the gangplank at a double rate of knots; then greeted Jenner-Fust, before that worthy had a chance to explain our leave concession, with the crisp command, "Clear lower deck at five past twelve!"

"It's good," he gloated, "to see everything so shipshape, and I would like to talk to the ship's company while they are still all here."

"So what the devil do we do?" I asked, as Sammy dashed off to his cabin.

"That crafty old buzzard," said Number One, with commendable restraint, "must have seen some of the libertymen ashore."

A steely glint showed in his eyes. "Well, blow that," he exclaimed with a rare lapse into the vernacular. "Send for the Coxswain and the P.O.'s, Guns. Rake them out quickly; I want to speak to them!"

*   *   *

The subsequent stratagem of Lieutenant Richard Jenner-Fust O.B.E. was by no means the sort of thing one would have expected from a product of Dartmouth, and contained elements of risk that made my blood run cold. In short, he planned to play Sammy at his own game. He told the Petty Officers to go round the other ships, and collect as many ratings as they could. These, he pronounced, would be our Second Watch.

"Shanghai 'em if you like," he said, "but make sure they fall in behind the returned libertymen, the genuine First Watch. For when Clear Lower Deck is ordered I shall want to see *a full ship's company*!"

*   *   *

Twelve five, and the ersatz Second Watch was mustered . . . some of them in the plot and delighted to help, some only partly in the plot but anxious for a bit of a lark, and some—by no means least in numbers—knowing nothing at all about the plot, and quite hurt by the way in which they had been whipped in.

Quite candidly I had no stomach for the masquerade which appeared to be completely crazy, and my flesh literally creeped when Sammy eventually showed up. Some of our P.O.'s had obviously taken Number One's remarks about "shanghai-ing" far too literally, so that there were sulks and scowls on some of *Electra*'s brand-new faces. But worse was the fact that the others, the "informed" elements of the draft, found it so difficult to keep back their grins that they'd even ceased to try. In any case, I thought despairingly, our Sammy had a memory like an elephant's, so far as his ship's company was concerned. We didn't stand a chance.

Yet Jenner-Fust's aplomb remained completely undisturbed. A crisp salute preceding his report that the Lower Deck had been duly cleared, he now stood at attention, grave-faced, respectful, as the Captain took the "chair".

For a moment Sammy gave the troops a long, hard stare, a very penetrating stare, and then he spoke, But to my astonishment his words were uttered quietly, almost gently, and not for a moment did he refer to anything untoward. Instead he delivered a benign little homily and said at its conclusion, with a gesture to Number One: "Get the Second Watch on leave as soon as possible. They deserve it!"

The crisis was over.

It was not until some months later that I heard Sammy's side of this astonishing affair. He had not only *seen* some of our libertymen start on their journey, he had actually *spoken* to a couple of them; and they, not knowing for a moment that Jimmy was sailing so close to the wind, had confided that they were going to London as a result of "special permission". Now Sammy was all in favour of the move, but just for the devilment he had decided to call his snap parade and see how his usually imperturbable First Lieutenant would cope.

"To say that I was surprised when the anticipated blushing apologies did not arrive," said Sammy, "would be to put it mildly. But when I saw how that ruddy villain had organised his bogus parade well—I was shaken, absolutely shaken. Caught me for once, flat-footed."

Yes, Sammy was Big . . . big in spirit, as well as in physique. He was incapable of bearing petty malice and, with his down-to-earth psychology, he reckoned that Jenner-Fust's prank would do no harm but would actually be good for the men's morale. And in this he was right, for the troops talked about it, and chuckled about it during many a dreary watch in the long, grey months to come. A smart ship, *Electra*, to put it across one so wily as Lieutenant Commander Buss.

*   *   *

April 5th was much like any other day save that the battle-cruiser *Renown*, flying the flag of Vice-Admiral W. J. Whitworth, and accompanied by a minelayer and four destroyers, steamed out of Scapa and proceeded towards the east. Operation "Wilfred"—much debated, much postponed—had at last begun.

For months past the Germans had been taking full advantage of the Allies' conscientious respect for Norwegian neutrality. By using the Leads—the long stretch of territorial waters that formed a "covered way" from North Cape to the Baltic—they had been able to pass their blockade runners unmolested into the North Atlantic and bring their vital iron ore convoys safely home.

In January the *Altmark* incident—although resolved by the brave and unorthodox action of the *Cossack*—had served to spotlight the dilemma in which the Allies found themselves, a dilemma created not only by geography but by politics as well. On the one hand they were pledged to uphold the rights of the small nations; on the other, their opponent—far less "nice" than they—was exploiting their strict observance of international equity. Their published morality had become a weapon in the hands of the enemy.

Hence the emergence of "Wilfred", as a compromise between those who felt we must completely disregard Norwegian neutrality, however much such a policy would have conflicted with our principles, and those who wanted to leave the situation unchanged, despite the fact that it was costing British lives. For "Wilfred" had a strictly limited objective.

Neutrality was to be infringed, but not to the extent where an armed clash with Norway would become inevitable. The covered way was not to be forced open, but obstacles were to be placed inside it; the Leads were to be mined, and the mined areas declared.

First intimation that "Wilfred's" life might be somewhat more exciting than the planners had envisaged, came when the destroyer, *Glowworm*—detached from the main force to search for a rating who had fallen overboard—encountered suddenly a large warship, the German heavy cruiser *Hipper*. With tremendous gallantry, and evading the enemy escorts, the lone destroyer went into the attack, damaged her opponent, and then was sunk. Fresh "enemy" reports came to hand a little later. The *Scharnhorst* and *Gneisenau* had put to sea, German transports had disappeared from the estuaries of their homeland, a large force of destroyers had passed through The Belt, a convoy of "merchantmen" had arrived off Narvik . . . by the morning of the 8th the scattered units of the "Wilfred" force were regrouping around the flagship; by the afternoon the Home Fleet was approaching Norwegian waters.

To us the meaning of this flap was anything but clear; for the strange coincidence that had caused the minelaying force to commence operations on the very day that the Germans had sailed on their (long planned) invasion of Norway was still unguessed at. But enlightenment was imminent.

On that same evening, in the waters of Oslo fiord, the Phoney War came to its abrupt and violent ending—an ending accompanied by the thunder of the German guns, and lit by the flames from the German cruiser *Blücher*, torpedoed by the betrayed Norwegians in a fierce, brief agony of defiance, a gallant resistance to an implacable fate.

At 4.30 a.m. on the 9th—six hours after the attack had begun—the German Minister in Oslo presented the Norwegian Government with a demand for surrender. It was refused; and meanwhile, in the middle of a snowstorm, the twenty-one-year-old *Renown*, was delivering the first return blow of the Allies, engaging the two new German battle-cruisers and inflicting damage on the *Scharnhorst*, forcing her to turn away. Yet, heartening though it was, Whitworth's success had but little effect on the progress of events. German forces had already landed at Trondheim and Bergen, and German destroyers were occupying Narvik, "the bastion of the North". From Denmark to the Finnish border the front was now ablaze.

3

Full Astern!

OUR first trip to Norway was uneventful, producing nothing more menacing than a German patrol plane. On our second voyage, when attached to the naval force escorting a troop convoy, we had our first encounter with Goering's bombers.

It was a heavy attack, pressed home with great vigour; and by the end of it an ex-Polish liner, crammed with soldiers, was fiercely ablaze. Yet despite the risk to themselves two destroyers ran alongside her and actually succeeded in rigging gangways to her decks, while the pongoes, I was later told, *marched* off the ship as though parading before a General.

This excitement over, and the remainder of the convoy safely delivered, we picked up two army officers and landed them in a desolate spot a hundred miles to the north. Then, while we were waiting the boats' return, two German planes appeared, flying very high and crossing the head of the fiord.

Electra's luck was in. Results had been discouraging when she had popped off her guns before; yet now, when the chances of her hitting anything appeared to be 20,000 to one against, the Germans, all oblivious to her presence, happened to swim into the sights of the Director-Layer. Jenner-Fust only a moment before had ordered the four-inch guns to load, and as Watkins pressed the trigger the effect was sensational. One of our guns was "wooded", the planes being shielded by the structure of the bridge. And another threw up a shell which, faultily

fused, gave up when only halfway to the target. But the others?
Twin bursts of smoke and steel exploded on each side of the
nearer aircraft. It banked steeply, then part of its wing dropped
off. A cheer went up from the troops, almost drowning the
bomber's despairing wail; and the enemy dropped like a stone,
and was lost sight of behind the mountains.

It was a most encouraging event, and when she left the fiord
Electra's tail was high.

* * *

Events on the Norwegian front were moving with bewildering speed. As viewed from our small destroyer the affair
seemed chaotic.

One dirty grey morning, with *Electra* digesting the local
mixed grill—driving rain, an overcast sky, and a heavy sea—
our routine was enlivened suddenly by the report: "Ships'
masts on the port bow." Then, almost immediately, another
lookout sung out: "Ships' masts on the starboard bow." We
had received no report of any of our ships being in the area,
and Sammy's hobnails disappeared as if by magic. There
would, he prophesied, be blood for supper.

"All guns load with armour-piercing shell. Follow Director."

The gun crews jump to it.

"Gunner to take over foremost tubes in local control. After
tubes will be fired from the bridge."

I take over the firing position. "All tubes ready!"

A calm voice crackles through the headphones.

"Ships ahead are cruisers, believed to be enemy. So fire when
your sights come on, and make sure of your target. We won't
get a second chance!"

Now through the mist and the murk we see them—two
huddled grey shapes, their guns trained fore and aft. But suddenly the turrets begin to turn . . .

"Twenty degrees to go." Crouched over the sights I am gripped by the habit of the years.

"Twenty degrees to go." The leading torpedoman repeats the refrain.

In seconds, I think incredulously, I will be pressing the firing levers; shooting the torps in earnest. Oh God, let them run straight; then, almost as an afterthought—and please look after us.

My hand is actually on the lever when frantically comes the call of "Check, check, check . . ."

The cruisers are two of ours. Only no one has thought to tell us—not until now!

The flap over, Mash reports the after tubes secured, and says: "Crikey, that was a near thing; but the Old Man has certainly got guts."

"And in a way," he adds, "I almost wish they *had* been German. Think you'd have got yours, Sir?"

"Could scarcely have missed, but neither could they. And they might have got us first, although I'd have fired with the flash of their guns."

We come back to normal, to realise that maybe things could have been far worse; and Tiger grins, "Ah well, we ain't got much money, but we do see life."

*   *   *

A few days later Sammy's temper became almost unbearable. *Electra*, equipped with minesweeping paravanes, had been picked to clear the way for *Warspite* into Narvik, where lurked the remaining ships of the German destroyer force; then Admiral Whitworth had spoilt it all by deciding to risk the mines and by leaving *Electra* to patrol outside the fiord while he went in with Vian's large Tribals. Brilliantly successful though Whitworth's action was, I don't think that Sammy ever forgave him for it; and even we feebler souls were bitterly disappointed, especially when the ship was demoted to a convoy job, in typical convoy weather.

It was therefore a great relief to hear that we were to participate once more in a real Fleet movement, by acting as one of the escorts to *Ark Royal* which was to launch an air attack on Trondheim.

* * *

The aircraft took off at dusk, heavily laden planes that seemed to drop as they left the flight deck, and almost skimmed the top of the waves before hauling themselves up by their bootlaces, so to speak, into the darkening sky. They were expected back at first light, and as the German reaction was likely to be fierce, we turned in with expectations of fun and games to come.

It was just after four in the morning when we went to full action stations. The sea was calm, and as the *Ark* turned into what little wind there was, the destroyers, ready to defend her against submarine attack, formed a huge semi-circle with *Electra* on the outside edge. The first few aircraft began to come in on schedule, but no longer in neat formation. They came back in ones and twos, and some were literally limping home. Then, while we were counting them, a great bank of fog loomed up ahead of us.

"Ninety degrees starboard."

But even as the leading ships began to turn the fog overran them.

"As outside wing, *Electra* will increase speed to maintain position," I explained to the tubes' crew.

"And simultaneously the inside wing will start to slow down. It's a simple manœuvre really—rather like a drill squad wheeling on its marker."

We heard the whine of turbines, revving up. We felt the ship heel, as she altered course. And then the murk enveloped us. Minutes passed, we continued to travel fast, until suddenly, dramatically, H.M.S. *Antelope* appeared—less than a stone's throw away, and cutting across our bows.

"Full astern together." Sammy's voice seemed to ring through the still air.

"But it's too late, too late," registered my mind, appalled.

"Hard a starboard."

The propellers thrashed wildly under full power, striving to take the way off 1,500 tons of steel. But not even Sammy's skill could pull us through; not now.

We struck home, with a terrific crash. We had hit *Antelope* in the wardroom pantry. Steel screamed, men ran for safety, and *Electra* ploughed on until her foc'sle was level with *Antelope*'s X gun. We ground to a stop; our engines began to pull us slowly away: then we stopped again, to regard the damage. Our foc'sle was intact, but the deck below had been pushed back for nearly a quarter of the ship's length. And in *Antelope*'s side yawned an enormous hole. "*That* was her wardroom," someone said in awe.

Two figures swum out of the hole and into the calm sea. They took a quick look at *Electra*, looked back again at their own ship; then, evidently deciding that the latter was the better risk, they promptly swam back the way they had come, reappearing a few seconds later on *Antelope*'s quarter-deck.

A man I had never seen before came up to me.

"I'm from *Antelope*, Sir . . ."

"We seem to be getting a bit mixed up," I said.

"Climbed up the anchor chain . . ."

It appeared that the "stray" belonged to one of *Antelope*'s after guns. He had seen our foc'sle towering over him and, with a sort of shock reaction, had promptly swarmed aboard. He had burned his hands on the steel—red hot from the force of the collision—and was the accident's sole casualty. But we did not immediately appreciate this latter fact, for things looked as bad as they could be.

I went to the upper messdeck, to find it resembling a shambles. All the tables and stools had collapsed, the lockers had capsized; sprawled over a heap of debris in the corner lay a seaman.

I grabbed him by the shoulder. "Are you all right?"

A morose face looked up, "I've lost me blinkin' ticklers . . . I can't find me blinkin' ticklers."*

I left him to continue with his search.

The ship had been smashed as far as the after bulkhead of the stokers' messdeck. A great stretch of steel had been peeled from her nose and trailed its jagged edges in the water. The cable locker was gone completely, and our anchor chain hung like a mass of tangled knitting.

"Gather *Antelope* didn't receive the signal to turn," shouted Charles, hurrying from the bridge.

"Well, she's still in better shape than us."

For the rent in *Antelope*'s side was not as serious as it looked; but our own wound "faced the front".

The sharp bow that had enabled *Electra* to knife her way through the waves had disappeared, leaving only the one wide bulkhead to present its flat surface to the pressure of the water. Our first job was to shore up this uncertain barrier; our next was to rid the ship of the cable chain. Soon, with the exception of *Zulu*, who had been detailed to stand by, the Fleet was miles away. And even *Antelope* had begun her journey home. Time passed with extraordinary slowness. And, with the German bombers roaring overhead, our prayers that the fog would last were pathetically sincere.

The water was swimming over the wrecked messdeck, hitting our new "steaming bulkhead" at all sorts of odd angles, and creating an alarming noise; rather like the break of the waves

* Tobacco issue.

over a groyne during rough weather. And when, at long last, Sammy decided to get under way again, the mangled steel plating acted as a sort of forward rudder, making steering extremely difficult. Yet steadily the ship worked up, with Jenner-Fust and Tom Lee positioned to watch for signs of the bulkhead's collapse, and the loose plates clanging as mournfully as a passing-bell. Slowly the speed increased . . . to five knots, to five and a half, to six. And then—the bulkhead bulged! "The strain's too great," said Sammy.

He tried different tactics, and endeavoured to steam the ship stern first; but it was impossible to keep her on an even course; she veered around like a drunk. He decided to keep to five knots and hope for the best.

"Get *home?*" exclaimed Ted Mash, overhearing the misgivings of a new boy. "Of course we'll get home. You couldn't have a better bloke than Sammy, not for this sort of job. So cheer up my lad, and thank God that the galley's working."

We went to tea.

*   *   *

It was the fourth day of Sammy's battle for *Electra*'s life, but down the ship's side the tangle of twisted steel still sagged into the sea. Every movement caused *Electra* to sway and groan, as though in pain, and now and again, when the wind freshened, she would give a little lurch, and the scar would lengthen for yet another inch or so, exposing her flanks still further. Once let it extend beyond an upright riveted rib, the crucial point, and yet another compartment would be flooded. Just after the collision the sea had only two feet to go: since then each watch had seen the distance lessen, and now, to make things worse, the weather was deteriorating.

With the sea rising Sammy was forced to reduce speed still further, but although he tried once more to go astern not even he could hold the ship. Working one engine and putting the wheel hard over just wouldn't work. She kicked her stern straight up into the wind, and stopped there.

The crack had spread alarmingly when I handed over the watch, and I wasn't in my bunk an hour before I was called to the bridge again, to find that Sammy was preparing for the worst.

"You'll have to get rid of your ashcans and torpedoes," he told me, "in order to lighten the top weight of the ship."

I demurred at this, arguing that the sixteen-ton weight of the torpedoes was evenly distributed along the fore-and-aft line, and that I could not see that jettisoning them would make much difference.

"I know that you worship your wretched toys, Guns. But the safety of the ship comes first." He spoke tiredly, but not ill-naturedly.

I tried a different line of argument: "Then what happens if we get flushed by a German cruiser?"

"If *that* happens then it won't matter a damn whether you've got your fish or not. You surely don't imagine we could do anything in our present state?"

"Quite frankly, no, Sir—but that wouldn't stop you from having a damn good try!"

Sammy grinned. "You're an obstinate cuss, but you may be right."

So eventually we compromised—I guaranteeing to ensure that the tubes were ready for firing; Sammy agreeing not to fire them without first telling me.

Came four o'clock. The sea was still rough, and in the grey light of dawn we saw that the rent had at last worked back to the line of the rivets. The peeled-back plating, looking for all the world like the serrated top of an opened sardine tin was working backwards and forwards with the movement of the ship, and tugging at the all-important rib: the crisis could not long be delayed. Then, even as we watched, *another* crack appeared: but this one, miraculously, was going *down* the line of the rivets. We gazed at it, hardly daring to speak. A vertical line, it was cutting at right angles across the original tear; it was severing the mangled deadweight from the ship. And then, with hardly any warning, and as if ripped away by some mighty hand, the plates crashed loose from the hull, and plunged into the sea!

The difference could be felt immediately; it was expressed in the very movement of the ship. Relieved of the backward pull, *Electra* shook herself, and then began to ride more comfortably; her luck had held.

Looking five years younger, Sammy came away from the side of the bridge. "There are," he said, "two things a British captain can always rely on—the loyalty of his crew and the best built ships in the world."

Then, as if regretting this unusual flash of sentiment, he rushed below, to bawl out some of the troops for not moving fast enough.

In the middle of the forenoon, when all was well, the Captain showed me a signal, just deciphered. "Every effort must be made to save torpedoes. They are to be jettisoned only as a very last resort."

I waited for the congratulations; they did not come. Instead, Sammy blandly remarked: "Wise of me, wasn't it, to restrain you last night! If you'd fired those fish of yours I would have had to have given reasons in writing. However, you'll learn . . ."

In the Navy there is only one foolproof answer to a situation of this sort; and I gave it with a grin: "Aye, aye, Sir!"

*   *   *

Troon, where *Electra* was sent to refit, couldn't do enough to make us welcome. Yet, despite the blessings of Scottish hospitality we tended after a while to chafe at our inactivity;

for we had so often moaned about the hardness of our lot that we felt shamed by our present ease. Dunkirk was over and done. The Battle of Britain was beginning. It was not a good time to be out of things, and it was a relief to see the ship take shape again.

The yard in which she lay belonged to the Ailsa Shipbuilding Company, a small, old-established concern, noted for its craftsmanship and its successful yachts. *Electra* was the biggest repair job the firm had tackled, and Mr. Turnbull, the energetic yard manager, was determined to do us proud; an ambition that had pleasing, though sometimes unusual, results.

Given a free hand, he had the wardroom decorated in a natty shade of Royal Blue. And when we congratulated him on the effect, he told us: "Your ship is making history, I've given her the colours of a football team." Turnbull, we learnt later, was one of Glasgow Rangers' keenest fans.

But Sammy would gladly have dispensed with at least one of the Scot's "improvements".

The safe in the Captain's little day cabin was housed beneath a locker seat, an arrangement which irritated him intensely for it meant that whenever he wanted to get anything from the safe he had to lift the seat to get at it. A simple operation? Not the way that Sammy handled it . . . for Sammy was always busy, always in a terrific hurry. And thus he could never be bothered to remove the seat entirely, but would prop it back impatiently with his head while he rummaged; and suffer accordingly. For it was a ten to one chance that, having found what he wanted, he would forget all about his balancing act, withdraw his head suddenly, and get his fingers caught as the lid cracked down.

Thus, settled at Troon, the Captain decided he had had enough of this annoyance. "Get me a new safe, and install it near the fireplace," he ordered, ignoring, in his characteristic way, that safes were in short supply, and that we had already

had our quota. "And make sure it's kept clear of that blasted
locker seat!"

Sammy's demands, even when unreasonable, had a habit of
being met. So, somehow or other, I managed to get the job
done; and the Captain went on leave well satisfied. But, on his
return, he could scarcely believe his eyes. For there it was—*a
new seat locker*; a ruddy new seat locker; a seat locker that
squatted on top of his brand new safe, and would fall with a
bang on his unprotected fingers! He just stood there, *looking*.
And so angry that he was almost incapable of speech.

"See what I've done for you?" Mr. Turnbull was triumphant.

"*You!*" exclaimed Sammy, colouring up.

"Well, fancy him having to stare at that eyesore of a safe,
I thought. I wonder what we can do for him? And then,
Captain, I had my bright idea. Let's cover it up, I decided,
disguise it as a seat!"

Poor Sammy. He had a great liking for Turnbull, and thus,
although the words almost choked him, he had to express his
thanks for so ingenious a contrivance; and continue to bruise
his fingers until the day he left the ship.

*   *   *

Electra experienced many changes in her make-up, both in
the course of her sojourn at Troon and in the weeks that
followed.

Fred Castle, a nimble cockney reservist who had served fourteen years with the colours, was placed in charge of a new-
fangled Oerlikon gun; and soon, in the manner of all good
sailors, he had become intensely possessive about his charge,
the Oerlikon becoming "my gun". But one man's meat is
another's poison, and in order to make way for our increased
anti-aircraft armament, I had to lose four precious torpedo
tubes; and was not pleased!

There were changes in the ship's company, where several veterans were called away to give the benefit of their experience to other ships. There were changes in the wardroom—where Tom Lee was replaced by Engineer Lieutenant Frank McLeod, and Roger Price R.N.R., arrived as Sub.

The new "Chief" (a Scot!) had entered the Navy as a Boy Artificer Apprentice. Having risen through the ranks at a time when promotion was at its most difficult, he was a first-class engineer with a long experience of destroyers; and although entirely different in appearance to his jovial swashbuckling predecessor—Mac was rather slightly built—he soon found his place among us, becoming one of the family.

Roger Price—with his M.N. background—was less easily assimilated. An extremely likeable and outspoken young man, very keen on "moving with the times", he found our naval traditions rather stuffy on occasion, and did not hesitate to say so.

"For everything," he once exclaimed, "is the way that ruddy Nelson did it, every goddam thing! If Nelson had ever tapped the blessed weevils out of the ship's biscuits, and made them form fours on the wardroom table, we'd still have ship's biscuits as our staple diet. For where else could we get the traditional weevils from, to form them up in fours!"

But, despite such near-sacrilegious comment, Roger, a very competent and conscientious seaman, was well liked by us all; and only once did his rugged individualism offend.

This happened when, at dinner, he happened to catch an empty glass with his fork, causing the glass to ring. Swiftly Charles put a finger on the glass to stop the sound.

Roger looked up, indignantly, "Was that necessary?"

"An old naval custom," Charles told him, very gently. "For tradition has it that every time a glass rings a sailor dies . . ."

"Well, it *has* rung, and the sailor is dead. So you're a bit too late!"

"But if the ringing can be stopped before it dies out naturally," said Charles, "then the devil is prevented from taking the sailor's soul to hell . . ."

This was far too much for Roger. "Stuff and nonsense!" he exploded, and flicked the nearest glass with his fingernail.

An awkward pause. Then Sam's angry voice blasted down from the head of the table: "Mr. Price, while you are in my ship you will observe the customs of the Service, or else you will eat alone!"

Roger, in the end, was to be as great a traditionalist as any of us; but for quite a while he regarded the "Royal's" conservatism as "Bull, my good friends. Sheer bloody bull! A grand pretence . . . Boloney!"

*   *   *

"Pleased to meet you," I said. "And now you'd better come to breakfast."

The rain-drenched, but still dapper, young officer, who'd just climbed inboard from the mail vessel, looked a little worried. "But what about the Captain? Won't he think it strange if I don't first report to him?"

"Oh, Sammy won't be safe until after ten o'clock," the reply came pat. For hadn't I heard a similar conversation once before?

Dried off and tidied up, Henry Whitcliffe Davies entered smoothly into the team. Allied to a neat appearance, a friendly manner, and a great capacity for leg-pulling, he had an extremely brilliant brain, and intense powers of concentration. He was also my watch-keeping opposite number, which to me was important.

When you spend most of your waking hours with the same companion, sharing similar responsibilities, sharing good times and bad, you either learn to respect him as a true comrade, or else you grow to hate his guts. I am proud to say that Harry and I were soon firm friends, and remained so to the end.

Son of the Dean of Worcester, and graduating at Oxford, Davies was on the faculty of the University of Aberdeen when war broke out. Intensely idealistic, like so many others of his class and generation, he had volunteered immediately. He was extraordinarily well read, and many a black and miserable night-watch was made more bearable by his recitations, which ranged from "Alice in Wonderland" to extracts from the tales of Homer.

"I can't understand you two," said Number One. "You seem to regard watch-keeping as a pleasant pastime. If ever I want to make you miserable I'll split you up!"

But, of course, he never did; *that* was to be the prerogative of the Jap . . .

* * *

It was on New Year's Eve that *Electra* experienced her biggest change of all.

We had spent Christmas pursuing a false report that a German raider had broken loose in the North Atlantic: then, frozen stiff, we had crept back to the Sound, to tie up alongside *Echo* and thaw out with a party.

First hint of anything unusual was when the Yeoman entered the mess. There was an air of excitement about him, and going up to Sammy, he said: "Commander, Sir, the Promotion Lists!"

"All right," replied Sammy, unconcerned. "Just put them on the table, and I'll see them later on."

But Tingle, planting himself in front of him, repeated firmly. "*Commander*, Sir—and may I be the first to congratulate you!"

Sammy's head jerked back like an angry bird's, as he opened his mouth to blast the persistent yeoman; but no words came. For there before him, underlined with a dirty great red crayon mark, was the announcement: "Lieutenant Commander to Commander: S. A. Buss . . ."

"We want Sam . . ." Number One started it, thumping on the table with his open hand in the traditional naval manner of acclaim: in a second we'd all joined in. But when the Captain rose to his feet the noise grew even louder, and the refrain was changed to an even more distinguished signal of respect, that of "Up, Up, Up!" At this, which requires the person honoured to climb on to a chair, Sammy's weatherbeaten face was pink with pleasure, and a rare embarrassment. I don't think that he had realised, until that moment, the extent of the affection he had inspired among the men he had led so resolutely, and roughly; or how much they understood, forgave, and even admired, the foibles which had made him, a wonderful leader, so intensely human. But now . . . there was no doubt about it; the whole ship was pleased and happy for him. And when the Chief Engine Room Artificer called, to present him with a model of a Commander's hat, complete with laurel leaves, and made of brass, I thought for a moment that Sammy would actually break down.

*   *   *

Every promotion has its snags; and the snag about Sammy's, was that he would have to leave us.

"I expect that you will be glad to see your bad-tempered Old Man go?" he commented over a farewell drink.

"Oh, I don't know, Sir," answered Chiefie. "Very often the buzzard you know is better than the devil you don't."

Sammy guffawed. "An honest answer, if not very flattering; but perhaps my relief won't suffer from hobnails!"

Hobnails . . . and we had fondly imagined that he was the only man on the ship who didn't know the significance of the word.

In spite of the fact that there was to be no demonstration of farewell by the Ship's Company—Sammy had said he didn't want one—the troops were all on deck as the Captain left; and the Coxswain, the Quartermaster and the Chief Buffer had formed themselves into a ceremonial piping party. Therefore, his send-off was a worthy one, to the shrilling of the pipes, and the cheers of his men. As Sammy moved slowly down the gangway for the last time, one frank admirer bawled: "You're all right mate, a bloody good skipper. Now shake the next bunch up, and teach 'em to be as good as us!"

Sammy bared his teeth in that well-known tigerish grin. "Trust ME," he answered; then gently added: "Good luck, *Electra*, and God Bless you all."

He was killed two years later, in action in the Med. And the Navy, and the Nation, were the poorer for his passing.

*   *   *

Gathered in the wardroom, we awaited the advent of the new Owner; with interest but scant enthusiasm. All that we knew about Cecil Wakeford May was that, a fairly senior commander, he had come to *Electra* from the Admiralty, and had confided to Number One that he was glad to get back to the sea. Otherwise we had scarcely heard of him, and were sceptical about the chances of anyone adequately filling Sammy's empty place.

Two punka fans were suspended from the deck-head in the mess. Now, as May entered, he instinctively ducked to avoid them.

"Don't worry, Sir," I quipped. "They are six feet two inches from the deck."

A slow, friendly smile spread over a lean, rather thoughtful face; and very gravely he replied: "But how fortunate . . . As I am six foot one and a half inches tall, the fan will remind me when I need a hair-cut!"

Quiet in manner, blessed with a sense of humour, May— like Sammy—was a born "destroyer-man". But otherwise they were exact "opposites". After his predecessor's ebullience May struck us, at first, as being reserved, almost remote. But we soon got to know him better. Never familiar, he was friendly and sympathetic; yet his anger—very rarely roused—was to prove itself a thing to fear. His blue eyes seemed to contract as he froze the object of his displeasure; and although he never raised his voice in annoyance, his words could pierce the toughest skin.

It transpired that, only a few days after Sammy had left us, we were sent on a long sweep up into the Arctic, followed by a return through the Denmark Strait. In the course of the operation *Electra* had to refuel from one of the cruisers, and as this was a manœuvre requiring first-rate seamanship, and clear thinking, the highly critical ship's company turned out in force to watch their new owner's performance.

But May never turned a hair. Although there was a heavy sea running, and although the ships were proceeding at ten knots, working up to fifteen, he took our destroyer alongside as coolly as if he were parking a car in an empty street. His composure never left him, not for a moment; and even when one of the steadying wires suddenly parted like a piece of string he merely commented, with unaffected aplomb: "Don't bother to put another wire out, Number One. We are nearly finished now, and I can hold her till we are."

By the time the voyage was over, *Electra* had become reconciled to her Captain.

*   *   *

A new Doctor joined us, Lieutenant Seymour R.N.V.R. A dry Ulsterman, Seymour had an intense love of small boats, and a fund of knowledge that extended to the most unexpected subjects. On one occasion he astonished us by working out that the battleship *Rodney* would start to plane at 82 knots. On another he gave an off-the-cuff answer to a technical question that had been puzzling us regarding the reactions of a "tow". But although Doc's mathematical calculations seldom failed to bewilder us they invariably proved to be on—or near —the mark. A brilliant medico, Seymour had served with distinction during the blitz on Coventry, and was to distinguish himself still further during the fierce year ahead. But he was also an absolute natural as a sailor, and was seldom happier than when he was on the bridge.

Epitomising the way in which our newcomers had settled down, becoming part of the ship, was a conversation between Roger Price and an army officer friend.

Said Roger, having patiently explained just why our visitor should beware of "ringing" his glass: "Now don't you think that's a very moving tradition? Only the Navy could have thought of it!"

Electra was a united ship when she prepared to face the hazards of 1941.

4

We Steam against the Bismarck!

IT was February 1941. The Battle of Britain was over and done, and although Goering's raiders savaged the cities by night the very wildness of their attacks was symbolic of the bitterness of the enemy's frustration. The Luftwaffe had lost its chance of a decisive blow, and for the long-suffering Home Front the worst was over. From overseas too the news was good. In the Western Desert Wavell's breathless little army—a thousand miles of success behind it—had taken Benghazi and stood poised on the frontiers of Tripoli. In East Africa the victorious Empire forces, having chased the Italians out of the Sudan, Somaliland and Eritrea, had entered, with Haile Selassie, the kingdom of Ethiopia.

Such triumphs were phenomenal and completely unexpected. After six months, in which she had succeeded in "standing alone" against a cowed or hostile world, Britain, was no longer content with a static defence—she was everywhere advancing! Furthermore it appeared that she was reaping the fruits of her confidence and daring—and reaping them not only on the battlefield but also among the uncommitted nations on its fringe. For with British land and air power extending itself across the shores of North Africa and the Royal Navy reigning almost unchallenged in the Med., Spain was less tempted than she might have been by the generous urgings of the Axis—solicitously offering aid should she care to march against Gibraltar—while Greece was sustained in her struggle against the legions of Mussolini. Turkey, too, had been strengthened in her resolve to defend her neutrality, and there were signs that the French were beginning to stir from their morbid obsession with past shame to look with new optimism towards the future. Yes, all in all the New Year had opened on a distinctly promising note. Rommel was still unknown, the Japs looked like staying out of the fray for ever, the Americans were becoming more helpful every day: the Tide, it was felt, had turned . . .

*   *   *

To Jolly Jack, in Scapa, the change in the nation's fortunes was, however, a little less apparent. Nor did the climate do much to buck him up. Winter glittered harshly on the Flow's unsmiling surface, and the bald hills around the anchorage brooded sullenly through mist and sleet. The sun, on the rare occasions when it succeeded in breaking through, was a pale yellow. It looked remarkably like an underdone fried egg, and as regards its inability to generate heat lived up to its appearance. Convoy work, though vital, was tedious and harsh. Our feet froze in their seaboots, the thickest of balaclavas failed to warm our ears, leave was a bygone dream and drama was non-existent. In fact, as one of the lads put it, we'd lost our chance of flipping glory, and would probably peg out with pneumonia while playing Nanny to a collier!

For the Navy there could not be an all-decisive battle—not unless the Germans were bent on suicide. Nor did Hitler's designs on the Aegean States and Russia reduce by one iota his destructive designs on our ocean life-line. Thus there was no let-up in *Electra*'s chores, and although the demands on her valour were few the exactions made on her strength and patience grew ever more considerable.

At the beginning of the year the German surface fleet was ominously quiet. But the lull was not to last for long—on

January 22nd the *Scharnhorst* and *Gneisenau* were to make their celebrated two-month-long sortie into the Atlantic. And in the meanwhile the U-boats were increasing in numbers and improving in organisation. The "wolf-pack" system had begun to operate, and though the three German aces who had initiated it—Prien, Kretschmer and Schekpe—were soon to be disposed of, the losses from their depredations were (rightly) forecast as "severe". The long-range bombers were active too, sinking 90,000 tons of shipping in a month: for there were few protecting aircraft available and many of the merchantmen possessed only the most ineffective ack-ack armament. The Kondors and the Dorniers had an easy prey.

And lastly there had to be tackled our old enemy the sea, relentless in its pressure, impervious to threat of counter-action—the hardest foe of all.

Once, with the weather unexpectedly kind, *Electra* was heading back for Scapa after escorting a lone merchant ship as far south as the Bristol Channel. It was a lovely afternoon, we were in comparatively safe waters; it was time to relax.

A Coastal Command Anson had picked us up when we were still fairly close to the shore, and had bumbled around our masthead to pass the time of day by Aldis lamp before resuming its patrol; flying in ever-widening circles across the sea. At first there had been some interest in its progress, but the effort of watching another fellow working can, in itself, become fatiguing: and, as the aircraft dropped astern, we had lost sight of it, and turned to other things.

Yet to Allen, the gunlayer on X gun, that disregarded Anson was heaven-sent. A P.O. of the keenest type, he didn't take kindly to relaxing, and had hardly known what to do with himself on such a boring day. Then along had come the aircraft—a splendid opportunity to liven up his gun-crew; the ideal target for a laying and training exercise. Promptly—full of enthusiasm—he roused the men from their semi-torpor.

And the placid rhythm of *Electra*'s afternoon was shattered by a staccato volley of shouted orders . . .

Yes, Allen was keen; and a sight too ruddy keen, mumbled, disgruntedly, his reluctant crew. But Allen's eyes were sharp, exceeding sharp—so sharp that he was able to follow the manœuvres of the Anson when, to most of the men, it was quite invisible against the shimmering water. For, having got the aircraft in his sights, he held it there. In fact it was Allen, and Allen alone, who still had the Anson's movements taped at the vital moment when, wave-hopping on the far horizon, it suddenly faltered, tilted sideways, scraped its wing-tip on the surface of the water, and plunged like a plummet straight into the Drink . . .

One of the crew was missing; but we managed to save the rest—three men who owed their lives to a zealous and able petty officer who didn't take kindly to "relaxing"; the fellow they said was "a sight too ruddy keen".

*　　　*　　　*

Time after time had *Electra* rounded the Old Man of Hoy; snarling and straining in every plate, plunging her bows heavily into the rolling waters of the North Atlantic. Time after time, streaming green-white pennants of foam from her stem, had she swept upwards from the valleys of the wind-driven ocean before reeling corkscrew-wise into the seething turmoil of the trough, or else, on rare days of calm, skimmed with her wake like a snowy plume behind her, across the black surface of a sinisterly silent sea. Her spells in harbour were brief, her stint was in the wilderness outside; where the grey and rusty merchantmen struggled and clawed their way to Halifax, Nova Scotia, unseen by the folk on shore who relied on them for their bread and butter, and the oil that was the blood of the country, and the ammunition that was needed for its guns. She grew visibly older beneath the battering of the waters; her skin peeled and salt wrinkles spread around her hull, yet we patched up her scars and remembered her former beauty, and much though we cussed, we cared.

In October, having limped home after a bashing from the elements that had filled the sick bay with casualties, we had celebrated Taranto and the Fleet Air Arm's disablement of three Italian battleships. Now, in March, we were celebrating once more, and this time it was the victory of Matapan where Cunningham's men had sunk four of Mussolini's heavy cruisers and a couple of large destroyers. It seemed that we were *always* celebrating, said someone, with considerable exaggeration—and always the drinks were in honour of somebody else's victory. Why, even the *Scharnhorst* and *Gneisenau* affair, which had started promisingly enough with the enemy being sighted and chased, had ended in disappointment. We hadn't had a chance of firing a shot, and today, their ten weeks of raiding over, the Germans were home and dry in Brest. Poor old *Electra*, we snivelled—always the blushing bridesmaid, and never the blushing bride!

By the end of April the Mediterranean picture had changed. And changed dramatically. For while our ship still shivered in the blast of the northern winds, her sisters in the south were ablaze beneath the fury of the enemy. He attacked from beneath an emerald sea, he attacked from out of a sapphire sky. On land, the panzers had poured into the Balkans, and had dashed out of Tripoli into Libya. At sea, when the Navy intervened to save the remnants of the expeditionary force to Greece, it was presented with a bill that proved impossible to evade.

With neither cloud nor rain to give them cover, the much-tried ships ploughed grimly to the shore; to show up off sun-baked beaches like fine-drawn etchings. With every detail of them sharply defined to the questing Stuka crews, and with only the smoke of their guns to blur their outlines or give protection to their nakedness, they dared the impossible; and their loss was heavy.

Such altered fortunes in the South most certainly did not make us more fond of our uneventful daily routine. Nor did we feel very happy at being so far removed from what seemed to have become, quite suddenly, the fulcrum of events. The Navy, even when swollen to war-time size, is always very much of a family, and there was hardly a ship in the Home Fleet which did not have its own close link with one of the hard-pressed vessels in the south. Thus the losses sustained there, which included such readily remembered destroyers as *Wryneck* and *Diamond*, affected us in a peculiarly personal sort of way, and we were inspired by more than the usual military considerations in our desire to avenge them. And yet, though our tempers were high, the chances of indulging them seemed almost maddeningly limited.

Then May came, and the eve of the invasion of Crete. By the end of this battle—this conquest of an island from the air—there would not be a mess deck in our flotilla but had been bereaved of a former chum, not a wardroom but had not lost a brother. By the 22nd, however, we had problems of our own. The enemy surface forces had struck into the North Atlantic, and it seemed that at last we were to get our chance of action.

*   *   *

A Coastal Command Spitfire saw them first—two dark and menacing shapes, their camouflage blending with the shadowed water. A trio of satellite destroyers screened them from torpedo attack from seaward, the land enclosed their flanks in its protective paw, the black hills of Kors Fiord were at their back. The mighty *Bismarck* was ready to come out. In company with the cruiser *Prinz Eugen* the world's most powerful battleship was poised at the gateway to the Outer Seas.

Only later, when the planes of another formation dropped flares over the anchorage—by then deserted—did Group North begin to realise that the British had perhaps suspected that something unusual was happening among the inlets and islets of the Bergen coastline. But it was now too late for Berlin to intervene; the die was cast, and the operation must go on.

The squadron had sailed from Poland just two days earlier on the first lap of a journey that was intended to make commerce-raiding history. Its departure had been treated as top secret, and elaborate preparations had been approved to receive it on its emergence into the open sea. Seven oilers and supply vessels, several U-boats and two scout craft had been placed in strategic areas in the Arctic and the North Atlantic. Fighter cover and destroyer support had been organised to give maximum protection in coastal waters; long-range patrols of Focke-Wulf bombers were to watch for any signs of hostile preparation among the Fleet at Scapa Flow.

The operation on which the force was engaged had been christened by the disarmingly innocent title of *Rheinuebung* (Rhine Exercise), but it was certainly worthy of all the hard work that the planners had put into it. For if successful it would wreak mass destruction among the Allied convoys and cause complete disruption, for weeks on end, of the complicated network of supply on which Britain relied not only for her armament, but for life itself.

But, unfortunately for the Germans, three things had gone wrong with the enterprise at its start. The ships had hoped to escape from the Baltic undetected, but the Admiralty was informed of their northward move as soon as they appeared off the Kattegat. Lutjens had planned to get out in April, but had suffered a fortnight's delay as a result of the *Prinz Eugen* sustaining damage from a mine. It had been expected that wireless monitoring and air observation would alert the squadron to any British counter moves, but the Fleet received its news by telegraph, and bad weather kept the recce planes away . . .

On the twenty-second of the month a Maryland aircraft of the Fleet Air Arm confirmed that the Germans had left their temporary lair, and the bulk of the Home Fleet sailed a few hours later. But even before the Maryland's report the 2nd Battle-Cruiser Squadron had been ordered to the north. Six destroyers accompanied the *Hood* and the *Prince of Wales*, and *Electra* was one of them. The hunt was on, and we were ahead of the pack.

*   *   *

It was 11 p.m. and the Scapa sky was bare of stars. The signal to raise steam had just been received and Chiefie McLeod, conscientious as ever, was off to the engine room, without even stopping to finish his smoke. Not, on the face of it, that there was any need for such indecent haste. *Electra* was always being ordered to "raise steam", they seldom left her at rest for long, and the signal was of a routine nature—allowing the ship four hours to prepare for sea. But McLeod never wasted a moment. He could well have afforded to dally a little longer, could at least have treated himself to another pull on that battered briar. And yet he did not.

Now, as he hastened along the companionway, Mac wondered rather sourly what sort of damn dull escort job they'd given the ship this time, and spared a passing thought or two for the latest manifestation of that conversational chestnut—a "break-out" of the *Bismarck*. Wonderful how such rumours get about, he thought, and wonderful too was the gullibility with which the crew received them.

"Raise Steam With Despatch!" This second, far more imperative command—following the first within a matter of minutes—meant that the time available for *Electra*'s preparations had been cut by half; it meant there was Something Up. But Mac took the news with philosophic calm. No doubt, he reflected, they would be getting into a hell of a flap on deck; but here, in the familiar fug of the engine room, the V.I.P.'s of the ship—the workers without whose professional skill she couldn't hope to move—had merely to increase by a fraction the rhythm of their effort. They were easily able to meet the Owner's new requirements and he, McLeod, had no special need to drive them. Every inch of the gleaming mechanism around him was working perfectly: its functional efficiency was his delight. And his men were excellent too, although he would never tell them so. Now, recalling less disparagingly than before the rumour about the *Bismarck*'s sailing, Mac was appreciative of the consolations derived from his good conscience: the ship must be ready within two hours—yet still there would be time to spare. Then came another order, "Raise Steam With All Despatch."

Up top a youngster asked P.O. Tingle: "Just what does the latest signal mean, P.O.?"

"In language that YOU would understand," said the Yeoman heavily, "it's take your finger out and *get cracking!*"

*   *   *

The Captain felt that the importance of the occasion would excuse the mild excitement that had crept into his heart, and the quiet smile that he found impossible to conceal. For this time the news of *Bismarck*'s emergence from the Baltic was unquestionably genuine, and unless she chose to stay in Norwegian waters the only doubt remaining concerned the route she would adopt for her break-through into the Atlantic. She might risk a southerly run, passing between Iceland and the Faroes, or else she might sweep to the far north and then come south-westwards by way of the Denmark Strait. But either alternative would present peculiar problems to the hunters, and May had no illusions.

Should the battleship take the southerly course she would be nearer to the main British force at Scapa, but she would also be nearer to the convoys. And should she take the northerly route her capacity to manœuvre would be restricted—at the beginning of the Denmark Strait—to a 40-mile stretch of open water between the Greenland ice cap and the tip of Iceland. But the Strait widened very rapidly, and the weather, too, would prove useful to the Germans. There would be fog, ice, and mirage effects conspiring to confuse the pursuers, and perhaps extend a protective screen for *Bismarck* for many miles into the North Atlantic.

All in all, as May saw it, the chase would be arduous and the quarry, if cornered, would prove a cunning and ferocious foe. And yet, paradoxically, his spirits were serene; he felt as though a weight had been lifted from his mind. Better by far to have a *Bismarck* that was "out" than a *Bismarck* that remained in harbour, "a threat in being" and ready to pounce unseen. He was proud of this destroyer, *Electra*; he was pleased with her company, whom tedium could not spoil. He was modestly confident in his capacity for leadership and the ship, he knew, would do her duty whatever the call that might be made upon her. So in the meanwhile—very sensibly and not "fussing" anyone—he stood quietly at the apex of this pyramid of activity; a man who was apparently relaxed, a man who was not missing much, a man who was waiting for the company he led, and in whom he trusted, to show the results of the schooling that he and Sammy and the Navy in general had given them . . .

An organ loft of pipes, each in its white asbestos jacket, a row of gleaming turbines and brass-rimmed pressure gauges, an aisle of slippery steel plates . . . As McLeod, well satisfied with his domain's well being, cast one last sharp but affectionate look around, he sniffed nostalgically the warm moist air, then climbed almost reluctantly the narrow ladder that led him to the uninspiring world outside.

"Steam for twenty knots, Sir . . . the third boiler will be ready in the next half hour."

"Very good," said May.

Number One arrived on the bridge. He, too, had been busy.

"Ship secured for sea, Sir . . . Slip Rope Wove."

"Very good," said May.

He glanced at his wrist-watch. Only forty minutes had elapsed since the Flagship's signal; and only the Slip Rope—a slim wire hawser—now secured *Electra* to the buoy.

5

"Hood Sunk!"

AS *Electra* passed through the Gate and left the booms behind her all hands were occupied with the preliminaries of action—priming depth charges, arming torpedoes, checking the guns. "Ready-use" ammunition came up from the magazine, the Asdic staff sent out exploratory "pings", Doc Seymour went into sinister conference with the S.B.A. A tense expectancy seemed to pervade the ship, a sense of satisfaction too. The troops were in good form.

Admiral Lutjens, before sailing from Norway, had given his German crew the traditional hunters' toast of "Good Luck and a Good Bag", but we too were hoping for a successful chase and kill. The role of the Second Battle-Cruiser Squadron was to race ahead of the Fleet to a point off the coast of Iceland, and position itself to intervene in whichever of the two main approach lanes that the enemy might use. But even should Lutjens succeed in evading us, by profiting from the weather and the thinness of the cruiser screen, his situation would still remain unenviable: *King George V*, *Repulse*, and the carrier *Victorious* would have to be evaded, and we, once re-alerted, would be following in his tracks.

Such then, was the plan of action as seen to *Electra*. But our assessment of its absolute effectiveness was incautious, to say the least. For a needle is notoriously difficult to find when concealed in a haystack, and even the greatest of ships is reduced to needle-size proportions when you come to look for it in the immensity of the sea. Again, to stretch the same analogy a little further, a needle at least stays put, but a raiding force does not; and a needle cannot think, but your German "oppo" does! Yet we had waited too long for our opportunity to readily believe that it would pass us by. The ocean was wide, and the enemy was wily, but it was up to My Lords to fathom out the snags; for we were too busy. In fact, among the grey ships that now drove steadily into the northern night there remained only one fear to fret and fidget . . . Had the Germans at last appreciated the fact that we were aware of their presence? Were they likely to have second thoughts, and turn suddenly for home?

* * *

Bill Brayley grinned, then jabbed his thumb towards the dark shadow on our quarter. "Jerry's going to have a bit of a shock when he sees *her* ahead of him," he said. When it's *Hood v*. Hitler I back British all the way . . ."

"You've a discerning taste," I said.

On my way to the wardroom I ran into the Captain's steward: "Think we'll have luck, Sir, if we catch up with the blighters, I mean?"

"Luck? Of course we'll have luck!" The answer came pat. "But we won't *need* luck, Gretton, not with the *Hood* for company!"

Yes, we were proud of ourselves, and of the company we kept: with *Hood* to support us we felt we could tackle anything. *Hood* was our "chummy", there was no beating her . . .

Throughout the years—and twenty-four of them had passed since the date of her launching—*Hood* had become the living symbol of Britain's sea-power. She was almost legendary.

Nor was it difficult to assess why this was so, for her figure and vitality were so impressive that her age and her failings were all too easy to overlook. With a displacement of 42,000 tons she was reputedly the world's largest warship, and with a speed of 31 knots she was also one of the fastest—outpacing in rough weather some of the swiftest fleet destroyers. She had "classical" lines, she was good to look upon, and she carried a heavy punch—the punch of eight 15-inch guns.

Yet although such statistics were impressive, and true enough in themselves, the deductions to which they gave rise were both misleading and dangerous. It was said, with some truth, that the bitter lessons learned from Jutland, and the havoc wreaked there among the battle-cruisers, had been incorporated in *Hood*'s construction. But wishful thinking had carried the reassurance further, until it was popularly believed that she had a strength that matched her size, and that she was foolproof, invincible, and fit to beat all comers. And this was false.

For although a "capital ship", under the restrictive clauses of the Washington Treaty—limiting Britain to a 15-15 ratio in capital ships with the U.S.A. and a 15-9 ratio with Japan— *Hood* was never a *battleship*, despite her size. She was built for speed, not for a slogging match. *Nelson*, built only nine years after her, and only three-quarters her size, had six inches of deck armour to ward against bombs or steeply falling shells; and *Bismarck* and *Tirpitz* were even better covered. Yet *Hood*'s deck protection, even at maximum, was only three inches thick.

In short, *Hood* was a great ship—but she was also an old ship. Vast advances—both as regards protection and hitting power— had been made in warship design throughout the world since the date of her launching. And the fact that she had been years ahead of her time when first designed still could not compensate for the brutal reality, that she was years behind her time in 1941. Yet it was not only the layman who was dazzled by the apparent lustre of this Queen of the Battle-Cruisers for even those who ought to have been in possession of the facts, and ought to have known better, were similarly deceived. The misgivings of the few were ignored or derided as alarmist, and—with "economy" the catchword—several years went by before they gained official credence. But, by then it was too late! *Hood*'s belated reconstruction was promised for early 1939, but at the last minute it had to be postponed. The war clouds were gathering fast and the Navy needed every ship that could be mustered. Hitherto Britain had not been able to spare the cash —but now she could not afford the time . . .

It is all too easy, however, to be wise after the event and, to be candid, I must admit that few of us on *Electra* were endowed with a comparable wisdom at the time when, the prelude over, the curtain began to lift and the tragic players took their cue. For even those of us who had heard the grapevine rumours concerning *Hood*'s deficiencies did not seriously consider that those deficiencies might have fatal consequences. This was our "chummy"—considerate, protective, a friend of whose size and loyalty we could well be proud. We would have considered it inconceivable had we been told that she was soon to disappear for ever beneath the impact of three enemy shells— we would have refused to credit anything so dreadful as that her hospitable company—over 1,400 strong—would pass from all human knowledge in less than half the time it takes to smoke a cigarette . . .

Electra had worked with *Hood* in every type of weather and in every condition of war. But never had the battle-cruiser looked more impressive than she did today—as she drove towards Iceland and her destiny, as she narrowed by half a mile a minute the distance between her and the fateful German guns. *Hood*, when we steamed out of Scapa, was no longer the world's largest warship, for unbeknown to us, the new German battleships had exceeded their published displacement by 10,000 tons. But, as the cold dawn broadened over the slate-grey sea, and as *Electra* bucketed through the creamy fringes of the squadron's wake, we waited with confidence and pride the outcome of the voyage. With *Hood* beside us we felt we could tackle anything.

*   *   *

"Enemy to the north of the Denmark Strait!"

It was 7.22 on the evening of May 23rd when the County class cruiser *Suffolk*, equipped with the new search device of Radar, identified the Germans and sent her signal to the Fleet. But *Electra* didn't get the report until later, when it was relayed by *Suffolk*'s sister, *Norfolk*. The moment the buzz got round we had a hundred and one requests for confirmation, and when the news was declared official there was a sigh of relief so intense, so universal, that it seemed to come up from the straining fibres of the ship herself. Everyone went about his duties with a quite unusual liveliness, yet with a studied attempt at nonchalance that was anything but convincing. All but four of the destroyers had been sent off to refuel; so that we could count ourselves fortunate to be in at the kill.

Further reports arrived. We heard from *Suffolk*, succeeding so mysteriously in her equivocal task of keeping the enemy at arm's length and yet never letting go of him. And there was fresh news of *Norfolk* who, seeking visual contact, had approached within 10,000 yards of the Germans, and had come under their fire before taking evasive action, escaping unscathed under the cover of her smoke.

May believed in keeping all informed—to the best of his ability—of the progress of events, and each signal was no sooner plotted than it was "put into English" and passed on to the troops. Our interest was intense, so too was our admiration for the cruisers. We knew nothing, or next to nothing, of *Suffolk*'s "magic eye", and to many of us the fact that an enemy task force could be traced as two "blips" on a small black screen would have smacked a bit of witchcraft; but we did know what could happen to our distant friends should the *Bismarck* turn upon them, and thus, as the devoted cruisers continued in their classic function of "report and shadow", it was impossible for even the dullest to be unmoved by the occasion's drama, or to avoid reflections as to the strange manner in which the stage was set.

At the time of the first sighting, the distance between the squadrons had been equivalent to the distance between London and John O' Groats. Yet by now the gallant "Counties"—side-stepping smartly from their baited quarry's fire, hugging his flanks and never losing sight of him—were pinpointing the location of the enemy on this wide expanse of ocean as accurately as if the speeding ships were as stationary as church steeples set down on an ordnance map. The gap between the opposing forces was closing rapidly—at the rate of sixty miles an hour!

*   *   *

It was ten o'clock, and the start of the North Atlantic twilight when we went to Full Action Stations. Only one question was on everybody's lips—"Will we be lucky?" And there was only one reply—"Of course we will."

Admiral Holland had long since increased the speed of the battle-cruisers to 27 knots and had told us to follow as best we could. But we, anxious not to miss anything, had succeeded in building up to 31 knots, and were now disposed ahead of the Fleet. An artist would have found in the setting a subject worthy of his skill, with *Electra*, at maximum revs, slicing straight through the waves, the waters rising like green-white walls around her bows, and sheets of spray shooting up and over the ship like heavy rain. Our sisters, the rest of the destroyers, were often quite invisible beneath the water they displaced, and the battlewaggons rose and fell with the sound of thunder as they pressed majestically on, jettisoning great streams of water from around their cable chains, and steaming around their "nostrils"—the gaping hawse-holes that flanked their bows—like a pair of angry dragons.

The Admiral, we felt, was in no mood to waste time, and wished to close with the Germans at the earliest possible opportunity, and in the Strait itself, rather than risk them evading us in the broad waters of the south. This was, of course, pure guesswork on our part for we had nothing solid on which to base our estimates. But the theory seemed to make sense. Conditions were just right for a night destroyer action, and with "Our Old Man" as Senior Officer of the destroyers we felt confident of our ability to play a worthwhile part. We knew that the Germans might be fitted with the new-fangled R.D.F. and we knew that their crews were courageous, and that their gunnery was good. But such considerations did not trouble us: we would have been less than men if they had. What we could not know, however, was that Fortune had already swung against us, and that when the *Hood* and the *Prince of Wales* came up against the enemy, all the theoretical odds in their favour as regards weight of armament would be blown away in the first three salvoes. Nor could we foresee that, when the final testing time arrived for the too-old veteran and the too-young recruit, we of the destroyers would no longer be with them. Instead we'd be out of sight behind the far horizon; frustrated, bewildered, and powerless to help.

*   *   *

Midnight, and there are still five hours to go before the twilight gives way to the steel-blue glare of the northern sky. The wind is howling down the Strait, the sea is speckled by drifting ice, the glass is falling. *Suffolk*'s radar range is not very great— it's less than the distance that the German guns can span. And *Norfolk*, with an even more primitive radar set, relies on her sister's guidance, and the sharp eyes of her look-outs. The icecap to the west has ceased to distract and torment the watchers with its glare, but the night is unusually dark (by northern standards), and the enemy is doing his best to use it. Yet for five hours, despite the weather and the occasional attempt at reprisal from the *Bismarck* and her consort, the British ships have maintained their station, gliding like grey phantoms port and starboard of the Germans' wake, and dogging their every move.

They are highly vulnerable, the men of the "Counties"— the slightest mistake, or one swift reversal of the *Bismarck*'s course, can bring them death. And, with strict wireless silence, they are very lonely too; for Scapa is a thousand miles away, and they are unaware of the swift approach of the battle-cruisers. But they are perky, despite such snags. They know how well they have done the job assigned them, and they are confident that this time, whatever else may happen, there will be no repetition of the S and G affair.* They will keep in touch with the *Bismarck* come what may.

But five minutes pass, and the picture has tragically changed. Radar contact is lost . . . is not regained . . . and a sudden crisis confronts the cruisers. Deprived of their mechanical "eye" they must seek somehow for another visual sighting. But this is easier said than done, for down comes the snow! It falls like a great soft blanket, it blots out sea and sky, it makes mock of the men's devotion, it threatens all their hopes. As the weather worsens, the *Suffolk* and the *Norfolk* grope wildly to regain contact with their giant adversaries; but they grope like blind men, and they grope in vain.

*   *   *

To our silent squadron, now only a hundred miles or so from the enemy, the cruisers' loss of contact created considerable dismay, and a change of plan. It seemed reasonable to

* The *Scharnhorst* and *Gneisenau*, raiding during late January to March, evaded patrols and slipped into the shipping lanes.

suppose that Lutjens, having temporarily freed himself from the irritating surveillance of *Suffolk* and *Norfolk*, would have swung off his previous course in order to make the parting permanent. He could not go very far to the west because of the ice, but a south-easterly course might enable him, should we continue on our present bearing, to slip between us and the Icelandic shore and maybe double back for the north again . . .

Such evidently was the opinion of Admiral Holland, for he suddenly ordered a change of course and we turned to starboard, proceeding due north, with the apparent intention of intercepting Lutjens' force on its (assumed) line of divergence from the original plot.

Today, when its wisdom can be appraised in the light of its tragic consequences, this move has been criticised, but to us, at the time of its inception, it was a commonsense reaction to the circumstances then prevailing. We had an unbounded confidence in Holland, both as a leader and as a man. And, though we could not hope to know his intentions, his turn towards the north seemed to represent the logical counter to the move we thought the Germans would adopt. But at the conclusion of the sweep we were no wiser than we had been when it had first begun. There was no sign of the enemy, no news from the cruisers, and no hope of flying off a seaplane—the weather was too bad. We had steamed for some sixty miles, we had wasted precious hours: night, and the opportunity for surprise attack was fleeing fast, bright expectancy had changed to gloom.

From out of this period of confusion arose a dreadful dilemma for the Admiral, and a question of priorities that could not easily be resolved. For there were two possible explanations for his failure to make contact with the enemy . . .

One: that the *Bismarck* and the *Prinz Eugen* had not deviated from their original course, but had continued on it steadily, and might, even now, be escaping towards the south-west.

Two: that the Germans had rumbled our presence and,

deciding to avoid the risk of a decisive action so early in their cruise, had turned for home; with the idea of making a second sortie at a more propitious time.

But which possibility was the most likely to work out? And which enemy move should he best ward against—a break-out into the Atlantic, or a return to the north—maybe to base? Few, I imagine, would willingly have changed places with the man who, at the time such momentous questions had to be answered, had only guesswork to guide him. Nor is it very surprising that he should have been unfortunate in his choice of solution. For Holland's only fault was "to try too hard": he attempted to anticipate *both* of the enemy's alternatives, and in so doing was doomed.

It was on the morning of the 24th when the Admiral implemented the second movement of the tragedy that was to cost him his life and the lives of 1,400 of his company. First the battle-cruisers were turned about to counteract what he now quite rightly regarded as the most probable intention of the enemy, a break-through to the south. Next he ordered the destroyers to stay behind and continue with the search as a sort of insurance policy against Contingency Number Two— a getaway to the north.

Shortly after 2.15 a.m. Commander May opened formation and *Electra* and her sister ships, in accordance with Holland's latest order, spread out at fifteen-mile intervals to "search towards the north". A few minutes later the battlewagons were dipping their massive superstructures below the skyline and steaming at high speed towards the south. *Hood* was in the lead—it was the last we saw of her. Her fate had been decided—the squadron had been split.

*   *   *

An hour passed and the sea quietened; visibility cleared and the wind dropped; we had all the promise of a lovely day—

but only in respect of the weather, for the outlook, otherwise, was dim. We were still combing the Strait, without result; we were still doing our job, but without enthusiasm. The destroyers, pursuing parallel courses, could cover a "front" of some eighty miles but—"defeatism", "intuition", call it what you will—we had the feeling that the effort was not going to yield much profit: we were on to a red herring. We were convinced by now that the Germans were well away, and our memories of the high hopes of the previous two days served only to humiliate and mock. The escape of the *Scheer* . . . the escape of the *Scharnhorst* and *Gneisenau* . . . it seemed that the enemy, thanks to such accidents as the size of the sea, the unpredictability of the climate, and Britain's chronic shortage of cruisers, was always to have the last laugh. The prospect was depressing . . .

At break of dawn the ship's company, after being at full action stations throughout the night, were stood down and the Duty Watch took over. Davies and I were among these unfortunates, and thus while others—the lucky devils—were free to catch up with their lost sleep, it was our chilly duty to remain on the bridge and attempt to be alert. We were not very good company, not even for each other, for we were too disgusted with the apparent failure of the chase to want to talk much. We were brassed off, temperamental, and to be handled with care, and when McLeod, still in his white overalls after remedying some minor fault in the engine-room, came up for a breath of air he said he'd never seen such a dismal pair of crows in his life.

It so happened that Mac's arrival had coincided with that of Horne, bearing a jug of tea; so we had to stifle rude rejoinders —for the moment at least—while our Engineer, oblivious to our glares, began to review the tactical situation, pronouncing it as highly favourable. For once the optimist, he reckoned that we were on the best bet of all and that we should pick up either the *Bismarck* or the *Prinz Eugen* during the forenoon.

"And then?" I queried sourly.

"What do you mean . . . 'and then'?"

"Well, we won't have the battlewagons handy . . . so how fast can the Wee McLeod run?"

"Bloody Fifth Columnist! . . ."

We laughed, then I glanced at my watch. It was just six o'clock.

"Let's face it, Chiefie, we're going the wrong way. We haven't a hope in hell."

"I would'na be sure of that," said Mac. A second later there came from the Yeoman an excited cry.

"FROM HOOD. ENEMY IN SIGHT. AM ENGAGING."

*   *   *

It is the most dramatic moment we have ever known—and it takes us completely by surprise. For a fraction we stand stock-still—only half comprehending, wondering if we've heard aright. Then the picture springs to life again and the Yeoman is clattering off to tell the Captain. Davies is handing over the chart-table, and the usually phlegmatic Mac is hopping up and down like an excited sparrow: "How far off is she? Can they keep the party going till we get there? Give me the course and I'll fix the speed!"

The troops cluster around; grinning, backslapping, and I try to pour cold water from a great height on their enthusiasm, being vaguely conscious that it's a bit undignified. But I fail lamentably, for I myself am carried away by it all—it's impossible not to be. What's it that Chiefie says? "When the *Bismarck*'s hull comes up like a barn door—just burn the incense in front of your mouldies, Guns, then press the tit and you can't go wrong!"

The news has spread through the ship as if by magic. Never has the Grapevine worked so fast, nor the Captain (it would seem) so slowly. Where is he? What's detaining him? When will he give us the word to go? Then the Yeoman appears on the bridge, and his expression gives us a shock. For just what's happened to the feverish enthusiasm of five minutes earlier? And why the drawn face? He looks like a ghost. Impatiently I turn away. "Any further news?"

In a dull, flat voice he says:

"From *Prince of Wales*, Sir . . . *HOOD* SUNK!"

There is a stunned silence. Then the blood rushes to my head and I flare at him in anger: "You can keep your sense of humour to yourself!"

Another pause. And there are tears in his voice as he answers: "My God, Sir, but it's true, Sir. It's just come through—I have told the Captain."

May's calm voice breaks through our bewilderment: "What's our course to her last position, Davies?"

Harry, working like an automaton, gives the plot and adds: "We have sixty miles to go!"

"Then bring her round."

My hand rings down—hard—and May turns to other business. Yeoman Tingle's face has gone chalk-white but his pencil is poised efficiently over the message pad—"Make immediately our course and speed to the others and tell them to conform . . ."

Hood sunk? But it can't be true! Mac leaves the voice-pipe. "Are we sure there's no mistake?"

"Sorry, Chief. It's true enough. *P.O.W.* says that *Hood* is sunk, and that she herself is continuing with the action. And that's all we know." His voice is cold, expressionless: then he warms up. "In the meanwhile, we've work to do and I shall need everything you can give. I want to get to the scene as soon as we can. We'll still be needed to pick up the survivors."

Electra's bows begin to veer to port: the stern water froths and hisses beneath the screws. I look at my watch: the damn thing must have stopped. It is now only ten minutes past six, according to the dial, and thus only ten minutes have passed since the receipt of the first signal, giving us the news of *Hood*'s opening fire. Only ten minutes? Impossible! I mumble to Davies: "What's the time?" He squints downwards abstractedly, then says, astounded: "Good God, its only ten past six."

Our watches are still ticking . . . and the *Hood* is dead.

*   *   *

As *Electra* turned at speed towards the south we began to concentrate once more upon the practical—working out the time of our arrival in the area of the sinking, and seeing what effective action we could take. The motor-boat and a whaler had been stove-in during the night and thus, with only one boat still serviceable, the First Lieutenant and the Chief Buffer had to prepare alternative aids to rescue. Anticipating hundreds of survivors, the troops got to work with a will. Scrambling nets were rigged, heaving lines and lifebelts were placed handy on the deck. Doc, too, made preparations. His sick-bay was always ready for most emergencies but now, in consultation with the Coxswain, he planned to turn the mess deck into a hospital, in order to cope with the expected overflow of patients, and instructed Gretton to make sure that the officers' bunks were made up, in case they, also, were required. The steward looked a little worried. "But shouldn't I tell the officers about it first, Sir?"

"*Can* do . . . if you really want to," answered Doc, at first somewhat puzzled. Then light dawned: "Good gracious, Gretton. They won't expect to be *asked*!"

The destroyers were whipping through the water at maximum speed, and at times were identifiable only by the "white moustaches" which flared house-high around their noses. Their ensigns were straining and hammering from the stays; green waters foamed behind them. We had estimated, originally, that we would be in position by eight-fifteen, but thanks to Chiefie and his men we were improving on this forecast, and shortly before eight o'clock our hopes were raised by the sight of smoke, blown like a plume against the south-western sky.

Doc, always solicitous for the well-being of others, pulled me aside and whispered: "Guns, don't you think we ought to send some of the younger chaps below? Many of the survivors may be wounded; it won't be a pretty sight . . ."

I answered abruptly, all on edge: "Bloody nonsense! We'll need everyone we've got to help the poor devils inboard!"

But we were arguing on a hypothesis that did not exist; for as *Electra* closed we realised that our "clue" was false—the smoke came from the dirty funnel of a solitary merchantman, scurrying desperately for home. But otherwise? The sea was empty—or so it seemed. Our journey had been in vain—or so we felt. Yet, even as the horrible thought occurred that *Electra* was off course, the Masthead sang out and the first grim proofs of Harry's navigational accuracy appeared, quite suddenly, on the rolling swell—a large patch of oil ahead, a tangled pile of small wreckage . . . *and that was all.*

But where were the boats, the rafts, the floats . . .? And the men, *where* were the men? I thought of how we'd last seen *Hood*; and I thought of her impressive company. Like a small army they'd looked as they mustered for divisions. Then I thought of my words to Doc . . . "We'll need everyone we've got to help the poor devils inboard."

But, almost immediately, came another hail, and far over to starboard we saw three men—two of them swimming, one on a raft. But on the chilling waters around them was no other sign of life . . .

Chiefie exclaimed incredulously as we looked again: "But there *must* be more of them—there can't be only *three* of them! Where the hell are all the others? "

But there were no "others" . . . those scattered specks were all that remained of the *Hood*'s brave complement. Just three men now remained, three out of 1,419; three men who had lived through a catastrophe that had destroyed 42,000 tons of steel in less than four minutes of flame and shock.

It was a moment never to be erased from the memory. It was a revelation of horror.

We began our rescue work. The sea-boat was dropped and, with Coale in charge, went away on a forlorn search among the wreckage, while *Electra*, in the meanwhile, closed the swimmers and our chaps plunged into the water to help them inboard.

The survivors were a remarkable trio.

As the first man was hoisted on to the deck, and found himself surrounded by an audience of gaping and sympathetic matelots, he shook himself angrily, as though freeing himself not only of salt water, but also of bitter memories. "And what's up with you—you poverty-stricken crowd," he said. "Ain't you got no bloody boats?"

The second to be saved asked what ship we were, and when told *Electra* commented in disgust: "Now isn't that just my rotten luck—to be picked up by a *Chatham* ship!"

And then his eyes filled with tears, and he turned away. "My mates," he said. "Oh God . . . my mates!"

But the third survivor was the strangest of them all; I never saw a man more nonchalant, or less put out by his unexpected circumstances.

His raft was about the size of a dining-room chair, and although he was wearing a lifebelt he made no attempt to precipitate his rescue by trying to swim, but sat there quite calmly waiting to be picked up. Heaving lines flew at him from all directions, and a cuss or two as well. Yet he waited there as though taking his ease, until the end of one of the ropes fell directly into his lap. Only then did he graciously permit

himself to be pulled inboard, and, when confronted by Number
One, said with a smile: "So sorry I can't salute, Sir . . . I'm
afraid I've lost my cap!"

He was a midshipman, he added, and probably *Hood*'s
Senior Surviving Officer; and at this, quite suddenly, his sang-
froid seemed to vanish. He tried to stand, but could not; then
Doc briskly intervened: "You've damaged your ankle, and
you're badly shocked as well." He popped him on a stretcher
and had him carried off to the Sick Bay—protesting he was all
right.

May, pondering on the behaviour of his guests, gave us the
first pale smile of the day. "There's one thing the Hun forgets,"
he said. " . . . he'll never beat men like these!"

*　　*　　*

As *Icarus* and *Anthony* joined in the hopeless search for more
survivors, fresh evidence of the violence of *Hood*'s ending was
supplied by the nature of the scanty driftwood debris that now
remained as her only monument.

A desk drawer, full of ratings' documents, came floating
along *Electra*'s side. Such clerical records would have been
"well below", so that the drawer must have been blown
straight from the bowels of the ship by the force of the explosion; and yet when we came to examine our find we discovered that it was completely unscratched, and the documents
were intact. As we studied this useless piece of furniture it
seemed bitterly ironic that the blast had not used its human
victims with an equally freakish tenderness. And this reflection
was to grow upon us when we heard the stories of our rescued
friend; stories of miracles that, alas, were not more widespread,
and embraced but three souls among so many . . .

For at last we had to give up our attempt at further rescue
work as fruitless, and then, with the chase having receded into

the south, and with *Electra* and her sisters most desperately short of oil, we were left with no recourse but to turn gloomily for Iceland—there to refuel and wait for further orders.

We were depressed, and low in spirit, we were cold and extremely tired. But our thoughts—as we heard from the survivors of *Hood*'s last battle—gave us more discomfort than the climate, and our hearts were far heavier than our swollen eyelids . . .

6

"All Sorts make a Navy . . ."

THE first man we got inboard, an Able Seaman, had belonged to the crew of one of *Hood*'s four-inch anti-aircraft guns. Positioned on the boat deck during the opening of the action he could tell us very little—the exchange of fire had lasted for eight minutes, he'd been unconscious for three of them.

When the enemy ships were first sighted he and his mates were so keen to get at them that they had almost broken into a cheer, then they'd waited tensely for *Hood*'s opening thunder,* which followed a quarter of an hour later. But even as the battle-cruiser rolled from the blast of her big 15-inch guns, the *Bismarck* too had fired—hitting home and hitting hard, at 15 miles range and with her very first salvo!

In a flash it seemed to the A.B. that the vast well-ordered world that had been the *Hood* had turned upside down and was falling about his ears. One of the German shells had ripped through the deck beside him, hurling the smooth and spotlesss surface into a jagged confusion of upturned and twisted steel; deluging him beneath a hail of splinters. He hardly knew what was happening, he was deaf from the noise, and still dazed from the shock wave. Only one thing was clear to him—the *Hood* had taken a mortal blow. Then, as he scrambled to his feet, a cloud of dense black smoke poured suffocatingly from

* Said to have been misdirected, and aimed at the *Prinz Eugen*, of similar silhouette.

the hole that the hit had made and was followed almost immediately by a sheet of roaring flame. On one side was a
furnace, on the other the broad Atlantic. So what to do? He
hesitated, then looking upward saw an ammunition locker
come hurtling from the sky towards him, and, quite instinctively, he chose the sea.

No, he told us, he hadn't a clue as to what had happened
after he hit the water. In fact, considering the speed at which
the *Hood* was travelling, and considering the height from which
he'd jumped, it was a wonder he hadn't broken his neck. All
that he did know—and he couldn't get over the horror of it—
was that when he came to on the surface and looked round for
the ship, he found that she had gone. Then he'd had to duck
again as *Prince of Wales*, her guns blazing, came charging up
from astern . . .

The second survivor was a Signalman, who said that *Bismarck* and *Prinz Eugen* had opened fire together, and had
evidently concentrated upon the *Hood*. He couldn't remember
much more, except that there had been a terrific explosion
behind the funnel and that he'd woken up in the Drink.

But Snottie had the strangest adventure. On duty in the
spotting top, about 140 feet above the sea, he had actually been
washed out of one of its windows as the battle-cruiser plunged
into her grave. He told us—if I remember rightly—that he
had been carrying a cup of cocoa to his betters when the ship
received her first blow; then other shells arrived. He had been
"flung about a bit", and didn't know what the hell was happening, save that the compartment was filled mysteriously with
water. But he had no time to wonder, for a moment later he
was struggling for life against the suction that followed the
Hood's death-throes.

I said rather weakly, at the end of his story: "Well, what an
extraordinary escape."

To which he replied, very simply: "Yes . . . I *was* rather lucky."

Many years were to pass before I met Snottie again; only this time he was no longer a Snottie, but a Senior Officer with a distinguished record. We had only a few minutes in which to yarn, but I learned later that he had had three ships sunk under him during his war-time service.

Quite obviously a chap like that is destined for a ripe old age!

*   *   *

When *Electra* arrived in Iceland her tanks were almost empty; but no sooner had she oiled, and landed her survivors, than she was ordered to sea again, this time to escort the *Prince of Wales* to harbour. It was a miserable meeting. The battle-ship—newly commissioned, hardly "worked up", and with technical faults preventing four of her ten big guns from firing—had been in an unenviable position after the disappearance of the *Hood*. *Bismarck* and *Prinz Eugen* had been free to concentrate their full fire upon her, and had done so with deadly purpose. Yet, though temporarily forced to break off the action, the *P.O.W.* had accompanied *Suffolk* and *Norfolk* on the subsequent chase until she had barely enough fuel left to make the trip home.

It was easy to see—as we came up to her—that she had taken heavy punishment. Worse, contact had now been broken off completely and the German task force had, once again, disappeared into the blue. Morale was at zero in the presence of such disaster, for we were not to know that Admiral Holland's tragic endeavour had in fact achieved its main objective by planting in the temporarily victorious *Bismarck* the germ of her own destruction. The *Prince of Wales* had hit the enemy much harder than was thought, and Lutjens, confronted by a heavy loss of oil after the holing of his ship's tanks, had been obliged to abandon his sortie into the West Atlantic. Still further harassed by the attacks of the gallant Swordfish from *Victorious*, he was now wholly absorbed with the problem of returning to base.

Our first intimation of this more favourable turn of events came on the 26th, when a Coastal Command aircraft located the Germans off the Bay of Biscay, and reported that they were steering, to the east, and France. With contact re-established, "Enemy" reports, and signals concerning the dispositions of our own ships commenced to follow each other in quick succession, and once again, though this time as somewhat wistful spectators divorced from hope of action, we found ourselves crowding around the chart to pursue the progress of the hunt. At first, events were confusing, and as each signal was deciphered by Doc and Davies our hopes and apprehensions fluctuated.

We learned that the cruiser *Sheffield* was racing northward, then that she was making contact with the *Bismarck*. We heard that the *Ark Royal* was launching an extremely long-range torpedo attack, in the hope of slowing the enemy while the Home Fleet doubled back to the south. But later came the news that the aircraft, operating in filthy weather, had missed their target, and a general groan went up from we armchair critics—until it turned out that owing to faulty identification, the "target" was not the *Bismarck* but the persevering and patient *Sheffield*! Relieved, we continued to speculate upon the future until, slowly at first and faintly, like the white of an egg in a hot frying-pan, the outline of the giant operation that was being conducted by Admiral Tovey began to take shape. And, as the heat increased, the shape grew firmer—with the *Bismarck* as the yolk.

It seemed on that tremendous day that practically every major ship in the Navy was marching on the Germans. *Rodney* and *King George V* were hastening from the north, and veteran battleships that wouldn't have stood a chance of victory—but were willing to be sacrificed in order to buy time—had abandoned the convoys, and were approaching from west and south. Then the *Ark Royal* struck again; and *Bismarck*, twice hit, had her steering damaged. Soon she was reported to be proceeding at low speed, and on erratic course.

Yet, when night fell, the issue still seemed unresolved, and we waited with impatience as well as envy the outcome of the attack that Vian, with his big Tribals, was to launch during the hours of darkness. This, we reckoned, was the sort of show in which *Electra* could have excelled, and our jealousy was expressed in the slightly spiteful chuckles with which we greeted the signal that *Bismarck* was "still capable of sustained and accurate fire". Soon, however, such unworthy sentiments were replaced by admiration at the ferocity with which the destroyers pressed home their assault. When dawn lit the sea the chart revealed that the hunted German was at bay. The hounds were ready for the kill.

It was just before nine o'clock when Tovey's big guns opened fire. By 10.36 the fight was over. The *Bismarck*, her *coup de grâce* administered by *Dorsetshire*, had concluded her short, but spectacular career by heeling over, a blazing hulk, into the self-same merciless ocean that had so recently seen her triumph. And Lutjens, who had given the Navy such a good hard run, had met his end when on the very threshold of Occupied Europe. Another two or three hours' steaming would have brought the German battleship under the protection of Goering's bombers and the U-boat screen; but such fortune was not to be. Retribution had overtaken her, and very gallantly had she suffered it; fighting to the last. *Bismarck* had outlived our friend the *Hood* by just three days. To us the time had passed like an eternity.

*   *   *

They were on night leave, their first for many months. They had left *Electra* at Rosyth—where she'd arrived as escort to the damaged *Prince of Wales*—and had made a bee-line for Edinburgh, getting hopelessly jugged up. Old Stripey—needless to say—was the worst of the lot, and now the silly so-and-so had passed out on them; gone out like a light!

Fred Castle, he of the Oerlikon, took command. "Lay him out on the deck," he said, and then, this done and Old Stripey none the better for it, he added with resignation: "We'd better find a taxi!"

But this, they discovered, was easier said than done. The blackout confused them, and taxis were hard to get. They made their enquiries at various ports of call but no one seemed able to help, and finally after they'd braced themselves up a bit by an extra mixed or so—to keep out the night air—Fred had to tell them: "Well, mates. There's nothing else for it . . . we'll have to get back to Old Stripey, or he'll die of exposure or get pinched by the coppers."

A fallen comrade, that's what Old Stripey was, they said, and it was high time they put him on his feet. But their senti-mental journey, however praiseworthy, had unexpected com-plications for they'd tucked the corpse away in a fairly quiet spot, and when they emerged from the pub they found that they'd lost their bearings. What was the name of the street? No one had noticed. And in which direction did it lie? To port or starboard of the public bar? After some argument they went due south for a bit, but without result. So then they turned about and headed for the north; but still no good. It was rather like looking for some precious object that you had put away "for safety" in case you lost it. There were times when you could put away a thing *too* safely, so safe in fact that you couldn't find it.

It took them ages to uncover Old Stripey, and when they did eventually catch up with him it was to find that others were busy in the area of search. Two policemen were approaching on a rapidly converging course and, making knots fast, they reached the objective first.

"*That's* a bit of a facer," said Fred, and he and his comrades came to a halt. For, while desertion was unthinkable, they needed time to think; more time than usual, for their reflexes by now were slow.

The policemen bent over Stripey, shaking him vigorously with the obvious intention of bringing him back to life, and Fred was just about to move, apologise, and try and see if they couldn't go bail, when an extraordinary thing occurred . . .

"Before we could do anything," said Fred, explaining it all to his cronies later on, "before we could as much as say a word . . . out of a side street came some civvies, rough types you know, and proper lit up. One of them takes a look at the coppers, then shouts out to his mates: 'Look lads—a couple of bloody bluebottles.' And 'Holy smoke,' another says, 'they're beating the sailor up, the bastards.' And with that there's a proper free-for-all between the cops and the civvies. We stand there for a bit, just watching it all, and then a police whistle blows and more coppers arrive, and I say It's Time To Go, Mates, and we pick up old Stripey and get the hell out of it as fast as our feet can carry us."

So far so good. And *Electra's* luck had held; but although they'd escaped the police they had other problems to contend with . . . they'd no means of getting back to the ship; they'd no place to lay their heavy heads. By this time Old Stripey, pummelled, punched, and doused with cold water, was beginning to look more or less respectable—or so they thought —and they themselves had reached the stage when they were convinced that they were as sober as judges, and that it was only the perverse texture of the Edinburgh pavement that was making them slip and stumble in their progress. But where to spend the night? At last it was uttered, the inevitable suggestion . . .

"The police station," said some bright spark. "Let's try the police station. I've read somewhere that they're bound to offer you a bed, you just sort of tell them that you're distressed British Subjects, and they can't refuse you."

"Poleesh!" said a voice that was thick with emotion. "Poleesh, now why didn't we think of thash before."

*   *   *

It was early in the morning. *Icarus* was short of nine of her complement. *Electra* was short of twelve. Then the telephone bell rang.

As Officer of the Day I answered it, and was told by a police-sergeant whose name sounded like a series of rolling R's: "I have a dozen of your chaps here. They have missed the train and will be put on the bus."

"Thanks very much, will you be sending the Charge along with them?"

There was a Scots chuckle. "Oh no, Sir. We understand that they had good reason to celebrate, and they were no trouble really . . . just a wee bit tired, ye ken, and in need of a bit of comfort. So please don't treat them too harshly . . ."

Our strays were completely unabashed when they returned to the ship in the forenoon. Two of them had black eyes, and one had a cut lip, and Old Stripey had the father and mother of hangovers; but nothing could diminish their cheerfulness. As they came aboard they presented me with a note from the police-sergeant excusing them for being late, and his signature was as incomprehensible on the paper as his name was over the phone.

A few days later I heard Fred Castle telling the envious duty-watch of the fine time that he and his pals had had ashore.

"But the thing that really tickled us," he said, "was when we went into the cop-shop. For there they were, the civvies who had been fighting over the corpse of poor Old Stripey!

Oh, we were far too fly to let on that we'd recognised them. And they were far too tight to care. They'd been pinched, every one of them. They were to get weighed off that day."

There was a pause as the watch vaguely ruminated on the smallness of the world, until Fred added virtuously: "And serve 'em ruddy well right, and I hope they get a packet. Just imagine a bunch of disgusting drunks like them assaulting those nice kind coppers!"

*   *   *

It takes all kinds to make a navy, and the men of a destroyer are by no means of standard "type". They are noted for their diversities in temperament; no two of them are alike.

Shortly after Old Stripey's rescue I was standing by the tubes, chatting to some of the torpedomen, when I suddenly remembered that one of them, newly joined, had a rather remarkable detail filled in on his "personal document". It was this: "Did improperly discharge a firearm, thereby wounding Stoker Smith. Penalty, one day's leave stopped."

This had struck me as a very light punishment, considering the serious nature of the "crime", and as we were all a little informal and relaxed I thought I might ask young Paddy Reilly exactly what had happened. "There's no need for you to tell me, of course," I hastened to add, "but you seem to have been jolly lucky, and I'm just a little curious . . ."

But Paddy was quite pleased to spin the yarn.

Before joining *Electra*, he told us, he was with a trawler, a rust-streaked veteran, commanded by one of the toughest and crustiest of skippers, an East Coast fisherman with a tongue as jagged as a flail. But this was not the old boy's only attribute; he was also a bit of a gourmet, and a stickler for being served with his grub at the right time. As the complement of a trawler seldom includes such a refinement as a qualified cook, it is customary for the company to buckle to and take turns for the job, but according to Paddy this apparently straightforward routine always produced on *his* ship the most complex of complications.

For woe betide he who kept the skipper waiting, and woe betide them all if his meals were not well served and plentiful; especially at breakfast. The Old Man loved his breakfast. If his chow wasn't right in the morning then it would be "rough weather" for the rest of the day!

The chill morning of the crime found the trawler in harbour, with Paddy acting as quartermaster cum sentry cum knocker-up of the Duty Cook. He couldn't be said to relish any of the roles, but least of all did he like the last which, as five-thirty approached, was the most important of the lot. For Smith, the cook of the day, was a chap who hated early rising, and Paddy had no desire to brave the skipper's wrath. It was, therefore, with acute anxiety that, abandoning his guard duty and leaving the ship to look after herself, he went into the mess deck to shake his comrade into wakefulness.

"Rise and shine, man, or else there'll be hell to pay!"

But Smith, opening a clouded eye, was quite indignant at this excessive solicitude.

"Okay . . . okay . . . keep your hair on, Cock. I'll be along."

Well, it was a reassuring start, but when five-forty-five arrived, and there was still no sign of life in the galley, the Irish lad was again assailed by qualms. Something had gone wrong, he thought; and so it had; for Smithy had returned to his slumbers. Worse, he was not willing to be reclaimed from them, for every effort of Paddy's was completely unsuccessful. He pleaded, he prayed, he cajoled, he cussed, but only twice did Smithy show any signs of consciousness; once when he turned over to go to sleep again, and once when he used two words which, though forcible, are not printable. Finally, when 6 a.m. came round, Paddy felt that he had stood enough:

shock treatment, that's what Smithy needed, and shock treatment was what he'd get.

It happened that as the ship was alongside the quay young Paddy had been temporarily endowed with a third of the ship's armoury, namely one revolver. Now, plucking it out of its holster, he brandished it ferociously over the laggard's recumbent form.

"If yez don't turn out sure I'll blow yez out!" he bawled. And then . . . Paddy turned to me, with a childlike awe spreading over his face at the recollection of it all.

"And then by the holy angels, Sir, me finger slipped, and the gun went off like a clap of thunder. Smithy jumped to his feet but he didn't stay there long. In a second he was back in his bunk again . . . *for I'd blown his blessed toe off*!"

There was a roar of laughter at the end of Reilly's story, which appealed so much to our quaintly British sense of humour.

"But so far you've only given us half a tale," I said. "We're still waiting to hear how you got off with it so lightly."

"Well, Sir, 'tis a queer old yarn, but may I never move from here, Sir, every word of it is true . . ."

Apparently when our "criminal", expecting all hell to break loose, had loomed up in front of the skipper, he had found the old rascal in sympathetic mood. For Paddy, he emphasised, must not "fret himself" unduly for a very forgivable accident, arising as it did from "a well-meant desire to enforce Ship's Discipline"! And Smith was a pretty bloody cook, they might as well face the fact . . . a good seaman mind, but a bloody atrocious cook. In fact, to sum up, the skipper was convinced that Providence had done its best for all. Smith, he had felt, had never been very happy regarding the galley duty and now perhaps they'd give him a berth in a battlewaggon, or maybe even his ticket . . . the whole thing was really a blessing.

Punishment? It would be quite unthinkable, but there'd be a form to fill in to explain the expenditure of one round of revolver ammunition, and Paddy would lose a day's leave to attend to it himself; the skipper hated paperwork.

"We blew our stern off a couple of days later," said Reilly reflectively. "Nobody got hurt but they paid us off and I had to come back to the Real Navy.

"A pity," he sighed. "She was a queer old ship, that trawler . . . But I was just beginning to like her . . ."

*   *   *

Well, I couldn't say that I had not been warned . . .

I had the morning watch, next day with Paddy and his bosom chum Jasper, another of my torpedomen, acting as searchlight manipulators. Then, at six o'clock, the weather turned sour on us and as the rain belted down I sent the two youngsters to seek shelter in the cross-passage below the bridge; although, to be frank about it, I should have known better . . .

There are two stripped Lewis guns in that passage. Both of them loaded, they are ready for action against low-flying aircraft, and the sequel is inevitable. For no sooner does Paddy set eyes upon the confounded things than he has to explain to Jasper precisely how they work, and Jasper, as luck will have it, doesn't immediately understand, and so Paddy of course has to demonstrate. Then the ship lurches (just Reilly's goddam luck!) and his fingers happen to slip and a burst of fire goes soaring through the deck . . .

One of the bullets carved its way into Doc's cabin, ricochetting all over the place and finally burying itself in the woodwork of his bunk. Others slid wildly over a metal bulkhead, ripping into the silence like a battery of circular saws. And yet another, by a chance in a thousand, carved through the leads that carried the power to the Sperry compass repeats, causing all the alarm bells to ring.

In a moment all was undignified confusion, with half of the ship's company convinced that we'd gone to action stations, and the other half equally convinced that the bridge had gone off its rocker. I cussed the culprits at the top of my voice, Paddy dropped his gun beneath Harry's hurrying feet, the Doctor came up the ladder, breathing hard, the Captain arrived on the bridge . . .

I am afraid that when our two young seamen were subsequently paraded as defaulters they found that Commander May's punishments, though infrequently applied, were of a very different nature from the one imposed by the eccentric trawler skipper. They came away with fourteen days' extra work and drill, and yet, as Paddy put it, they had no "weed" against the owner. For Paddy Reilly had a brand-new nickname. Henceforward we were to know him as The Gunman . . .

Doc alone was a little worried about the severity of the "sentence".

"If they get fourteen days for missing me," he speculated, "what on earth would they have got for hitting me?"

Back came the answer in a flash: "Seven days' leave and a ruddy great pat on the back!"

*   *   *

In the sea-war against Germany our fortunes ebbed and flowed like the tide of the fickle ocean which formed the sepulchre of the fallen. In the Battle of the Atlantic there was no fixed front, no area of rest, no time of stalemate; a thrust off Greenland would be followed by another off Dakar, and a convoy successfully running the gauntlet of the U-boat packs in Biscay might still be annihilated by an offensive off the Cape. On several occasions it appeared that Doenitz and his sea wolves had produced the perfect offensive tactic, the argument to which there could be no answer. But each time came our counter measures—each of them also the "last word" in technique, until the enemy changed his style again, and until the next attack. In May the U-boats had sunk a third of a million tons of shipping, and there had been costly diversions of routing owing to the *Bismarck–Prinz Eugen* raid. And then, to complete this sombre picture, the bombers had ravaged Liverpool, the convoys' main port of reception.

Until mid-1941 the movements of *Electra*, a minute particle in this ever-changing pattern of the ocean conflict, had been governed by all sorts of day-to-day requirements.

Off Norway she had operated in the classic role of the fleet destroyer—to "destroy" light enemy surface craft that might attack the carriers and the cruisers. In her adventure against the *Bismarck* she had been scheduled to act offensively—a David against Goliath. But, notwithstanding such military excursions, most of her life, her wartime life, had been spent as the faithful shepherd of the merchant flocks and, while engaged in this occupation, she had been switched from coast to coast and route to route with a rapidity that had at least provided her with a variety of experience though few opportunities for heroics.

Thus, in the space of a fortnight, we had gone from Iceland to Rosyth, and from Rosyth back to Scapa. From Scapa we had indulged in a run down the West Coast, and from the West Coast we'd gone over to Ireland. Then, on the fourteenth day, we'd topped up with oil in Londonderry and started on a long haul out into the Atlantic, escorting a troop convoy to a point some 1,200 miles off the north-west coast of Ireland.

Considering that the Germans at this stage of their underwater offensive were doing well, the voyage was remarkably uneventful. The transports were fast, the escort was formidable, the weather was good, and yet, to *Electra*, it was noteworthy, an occasion to get excited about, a red-letter day. For it was in the course of our return trip that the Captain called the officers into his day cabin and said: "Well, gentlemen, I have news for you. I am to tell you that we are going back to Scapa and from there we are going into dock for a refit and a spot of leave . . ."

A pause, and then he added with a smile, "Oh . . . but I'd almost forgotten, we are going to refit in London."

7

Home is the Sailor!

A LONDON refit—it was our biggest break. Doc and Davies were already in the plot, having deciphered the order when it first arrived, but to the rest of us it came as a complete surprise, and a buzz of self congratulation broke out which was silenced by a gesture from the captain.

"We have five days to go before the start of our refit," he said, "and a lot can still go wrong. Our masters may change their minds, or a ship may get holed near London and take our berth—as the one that's most convenient. So, just for once, I shall require you to keep our destination from the company, to ward against disappointment.

"I shall merely announce that a refit will start in five days' time, and that its duration and place will be given when confirmation is received. But in the meanwhile . . ." He smiled. "Well, no discussions in the wardroom, gentlemen, for stewards have ears you know."

So began a complicated battle of wits, a guessing game between the officers and the matelots who, though highly delighted to hear of the ship's refit, had a very shrewd suspicion that the venue was known to us, and did their damnedest to pump us dry.

*   *   *

"Stewards have ears . . ." and Gretton's needed no deaf-aid. Never before had he been so solicitous for the well-being of his charges, and he hovered around the wardroom with an attention that was almost embarrassing. For every conversational crumb, we felt, was being carefully gathered up—for subsequent microscopic examination in the pantry. But if Gretton's role was a silent one—to observe and report rather than make a direct attack—there was no doubt that the mantle of Inquisitor-in-Chief had descended on the shoulders of Yeoman Tingle, who displayed a surprising subtlety in his questioning, and an indefatigable zeal.

Because of his duties it was inevitable that Tingle should spend many hours on the bridge, and as a result, be closer to the officers than most of the others. He was a first-rate man at his job, and well liked by us all; a chap who—like Gretton— would never presume in the normal course of business to profit from our idle gossip, yet a chap who, on this occasion, we had to guard against. For it soon became obvious that the Ship regarded the location of the refit as a major issue—and Tingle, after all, had a loyalty to his chums.

"Jolly good news this docking, Sir . . . are you going to bring the family up to *Grimsby*?"

"Grimsby?" I nearly fell for it, then regained balance, just in time. "Well, I just don't know. I dare say they'd be happy at Grimsby, but I suppose they'd like other places just as well. Brighton's quite nice for instance, and so too is Penzance!"

But the Tingle intelligence system, with its apparently innocent small talk, stood up to its initial rebuff and was indeed extended.

Thus.

Tingle to Davies: "Have you ever been to *Liverpool* before, Sir?"

Davies: "No, but I believe it's a very interesting place—and so convenient for Blackpool!"

Tingle to the First Lieut.: "The Gunner seems to be very happy to be going off to *Portsmouth*, Sir . . . but I suppose it's only natural—him with his wife and kids practically living on the spot."

Jenner-Fust, with well-bred austerity: "I also like Portsmouth, Tingle. But I live a fair distance from it."

Tingle was certainly tenacious, and he was abetted by many of the others, among them Ted Mash and most of my torpedomen. But not once did they ask a direct question, for that would have been contrary to their code; to trade on an officer's good nature was not included in the rules. Hence, when the Yeoman tackled Charles, the question was not presented as a blunt "Will we be docking at Cardiff?" but, "I suppose that once you get to Cardiff you'll be seeing your old shipmates, Sir?"

Charles: "Old ships are often leaky, Yeoman, and it is sometimes as well to keep clear of them."

But Tingle's most misguided effort was directed at the Doctor.

"*Belfast*," he said, "will be all right for *you*, Sir, but it's a bit out of the way for the rest of us . . ."

Doc answered sweetly, with his usual quiet smile: "I no longer reside in Belfast, Yeoman . . . and I have lots of friends in England whom I would like to visit.

"But so far as I know," he added regretfully, "there just aren't any docks in Birmingham."

*   *   *

A night in Scapa, and then with the ship secured for sea again "Clear Lower Deck" was ordered. The guessing game was over.

"We are leaving for our refit, and a well earned rest," said the Captain. "We are leaving today. I can promise you that I will give as much leave as possible, but I think you will appreciate that I can't fix the final details; that side of it must wait until we get to dock."

A pause. "Well, I don't think there's much further to say

except *don't go to sleep on the way down.* For remember, we want to get there in one piece."

He turned to Jenner-Fust. "Carry on to Harbour Stations, Number One, if you please . . ."

There was silence, the silence of embarrassment, from the trimly ordered ranks before him; and then the Chief Coxswain spoke up. Gould's chubby face was even pinker than usual and a bit perplexed: "May we know where we are going, Sir?"

The Captain regarded him in mock surprise. "Oh! But didn't I tell you? How very remiss of me. But surely the news is common property by now?"

Another pause. "Well, I hope the move will be popular, for we're going to *London!*"

The spontaneous and startled cheer that followed could have left him in no doubt that the secret had been well kept, and with a broad grin he moved away to the bridge, happy in the success of his little joke and with the obvious pleasure of the ship's company.

Today, in this era of the Sputnik, the Guided Missile, and all the rest of the scientific wonders, May's humour may appear to have had rather a childish flavour. But seamen are rather childlike people, and *Electra*'s was a happy family.

*　　*　　*

"We want to get there in one piece." That's what the Owner had said, and that's the way we felt about it, too. Normally *Electra* would have been keen enough to look for trouble, but this time we wanted her to take things with a pinch of bromide —no heroics for us, we wanted to get HOME.

Combining our holiday trip with business, we moved down the East Coast to pick up a southbound convoy and help escort it through the danger area to Sheerness. All went quite smoothly until, not far from Flamborough Head, we met one of the old W destroyers; a veteran of the first war but just out of dock and on her way to join the Fleet. She'd had an excellent face-lift, and looked about half her years, or less; but much though we admired her unwontedly smart appearance, we couldn't envy her destination. Idly we watched her cross into our wake, and follow along its path towards the north. Then she dwindled in the dusk and was lost to sight—and mind—until we picked up the rumble of an underwater explosion.

We plotted its location and assumed that our rejuvenated sister had dropped a depth charge, but as the bang was not repeated, and as there was no yell for assistance, we thought no more about it, and continued on our way. Only later did we discover that the W had run over an acoustic mine, although mercifully there were no casualties. We must have passed within yards of it!

The night that followed was fine, with a full moon and a tremorless sea; but we'd have much preferred a storm. The wind from the blacked-out shore was soft, and the silver trail, widening V-shaped from the quiet ship's stern, seemed to reach to the ceiling and the low-hanging stars. It made us a wonderful target. Around the guns and torpedo tubes our band of nomads, their shapes grotesque in duffle coats and balaclavas, strained their eyes into the half-light, more treacherous than any shade of storm, and made pessimistic forecasts. It would be a good night for the E-boats, lurking in the patchy shadows between the darkness and the light. It would be a good night for the Luftwaffe, guided in by the Bomber's Moon. It would be a good night for the U-boats, and the minefields too. Windy, that's what we were; windy at the horrible suspicion that something would ruin our leave.

We came on the southbound convoy in the early hours of the morning. But, when we made the challenge, our courtesy received a rude reply . . .

For scarcely had the lamp ceased flickering than we found ourselves the target of the entire convoy. First, one of the escorting Hunt class destroyers hurled over a salvo of four-inch shells, that wailed like demons above the masthead, and crashed like stones into the sea: then, as the splinters flew, and a fountain of water, rising steeply ahead, broke and cascaded across the deck, the trigger-happy gunners in the merchant ships joined in. A stream of coloured tracer came racing towards us, and other streams, mis-aimed, plunged straight across it, in a criss-cross effect of red, white, and blue. A regular Brock's Benefit!

May's hand rang down hard on the engine-room telegraph, and we beat a speedy retreat; zig-zagging wildly until the ship was out of range. A silence fell.

"Yeoman," said May, with admirable restraint. "If you are sure that you have the challenge right, please make it again—but this time on the big lamp. I didn't bargain on so enthusiastic a reception."

But the convoy had ceased firing, and the escort was already calling us up. "Sorry," we read, " . . . just one of those things. Welcome to the party."

Mollified, *Electra* answered: "Thank you for the warmth and vigour of your greeting . . ."

* * *

On arriving at Sheerness, with all his aggressive sheep intact, and ready for the fold, the captain of the Hunt destroyer came over to *Electra* to express his apologies in person: "I'm afraid that my Gunnery Officer was a little too quick on the draw, so I've brought him along with me so that you can jolly well beat him up."

"Sorry, chaps," explained the villain of the piece, "but it was such an *unfortunate* rendezvous. The place where you met us is usually the E-boats' favourite place of ambush, and some-times a fellow gets impulsive!"

Later, over a glass of gin, the Hunt officers told us that the convoy was the only one they'd brought south in recent months without experiencing attack . . . "We could make use of Lucky 'Lectra. She'd bring luck to the flotilla."

*   *   *

"The job will take six weeks," said May, "and I shall want as many bodies as possible sent on leave . . . to get out of the way of the dockers."

Electra was safely tucked up in the London docks. We were gathered in the wardroom. May had returned from a conference ashore.

"Personnel will be retained to man the light anti-aircraft weapons, and to provide a fire-party," he continued, " but no more, if you please . . ."

Our little group broke up, feeling very satisfied with itself. The leave arrangement was even better than we'd hoped; with a bit of wangling we could fix everyone with a month ashore.

"Now don't forget," murmured Number One . . ."no soft sentimental lingerings . . . no gentle surrender to nostalgia . . . for if I catch anyone loitering about the ship when he needn't, I'll get him certified!"

By the luck of the draw my own leave period was fixed for the latter part of the refit, and I was left to hold the fort with young Eric Coale, who had picked up his second stripe and was now a full-blown lieutenant. As Coale lived in London we worked watch and ward together, standing-in for each other for brief visits ashore. We were also able to contrive the odd week-end, and Coale, a firm favourite with my two small sons whom he had met some months before, insisted on doing the first stint so that I could run down to Midhurst and see my family without delay. Furthermore, as though this generosity was not sufficient, he loaded me with his precious chocolate ration: "More useful to the kids than to a grown man," he grinned.

A small point to mention, this good-natured offering? I do not think so. A ship, or a tradition, is made or marred by the so-called little things; for only a candidate for a lunatic asylum would expect Nelson's Column to stand without cement . . .

*　　　*　　　*

It was now July, and while Russia, so recently the servile collaborator of Hitler's Germany, was reeling before the unleashed fury of the panzers, the land and air defenders of the stubborn western islands were enjoying a well deserved break. Over London the barrage balloons hung placidly against a hot blue sky, while the crews of the ack-ack guns, free to snatch a little relaxation for the first time since the Blitzkrieg's opening, were sunbathing on the sand-bagged sites above the fire-scarred city, egging-on the Dig for Victory enthusiasts in the parks, or keeping vigil among the droning bumble-bees on the hills of Kent and Surrey.

Down on the South Coast too there was a comparative tranquility. Barbed wire in rich profusion, and concrete pill-boxes, which had sprung up like mushrooms, still served to emphasise the exigencies of the era; so, too, did the condition of the holiday beaches, naked of trippers' litter but speckled with the ugly brown of fuel oil, which rolled in on every tide. The shells from Cap Gris Nez, the sneak raiders from Abbeville, the flares that rose to seaward following a pulsing in the night . . . all these were visible reminders of the unpleasantness of war and yet there was a feeling of well-being and confidence abroad, which we had noticed in London immediately we docked, and noticed wherever we went thereafter.

At sea there was no lull in the battle, no abrupt transition from shade to light, but, ashore, the threat of present or future dangers was making a far less impressive impact on the minds of most of the people we met than the memory of the way in which their recent and mortal peril had been so resolutely tackled, and so spectacularly overcome. In general it was all very encouraging, and yet, in some respects, it was also a little alarming.

A friend of mine, writing from the Kentish countryside, summed up the prevailing sentiment in these words: "Convalescence has succeeded the ordeal of the operating table, the worst is over and we are getting on to our feet again . . ."

I hoped he was right, but speaking for myself, there were times when I rather wondered if some of the patients weren't overestimating their strength . . .

Although *Electra* was noisy with the hammering of rivets, the snarl of drills and the thud of dockers' boots; although the red lead dripped all over her, and the oxy-acetylene lamps flared angrily through the salt and the sea-scars on her hull, we managed to keep her as our "own", a living ship, even though, at the beginning of the operation we felt rather like a dispossessed family, apologising, when entering the sitting-room, for their intrusion on the bailiffs—busy removing the carpet!

We were strange to the ways of the Shore, and at first felt rather out of tune with them, knowing very little about the traditions of London's dockland, or the historical roots of its radical outlook. Both Coale and I had what the landsmen would call a working-class origin, but we had long been with an organisation where "Class" was never mentioned, and did not matter; and where the bosses endured the hardships of their men. We were vaguely familiar with trade union procedure, but we hadn't much knowledge of their more exclusive practices, and the fact that such practices should be maintained during a period of total war appeared to us at first to be more than a little quaint. Thus snags arose inevitably and, in ironing them out, much tolerance was required until each side was better acquainted with the other's viewpoint.

One day, while I was sitting in the mess working on some

of the accounts, Tiger Mash came along, looking rather worried.

"There's a chap who wants to see you, Sir. And I think you had better handle him as tactfully as you can . . . if you get my meaning."

Handle him tactfully? Strange words these from my tough T.G.M.

"No, I don't get your meaning, but just show the gentleman in. I'll do my best to behave . . ."

Tiger withdrew, though not before adding the sibilant hint: "Sorry, Sir, but he's all right really . . . just needs *handling*, Sir, if you take my tip."

Awaiting with some impatience the appearance of this formidable personality. I wondered what the devil was up. Couldn't be a member of the top brass—Mash was not one to take fright at a mere Admiral. Couldn't be a V.I.P. of the civilian branch—Mash scorned 'em, every one of 'em. But who then . . .? Some thug or other who didn't like my face? Or a casual drunk—merely spoiling for a scrap? The very idea was ludicrous. "Tiger" would have sent him off, stone-cold, by the first available ambulance.

"Morning, Sir . . . Now *I* am the Stooard!"

A pink-cheeked and sharp-eyed little workman stepped briskly up to the desk.

"Good morning to you," I became even more confused. "A steward? Well, I don't think it's me you want to see, the chap you'll want is Gretton. Gretton is *our* steward—it's he who deals with all the mess shopping and so on. So if you like I'll put you in touch with him."

But I realised that I'd dropped a brick, an outsize one, even before I'd finished the sentence; for the newcomer had a very expressive face, one of those very expressive faces that can register to perfection practically every emotion to which the flesh is heir . . . Surprise, humiliation, indignation and fury—

all had taken their turn during my "tactful" speech, a wonderful transformation and effected in less than ten seconds.

"*Mess shopping*!" he almost choked. "*I* am not that kind of stooard. I am a *Shop Stooard*, and here's my card . . ."

I looked at it, still at a loss. "Well, it doesn't mean very much to me, but if you think I can help in any way I will be only too happy to do so. What's the trouble?"

"Now look here, Mister," he complained. "I have caught some of your blokes—and I've caught them *working*!"

"Congratulations," I replied. "I wish I could say the same. Since we've entered dock they don't seem to have done a stroke."

The Shop Steward looked at me incredulously, almost pityingly.

"But don't you see, Mister, it just won't do. That's what I'm trying to tell you . . . *it just won't do.*"

"Cigarette . . .?" Restraint was needed.

"Thanks. But I tell you straight—there'll be trouble if this continues."

"Light . . .?"

"Thanks, but you still don't seem to understand. Your blokes are trying to take away our work, Mister, for it *is* our work whether you like it or not, and if your blokes do it then I shall have to take my chaps out. *All out*, unless you do something to stop it."

"Stop what?"

Only when we arrived on the foc'sle, and found three or four of the ship's company exchanging scowls with a similar number of workmen, did my mental fog begin to clear. One of our A.B.'s, having chipped off a square yard of paintwork to while away the time, had commenced in all innocence to follow up with a coat of red lead, but, when "red-handed" as it were, he had been spotted by the Steward who, representing the painters, had immediately gone up to him and told him to desist.

At first, the A.B. had merely enquired: "Have I heard you

right?" But then, on being reassured as to the efficiency of his ear-drums, and having had no briefing on "tact" from Tiger Mash to guide his tongue, he had pointedly asked whose bloody ship did the Steward think he was ordering about, and who the bloody hell did the Steward think he was? At this a warm discussion had ensued, with the A.B. telling our friend precisely what he could do with his "visiting card".

"I bear no grudge," said the Steward. "But you do see what I mean?"

I grinned, then intercepting a sudden warning flashed from Tiger, refrained from saying what I was going to say and went full speed astern, to explain that the procedure prevailing in the London Dock was different to the procedure we had encountered elsewhere. In the Royal Yards only items covered by our defect list were handed over to civilian labour, and we were accustomed to doing all the smaller jobs ourselves: so that our sin, if sin it could be called, was one of ignorance, and would not be repeated.

The opposition thawed.

"Well, don't start *worrying*, just tell your sailors that if they want any painting done while the ship is in this dock then they can come and see me and I'll get it done—in record time. But they mustn't do it themselves, *see*?"

I saw.

"Because if they do," he added, "then they will be doing work that belongs to US, and as I've said before, I shall have to take my blokes out . . . *All Out*. But believe me, I don't want to have to do it."

"And *I* don't want you to have to do it, so that makes two of us!" I replied.

The last I saw of the Steward was when he was happily drinking tea with the self-same A.B. whose action had pre-cipitated the rumpus.

*　　*　　*

Tiger had been proven right, of course. It would never have done to have delayed *Electra*'s rehabilitation, and small thanks would I have received had I touched off a dockyard strike. All the same, considering there was a war on, the situation struck me as faintly ludicrous, and rankled a bit, though not for long.

For as the days went by and we witnessed the things they were doing to our battered destroyer, we began to look at the workmen with a more tolerant eye. They were craftsmen, and proud of their craft. They were efficient and worked very hard. They did the "little bit extra" too . . .

Rapidly new links of friendship were forged between the ship and the shore, the dockers in particular earning our respect. Warm-hearted, cheerful, and as pig-headed, in their determination to stand by what they thought was right, as any of our company, they began to take the troops to their homes, their clubs, their social gatherings. And daily the lists of would-be hosts increased. Soon, from being regarded almost as an alien intruder, suspected of talking a different language and thinking a different way, *Electra*, a London ship, had been "accepted" and made welcome, warmly welcome. For Dockland never does things by halves.

*   *   *

My home-leave went all too fast as home-leaves always do, and on my return I met some of the ship's company at the station and we walked back together to the ship. We were all rather down-in-the-mouth and thoughtful, and preoccupied with the usual disturbing thoughts that war-time partings bring. And yet, as we came up to the dock, our melancholy was swept away by the sight of the ship, for she had changed so much that she had become almost unrecognisable.

When *Electra* had first arrived in London her Home Fleet coat of sombre grey—a practical but never inspiring colour—had been streaked with dirt and torn by the talons of the sea.

But proud though we were of her shabbiness, her "honourable scars," I am afraid that to eyes less prejudiced than ours the lady must have looked no better than a tramp. But now . . .? "Dolled up like a dog's dinner," said someone, whistling through his teeth. And we all stood back to take a second look, admire and criticise . . .

Oh yes, they'd certainly made a difference those chaps with the stewards, the union cards, the scrapers and the brushes; for beneath their ministrations the tough destroyer of yesterday had been transformed into a thing of beauty, as fresh as a debutante. The harsh wrinkles that had once spread outward around her nose and chin had disappeared, her figure had been restored to its former grace, and, most spectacular transformation of all, they'd bestowed upon her a party frock; had let fall over her once-tired bones a pattern of many colours, of lovely hues of blue and green, and delicate pastel greys . . .

"All part of the camouflage scheme," said Davies proudly as we came aboard. "And executed by Peter Scott, or so I've heard. Wonderful isn't it?"

But among the barnacled old salts there was considerably less enthusiasm. "Just fancy the wife having a face lift at *her* time of life!"

"H.M.S. *Sissy*," chanted a drunken matelot from the quay. "H.M.S. Sissy. Yesh, that's the name for you!"

*　　　*　　　*

New faces were evident among the ship's company and some very new non-substantive rates had been introduced. *Electra* had at last been issued with a rather primitive radar set and Leading Seaman Roberts and two other R.D.F. operators had been sent along to make it work. Frank Vincent, a young and fresh-faced wartime rating, had also joined us; with the intriguing title of Coder, and the job of deciphering the less highly secret signals, thus leaving the officers more time to devote to their ordinary duties. All of these "raw" reinforcements were to prove invaluable in the trying times to come: they adapted themselves readily to destroyer life and after the first week or so were as devotedly "*Electra*" as their shipmates.

There had also been a change in the population of the wardroom, where Charles had left us for a well-deserved promotion and a new Sub-Lieutenant R.N.V.R. had taken his place. The newcomer, Cruden, was rather reserved in manner and looked a little older than his age. Cultured, rather sensitive, he combined a taste for classical music with a dry Scots humour and—as we were later to discover—a treble dose of the usual allotment of courage and resource. But, when I first met him, only his shyness was apparent . . .

"And what do you do in Civvy Street?" It was the stock question, the well-meant attempt at putting a new boy at his ease.

But Cruden looked a shade embarrassed. "Well, I don't suppose you'd call it frightfully productive, but I sort of pottered around among ruins and things . . ."

"Oh, really? Civil Defence?"

A faint smile. "Oh no, nothing so spectacular, I'm afraid . . . the ruins were vintage. I'm an archaeologist!"

The news got around the ship, becoming a little distorted in the process, and the irreverent sailors were dubbing our Subbie "The Alcohologist", a title which was slanderous, but stuck!

*   *   *

Goodbyes are usually hateful things in wartime: the right words are so difficult to say, yet the occasion may be irrevocable. But the saddest goodbyes of all are those that are made on the dockside, when the water widens far too slowly between those who go and those who stay behind, and when the reluctance of each of them to part is coupled with an impatience to get the painful parting done. *Electra*'s departure for the sea was much lightened, however, by the rousing send-off we received from our new-won friends the dockers, who thronged the quay-side and, as the ship cast off, raised a terrific cheer followed by a chorus of individual good wishes, and much waving of cloth caps.

This incident bucked us up tremendously, and the Captain, reaching for the syren lanyard, was not slow in returning an appropriate reply. Three short pulls upon the lanyard preceded one that was lingering and long, at which, as the brave refrain of the V-sign was hooted raucously over London's river, there came another cheer from the dockers: a cheer that was even more formidable than the first. In fact, as regards its duration and volume, it would have been a credit to Labour Day.

*   *   *

It was quite a party, and *Electra* found herself involved in it only forty-eight hours after leaving London. Having reammuni-tioned at Sheerness she was ordered to the north again, attached as escort to a well-armed convoy, on passage through Bomb Alley. Then Jerry intervened, a few minutes after midnight.

Though first detected only as a gentle whisper to the east, the engine-note of his bombers increased very rapidly in intensity. Soon they were snapping and snarling around the fringes of the flock, until, having discovered a weak point, or so they thought, they came darting to the attack.

Unseen, save very briefly, and then as grey shadows only a shade or two removed from the blackness of the night, the enemy made the most of the advantages of the darkness. From the short-range platform I picked up for the merest second or two what I thought was the vague outline of a plane, but though we blazed merrily away with Castle's Oerlikon and the point-five machine-guns we were denied a kill. Nor was Cruden, joining in with the three-inch, any more successful, so we switched our fire, joining up with the general barrage which was extremely impressive and strangely picturesque.

For as the German attack developed, every ship hurled its

bricks in the general direction of the first shell bursts, until the tracers were shooting across the starless sky like lines being drawn by a score of coloured pencils across a sheet of black paper, on which as the four-inch and three-inch H/E cracked away, some clumsy hand was spilling blobs of paint. The ceiling was crackling with high explosive, and the sea beneath the bursting shells and the leisurely falling flares reflected a myriad colours.

Jerry still tried hard, we conceded him that, but the heat of the reception could scarcely have done much good to the nerves of his bomb-aimers. The bombs screamed down impressively enough, but the crump of their explosions was muffled, and very wide of the mark were the water-spouts that followed. Once only did we see traces of a hit, an ominous glow well over to our starboard quarter. And then, after a few more vain attempts to do us damage, the enemy turned away, the firing ceased, and all was quiet again.

In the first light of dawn we counted noses, and found to our satisfaction that the tally was complete. The ship that had been hit reported only structural damage; the fire had been put out, there were no casualties and she could maintain her speed. All in all, then, we reflected happily, *Electra*'s reputation still held good. For even though the chaps on the Hunts, the other destroyers, and the merchantmen themselves might feel entitled to a small share of the credit, it was, as we well knew, our own ship's good luck jinx that had really determined the affair!

As we parted from the convoy, by this time well out of the danger area and almost home and dry, the Senior Officer signalled: "Thanks for your support, whenever you get bored come down and join us."

"Many thanks for the entertainment," May replied.

And then, a little cockily maybe, *Electra* turned towards her old hunting ground and pushed off to Scapa and the frozen north.

8

Convoy to Russia

TINGLE must have been psychic. He had said as we entered Scapa that he sensed something was in the wind, and that they were earmarking *Electra* for a special show; now his prophecies looked like bearing fruit.

First the Old Man had been called over to the Flagship for a conference, and had been delayed there for hours. Then they'd sent for Lieutenant Davies, and *he* had come back looking as happy as a cat—a cat just presented with an extra large plate of cream. Nor did the portfolio, crammed with charts, that the Lieutenant carried beneath his arm escape the Yeoman's lynx-like gaze. *Electra*, he confided to a somewhat sceptical Fred Castle, was about to be fully employed—just wait and see if she wasn't. Yet, in the way of hard fact to back his hunch, Tingle could glean but little. Fancy knowing that there was Something On—but not having the foggiest notion what that Something was. It was enough to make a chap hopping mad!

"Come on, Harry . . . what's it all about?" In the wardroom too there was considerable speculation.

"Not to tell . . . *won't* tell . . ." Our friend maintained his smugness. "It's just a little secret, a secret between me and the Admiral . . ."

There was a concerted rush.

"Well, anyway," said Harry, breathless but bursting with the desire to uncork his sensational news. "The Old Man will be bound to announce it officially on his return, so I can't see much harm in letting you in on it now. This is a big occasion —for the owner, the ship, and for every one of us, as soon will be made plain. We're to be senior Escort to a convoy."

"A convoy! Senior escort to a convoy? Hell, if that's all there ruddy well is to it . . ."

But Davies shook his head. "It's no ordinary convoy, not this one. It's going to be the first of its type, and for all you and I know, it may well be the last."

He was suddenly serious. "Keep it dark, but we're off to Russia!"

*　　　*　　　*

In eight weeks the map of Europe had undergone yet another violent transformation, as the Germans, hurling their steel-edged onslaught against their late confederate, achieved one of the most spectacular initial successes in military history. Before the impetus of the panzer columns the gigantic Red armies had gone down like corn before the scythe; and, as disaster followed disaster the Kremlin's appeals to "imperialist" Britain for aid had grown as clamorous as her former vituperation. Yet though the situation was not without its ironies, it was obvious that something had to be done—and quickly—to meet Stalin's immediate need. Already, behind the defensive screen of Vian's cruisers, the carrier *Argus* had succeeded in flying off a group of fighter aircraft to operate from Murmansk. And now it was the turn of the convoys.

*　　　*　　　*

"Old Winnie should just take a dekko at us . . ."

"A Strong Force, they said . . . we're as strong as a weak cup of tea!"

My torpedomen, squatting round the tubes, were regarding the convoy and the other ships of the escorting force with the scepticism appropriate to professionals who must always conceal their keenness for fear that they be thought naïve. Yet, all the same, there was some point in their criticisms; for as a spectacle of Britain's maritime might P.Q.1. left much to be desired. Apart from *Electra* the total fighting force at May's disposal consisted of the destroyer *Anthony*, three Algerian class minesweepers and half a dozen trawlers. It wouldn't have frightened pussy. Then someone began to count the hybrid collection of merchantmen—and made the score thirteen!

"Thirteen! And what clot's responsible for such a damn fool notion as to fix on unlucky thirteen?" For once Paddy Reilly looked thoroughly upset.

"No need to worry," interrupted the well-informed Tingle. "If the big boys come out they'll find *Suffolk* in the way, and probably Vian's little lot as well."

"After all," said Fred Castle, "we've got the trawlers to support us!"

There was silence, then rude uncharitable laughter as one of the Shakespeare class, the subject of Fred's jibe, came into view. She was squat, she was lumpy, and as she laboured her way through the water it seemed improbable, to say the least, that she would be fit for anything more arduous than a journey to the junk-yard. The thick smoke poured from her skinny funnel, and a shower of black smuts fell dismally upon her bridge.

Then, as the men of the destroyer watched the trawler, which possessed a grace akin to that of Giles's "grandma", waddle determinedly past *Electra*'s swanky newly painted quarter, a penetrating whistle went up, suggestive and very vulgar; for they'd spotted the name on her blistered, peeling stern . . . "*Ophelia!*" . . . Could anything be less like?

*   *   *

Each day was colder than the day before, each night was

shorter than the night before. The sun, or the sun's reflection, on the long, slow swell of the northern sea, remained with the harshly silhouetted ships for all but a brief segment of the twenty-four-hour cycle, and, as the men's breath hung like steam in the thinning air, invisible pins and needles probed icily at their lungs. But they were lucky to get off so lightly, considering the time of the year, and every one of them knew it. It was late September when they started; it would be early October when they finished; but they had experienced far worse conditions further south, when hundreds of miles away in the roaring mid Atlantic.

Our orders were to skirt Iceland and keep well to the westward of the northern tip of Norway; thus making a wide sweep, so far as the ice would allow, in order to dodge the enemy bases at Narvik and Petsamo before turning eastward and then south and passing through the White Sea to Archangel, our destination. Intelligence had told us that the Germans sent out two recce flights daily and we were constantly on the look-out. But as the Luftwaffe men, with Teutonic punctuality, always started their operation at the same time, and followed the same route as that of the day before, our course and speed were neatly adjusted to take advantage of their timetable, and we saw them not—which was just as well. We also had to be on the alert against a German naval strike, but contrary to expectations, neither U-boat nor surface craft attempted to interfere and as each day went by we began to wonder if Hitler really cared about the northern life-line. Maybe he was anticipating that the Russians would collapse before our aid could become effective? Or maybe he didn't think that the British would bother to send the Russians aid? Or maybe . . .? Well maybe we were just plumb lucky—we just wouldn't know. And, while counting our blessings, we kept our powder dry.

*   *   *

One night, when *Electra* was well into the Arctic circle, Davies and I were sharing the first watch, from twenty hours to midnight. It was a pleasant enough stint, despite the cold. The sun had set, but the ship was bathed in twilight; the sea was silent, unworried by the slightest breeze; the Aurora Borealis no longer distant but seemingly almost overhead, was sending a myriad coloured lights to whirl and flash and dance in the cloudless sky and record their gyrations in the water's glassy surface. But even as we were congratulating ourselves on the sea's tranquility I picked up a pin-point of light— isolated, and fine on the starboard bow.

"What do you make of it, Guns?"

"*Could* be a small iceberg, catching the reflection of the sun . . . but it certainly isn't anything belonging to us."

The gun Director and the lookouts trained on the bearing, and the object grew rapidly larger. Its shape was difficult to distinguish. It seemed to glow internally, like the red-hot hull of a sinking ship.

"Making thirty knots, at least," said Harry.

"That's a wonderful calculation, considering we've nothing to go by. But when in doubt call the Captain! I think you'd better rouse him."

May arrived . . . but Harry, always quick at ship recognition, had come to a decision.

"Good God, it's an aircraft carrier. Now why the hell didn't I think of that before!"

"A carrier? How do you make that out?"

"It's simple really, Sir," expounded Harry. "The flight deck is catching the reflection of the Aurora and the humped effect on the port side is due to the island superstructure . . . they always look a bit lop-sided, these carriers, when seen bows-on."

"Oh, that's rather clever of you, Davies," said the Captain with a strange smile. "And of course if it *is* a carrier that would account for its speed?"

"Yes, Sir. Exactly so, Sir."

I butted in. "A carrier? But what the devil would a carrier be doing in these parts?"

"My dear Guns, why don't you use your loaf! We all know that *Victorious* has been busy around here: she's probably about to have another go against the Finnish bases!"

There was a snigger from the bridge look-out, and Harry, who had taken his eyes off the "target" while developing his theme, looked somewhat surprised.

"Well, what's so funny?"

"Professor," I gloated, "it is not unusual for aircraft to take off from a carrier, but this time the carrier itself has become airborne! Your 'carrier', my poor friend, just happens to be the Moon!"

And the moon it was—a quarter moon, that was rising at an almost incredible velocity, and was now well above the horizon. Our guffaws were long and loud.

Davies turned shamefacedly to the Captain. "Sorry, Sir, to have disturbed your rest and dragged you up just to look at the astral wonders."

"Don't worry. I'd sooner be called to nine false alarms than miss the tenth—the one that matters. At all events," May cast a thoughtful glance in my direction, "you seem to have made Guns happy—in fact a shade *too* happy for an honest man!"

Said Harry later: "Well, I must give you your due. You properly dropped me into it that time."

"Yes," I said, "I realised it just after we'd called the Owner—and that's a beer you'll buy me, and about time too."

Opportunities for "dropping each other" were not so plentiful now that Sammy had departed, but the draughts of victory tasted all the sweeter.

*   *   *

We were intensely curious as to what we might expect to

find at our journey's end. For though we had heard much about
the New Russia we knew but little. Utopia? Hell? Or a land
which, like most others, was a compound of both? The experts
differed strongly in their definition, and the very extent of the
so-called information published had served to confuse rather
than enlighten the simple sailor. Nor did the reports of eye-
witnesses help very much. For eye-witnesses, when visiting the
U.S.S.R. seemed prone to extraordinary attacks of blindness
—whether to fault or virtue depending on the side on which
their blinkers were adjusted, Left or Right.

Now, as the convoy entered the White Sea, even the charts
became appropriately enigmatic; and few of us envied Davies
his responsibilities as navigator, cheerfully though he bore
them. That the names of headlands and navigational points
should be practically unpronounceable was one thing; but our
dearth of up-to-date information concerning the waters off the
coast was quite another. One was to have been expected; the
other struck us as being gloomily significant. And then there
were those peculiar Russian lighthouses, which were unique in
their unhelpfulness. Hitherto we had quaintly imagined that
the role of a lighthouse was to act as signpost to the mariner,
but in the Soviet Union they evidently held different views; for
Russian lighthouses blend with their surroundings, and lurked
in the shadow of the land, as though afraid of being caught out.
Nor, despite the slenderness of the escort force and the ever
present possibility of German attack, did our allies go out of
their way to help the convoy's progress. Fighter planes came
out, but they were exclusively Royal Air Force; part of the
group that had been escorted by Vian. We saw no sign of
Russian aircraft, and the Red Fleet stayed well clear. In fact we
did not make contact with the Russians until we were boarded
by a senior pilot off the approaches to Archangel.

We were very glad to get there, for the supporting cast, as
Cruden had affectionately dubbed the sweepers, had been

giving cause for anxiety: and one of the skippers, on making
his daily fuel report, had revealed that he had only three shovel-
fuls of coal remaining. "Though don't worry about ME,"
he had added cheerily, in response to May's offer of a tow.
"I'll damn well sweep out the bunkers, and that'll do the trick!"

Throughout the long voyage the little ships had certainly
lived up to their tough nautical tradition, battling on without a
gripe. But it was with relief that we now sent them packing;
despatching them up-river with the rest of the convoy while
we patrolled with *Anthony* and the larger sweepers outside
the entrance—waiting for pilots and guarding against the pos-
sibilities of an attack that did not come off.

*   *   *

"Good Lord," said Number One, astonished. "It's Olga
Paloski!"

"Well, I'll be . . ." said the Signalman, but *his* comment
trailed off into a feeble whistle; like the sound produced by a
steaming kettle, when the gas is abruptly turned off.

The pilot who had just boarded the graceless freighter to our
starboard was enough to make any chap take a deep gulp, and
a second look. For the pilot was unmistakably feminine; a
blonde who—as seen through the glasses—could be justly
described as ravishing; the sort of girl of whom sailors can
never beware. Yet, much though we kept our fingers crossed,
in the hope of a similar visitation, *Electra*'s luck was out; and all
that *we* collected when the pilot-boat came alongside was a
seamed and weatherbeaten old gentleman in his seventies. He
spoke English fluently, and was a very competent pilot; but he
was—let's face it—no substitute for that "lovely Russian Rose".

Except for the brief appearance of the blonde, our arrival
was shadowed, to some extent, by a sense of anticlimax, and
came as rather a disappointment to the troops, many of whom
had caught the prevalent popular enthusiasm for the Russians

and their war effort. For the setting was sombre, and as *Electra* passed between the heavily wooded banks of the winding river that led to Archangel there was hardly a wave or a friendly hail to greet her.

At last even our own amiable overtures faded out in face of the general apathy, and a rather thoughtful mood descended upon the ship—a mood which was by no means dissipated at the sight of our resting place, an isolated jetty on which stood two greatcoated Red Army sentries. A pair of formidable characters, carrying rifles with bayonets fixed, slung over their broad shoulders, they tucked their hands into their belts and regarded us with stone-like eyes. But otherwise? No sign of dockers, no sign of spectators, no sign of life at all, and even the jetty itself appeared reluctant to receive us.

It was an extremely primitive affair, made of large rough baulks of timber. When we came alongside there were no bollards to secure our wires to, and when we threw our heaving lines ashore the sentries made no move to pick them up. Instead, with the lines lying almost at their feet they continued in their slouching stance, regarding us with slightly frowning faces, and budging not an inch until the pilot leaned over the side and blistered them in Russian, at which they were suddenly transformed into activity. By then, however, we had decided to do the job ourselves, and some of our A.B.'s, climbing like monkeys, had got up on to the jetty. But where to tie up? How to secure the ship? Then someone said: "Let's force the bloody floor up" . . . and the problem was solved. One of the planks of the jetty was ripped from its place, and *Electra*'s line was attached to one of the crossbeams beneath. We had arrived!

*   *   *

"I wonder, Professor, if my men could stretch their legs a little, and see something of your valiant country?" May had made the request at least six times before, but there was no harm in the polite pretence that this was the first time of asking.

The Russian liaison officer looked a shade more uncomfortable than on the last occasion; but he too was a diplomat. "But most certainly, my dear Captain. There may be delays of course—formalities due to the need to change money and so on—but I am sure that in the next day or so . . ."

"Thank you," said May gravely. Next week he would ask again . . .

It wasn't the officer's fault, this reluctance to grant us shore leave; we were sure of that. For he was courteous, affable and very eager to please. A professor of languages from Leningrad University he had come on board in the company of a Red Navy commander who spoke about as much English as we spoke Russian; but the Professor's tactful interpretation did much to bridge the difficulty of communication, and even though our guests' arrival had completely disrupted our living accommodation—Davies and Coale both surrendering their cabins—we had begun to find the Russians good company. They seemed to "fit", and though it may have been part of the act, they appeared to like us too.

And yet, on looking back, quaint contrasts in behaviour come to my mind, and assume a new significance as representing the fundamental differences that lay between the allies.

On the one hand was the fact that we were detained on the jetty, in what amounted to a state of quarantine. On the other was the fact that the Russian commander, accompanied by his interpreter was free to wander all over the ship, and used this freedom to the full. He was for ever asking questions—questions about our gunnery control, our torpedoes, our anti-submarine equipment. And we, for our part, were quite free with the answers; there were, after all, no orders to the contrary. But was he *really* an "ally", and "part of the family"? I sometimes wonder . . .

And then there was the attitude of the Professor. Even had we been able to speak their language it would have been impossible for us to have talked with the few Russian labourers with whom we came in contact; they seemed scared stiff of being seen with us. But no such inhibitions governed the conduct of the Professor, whose main task was to clear up any "misunderstandings" we might entertain about the Russian way of life. We could ask anything we liked, he said, and we would always get an answer.

He was an extraordinarily able man, and served his masters well. He made no overt move to turn us into Communists and —while his method of delivery would have made him a great hit on the old Third programme—the argument that accompanied his air of intellectual liberalism was usually couched in language that even we could understand. Yet, ever so occasionally, he let slip the odd unfortunate remark . . . to remind us, with something of a shock, that we were listening to someone who was temperamentally poles apart from the English dons whose "style" he so convincingly imitated.

Hence the Professor, a gentle soul, on the ethics of Stalin's purges: "But surely there's no need to fuss? Let's just agree, as friends, that we killed our quislings before they could do damage!"

Hence also the Professor, well-read in English history, when he commented: "We were delighted, but very surprised, to hear that your Winston Churchill had decided to *join* us in the fight against Hitler. We had feared that the British would make alliance with the Germans, and that both would try to crush us. *It seemed so logical!*"

"Expediency," he said on one occasion, "must govern the life of every man: even eating and drinking are expediencies, enabling a man to survive. Thus our occupation of Poland, and our *defence* against the Finns, and our *reclaiming* the territories of Bessarabia. A great nation must protect itself . . ."

At this I remarked rather bluntly that it was a pity the Poles, the Finns and the Rumanians did not see things the way the Professor saw them; and that so many should have been killed while attempting to resist. But he remained unruffled.

"Fascists," he said, "or dupes of the Fascists. Come, let us be reasonable lieutenant" (this with a droll good-tempered smile), "you English have a phrase for it, I think . . . 'You can't make an omelette without breaking eggs'!"

Timber is Archangel's biggest export, and stacks of it lay piled along the waterfront; but we were surprised to see gangs of women at work there, and tackled the Professor about it, asking if their employment as manual labourers was a wartime measure to release men for the Front.

"But of course not," answered our friend, in genuine surprise. "For why shouldn't they shift timber, as well as sew or cook? Didn't you realise that our Russian women have achieved a complete equality?"

To we poor sailors this point of view was novel.

*   *   *

We had British visitors during our stay—R.A.F. officers who had flown over the convoy as it approached the shore. They were most interested in *Electra*'s elegant camouflage; and told us that the first two flights had returned to base with the report that only one destroyer could be seen. This had caused some alarm, and a third flight had been sent to search for us. Thanks to Peter Scott's "decor", *Electra* had been identified by only one aircraft out of twelve.

Another visitor was the Air Vice-Marshal responsible for organising the R.A.F. in Russia.

"I was scared out of my wits, during my first night in Moscow," he told us " . . . not by the Germans, but by the terrific noise of the barrage. There was a gun on every roof and the shrapnel fell like hail upon the streets; I had never heard anything like it. There and then I came to this conclusion—no effective bomber force can ever possibly get through; the Huns will never take Moscow."

The following morning, he said, he had been intrigued to see two huge posters—depicting Mr. Chamberlain and the Archbishop of Canterbury as ferocious warmongers—on a hoarding outside his hotel.

"Then somebody must have suddenly woken up to the fact that Russia had changed sides, and that the view from my window was scarcely conducive to Allied solidarity. Just after breakfast a dozen chaps assembled, to strip the hoardings and replace the posters. Hitler and Mussolini were up there before lunch!"

The day after the A.V.M.'s departure we ferried two senior Red Army officers to a conference in Murmansk and when we returned to Archangel, and a belated breakfast, we naturally invited the duty pilot to join us. He spoke no English but applied himself to the meal with zest, and when Gretton placed the toast and marmalade in front of him he nodded his thanks, took a large spoonful of marmalade, plunged it into his breakfast cup and stirred it vigorously into the coffee ... but Gretton never batted an eyelid, and neither did Number One. Instead, with perfect dignity, Jenner-Fust placed *his* spoon into the marmalade, took an even large dollop than the pilot, mixed it even more energetically into his coffee and gulped the resultant brew with every appearance of relish.

*   *   *

"Call me George" was a lively young spark, a voluble junior lieutenant who soon became a favourite with us all. The Professor and the Commander had suddenly been recalled from their labours with us, and we were sorry to see them go; but "Call me George" was an even more agreeable substitute.

His English was quite good, though by no means impeccable, and the scholarly style of address adopted by the Professor was conspicuous by its absence: for George took to the English-as-she-is-spoke technique as a duck to water. In fact he was, if anything, just a little *too* eager to adopt our colloquialisms for, having taken a fancy to the sound of some particular phrase, he would employ that phrase as often as possible, bringing it out at the most embarrassing moments. On one occasion, after listening enthralled to the comments of one of Chiefie's gang, he came along to the wardroom and repeated the principal offending word—a forces' favourite—about a dozen times in two minutes, until the Captain, listening sympathetically, suggested with elaborate tact that "awful" was a word in more common use grammatically, and might serve George's purpose better. After that the atmosphere became a shade less blue, though "awful" developed an unsuspected versatility and became, on George's tongue, a verb as well as an adjective.

George had a deep-rooted love of Russia, and affected a great admiration for Winston Churchill and Admiral Vian. Thus, when he learned that the latter had dallied awhile on his voyage home, and had launched an attack on Petsamo, his delight knew no bounds. Slapping everyone heartily on the back, in the belief that this was a standard British expression of friendliness, he swayed round the wardroom, exclaiming at intervals: "What a man, eh! Oh, what a man! And those awful bastudds, the Germans . . . this has awfulled them up! I bet it has."

But, like many another chap who tackles a foreign language, our friend was often a bit put out by the differences between the sexes—the grammatical differences. And his tenses, too, were occasionally at fault. One day, after a U-boat scare in the White Sea had sent us out on an offensive sweep, George, on the bridge, was talking to me about his family. "My sister, he is a doctor," he explained, "but now she is driving a tank . . . though when this awful war is over he will go back to the hospital, where she will once again be a doctor."

We never found out whether George's "sister" was a he-male or a she-male . . . !

George was a confident sort of chap, and helpful, too. For when May resurrected his time-honoured request for shore leave and a visit to Archangel George said, "It will be done", and done it was. Though much to George's surprise I think, although he took the credit.

*   *   *

The town itself was some miles up-river from *Electra*'s berthing place and a Russian tug had been provided for our transport. Scheduled for twelve o'clock it arrived at two, but by Russian standards this was punctuality personified, and George was cock-a-hoop. In fact on the way upstream only one thing occurred to mar his happiness, and this only for a second; for he was able to waive the incident aside as an affair of no importance.

It happened when we saw a squad of about fifty women and two old men working on the road. They were wielding their pickaxes and shovels with an indescribable air of hopelessness, and whenever they flagged two burly armed sentries were ready to chivvy them on.

"Peasants!" exclaimed George with a flourish worthy of a Bourbon. "Mere peasants—nothing more." And then, noting our surprise, he explained that there was a black market in Archangel where the country folk were free to sell such food as they had surplus to their production norm. The system was under Government control of course, and if a seller disposed of more than his permitted share the Police arrested "everybody in the market".

"Everybody? Not just the offending party?"

"But of course everybody . . . unless they have helped the Authorities," said George, bewildered by our naïvety. "It teaches the rest to—how you say?—co-operate!"

He shrugged. "But it is not very serious. And you can't send people to prison for crimes of such a type; not when the prisons are needed for those other awful bastudds . . . the traitors against the Motherland!"

There was silence.

"And all they get, these peasants, is a week's unpaid labour. So they don't really mind . . ."

More silence.

"And anyway," said George, a note of defiance creeping into his voice. "It is—how do your sailors call it?" He groped for the words, then found them. "Ah, yes. *It's just their bloody rotten luck!*"

George was learning fast.

9

No Winter Woollies now!

"WELL, if anyone here knows English I should think that *she* would," said Harry.

"Good show!"

"Filthy beast—and you a married man."

Archangel, with its primitive roads, its lack of transport, its dour wooden buildings and its sombre-looking population, was extraordinarily depressing—or at least that's the way it appeared to Harry, Roger and I; losing our way while looking for the town's much vaunted general store. The children seemed to be well fed and warmly clad, but serious beyond their years. The women wore no make-up and the material of their clothes was as rough as the cut was shapeless. And then *she'd* swum into our line of vision, her high heels clicking along the wooden sidewalk, and her poise about as elegant as that of a model from Mayfair.

Yes, *she'd* know English, we said. And our hunch was correct. But the lady surveyed us as though we had come out of a dustbin.

"You English," she snapped at Harry, "are too lazy. Why don't you cease to act like lords, and take the trouble to learn other people's languages."

Well, fair enough, we'd heard the argument before. And chuckled over it, in our laziness. But somehow, coming from this wife of an official, or whoever she was, it annoyed. There was an indescribable spite in the way she spoke.

"Madam," began Harry, nobly attempting to put things right.

But she interrupted with a sneer: "You are living in the past, you so-called 'officers' of a doomed society—you must learn to speak the language of the future!"

This was too much. We hesitated, exchanged glances, then went into the counter-attack.

First Roger Price hit back, with a quotation in Urdu. Next Harry, following suit, murmured reprovingly a phrase or two in Greek. And lastly, after a pause, I too weighed in . . . with some patter I'd acquired from the cattlemen in South America. Full-blooded stuff, my contribution: and not to be found, I think, in a standard dictionary . . .

Our exhibition over, Harry stepped forward, and with a courtly bow said quietly: "We have between us, Madam, mastered many tongues—given just a little time and encouragement I am confident we will master yours."

A look of hate; for a moment we thought she was going to spit at us. Then, tossing her head, she clicked away.

*   *   *

Boosted by George into a sort of Selfridges of the Soviet, the Archangel store turned out to be disappointing and the prices were disappointing too. For despite all the ballyhoo about our shore leave having been delayed in order that we could change our money, we had been allowed eventually to exchange only a pound apiece; for which we had received ten roubles.

In its lay-out the shop was reminiscent of an old-fashioned "departmental store", of the sort that one sees in the more stuffy type of English country town But its wares were even less attractive. It was abundantly well supplied with plaster casts of Uncle Joe, ranging from models twice as large as life to cheap specimens of egg-cup size, but there was an astonishing dearth of less ideological commodities and their prices bore not the faintest resemblance to those which prevailed at home. Thus bamboo cigarette holders, which we could have bought in London for a humble penny, were priced at six shillings each. And yet, for the equivalent of twelve and six, I managed to buy my wife a pair of fur bedroom slippers that would have cost at least six pounds in England.

Doubtless, we reflected, the remoteness of Archangel was responsible for at least a proportion of the price confusion; but apart from my own bargain there was little we could afford. Yet our shopping, although not protracted, was made memorable by one pleasurable event; it led to us encountering our first, and only, "reception committee".

*　　*　　*

Children are children, all the world over. And Jack is a dabster at handling them. The matelots of other ships had already made themselves popular with the youngsters, and, the news of our presence getting around, the homely phrase of "penny please" was on the lips of half a dozen young Bolsheviks as soon as we stepped into the street. We were, needless to say, delighted to oblige, but when we sorted our small change, and began to hand it over, the kids insisted that we took Russian coins in return, and would not be content until we'd done so. This behaviour much impressed us. It was so dignified, we agreed, so moving; so unlike the materialistic attitude of western children . . . then George had to spoil it all by explaining . . .

The point was that the children were permitted to collect coins and other small tokens as marks of friendship . . . "But they must give something in exchange, for otherwise they will lower the prestige of their Motherland and become no better than cadgers."

And would a child cadger be punished? I asked.

George was quite horrified.

"Punishment! Of course there is no punishment, not for children. All that will happen will be in the interests of the child, his comrades, and the Soviet Union of Tomorrow."

"Goodness," I said.

"First the teacher will stand the anti-social one in front of his comrades, and point out the seriousness of his faults. And next the boy will admit his fault, and ask to make amends to the community."

I was fascinated. "But what happens after that?"

"Oh, perhaps he will be forgiven right away, but mostly he will be sent back to his place, and the rest of the class will shun him . . . until some day it is said by the teacher that he is fit to join the community again.

"In Russia," George added rather smugly, "there is always forgiveness. We do not cane the anti-social elements, not when they are only children. The cane is a barbarous relic of capitalism; we rely instead on the—how you say?—the social consciousness of the individual . . . it's better that way!"

He came back to normal. "But I must not make political talk, or I corrupt you—yes?"

"No, not at all . . ." the reply was ambiguous.

"Penny please, sailor," said the liberated urchin of the street.

*   *   *

Our leave in Archangel ended at 10 p.m. It was our only leave, for the invitation was never repeated. Yet, at the same time, I do not think that any of us were unduly disappointed; for Archangel did not impress us, except adversely. The people themselves seemed to have lost their early apprehensions of us, and some of the Red Army patrols who had helped round up the inevitable stragglers, the victims of over-exposure to the unfamiliar Vodka, were extraordinarily tolerant and human. But there was never any real attempt to make us feel "at home". Had a Russian convoy put into Portsmouth or Liverpool the clubs would have been thrown open to our allies, and there would have been countless invitations for them to see something of the people and the homes in which they lived.

It was all very different, however, with us in Archangel; where officialdom seemed most anxious to keep us at arm's length, and to frown on fraternisation. On the other hand, *Electra*, playing open host to such few Russians as ventured to come on board, did her best to establish good relationships; and despite the occasional reverse I think we had some success.

Not that the role of host didn't give us a headache or two; for Russians, it seemed, had no idea of time; and made their night "day", according to their whims. Thus it was by no means unusual for George to roll on board at two in the morning, a couple of cronies with him, and call on the Duty Officer to do the honours until reinforcements, aroused from slumber, tottered into the wardroom to help with false enthusiasm our allies "make a night of it".

Cruden's gramophone was a great attraction at the more decorous type of party, for Beethoven was a favourite and Cruden had a good selection of his music. But in general the Navy's gin and the Russians' vodka were the main aids towards our propagation of goodwill; and they served us well, except occasionally . . .

*   *   *

"I think that the time is right," said Doc.

He was eyeing the bottle with an almost clinical detachment.

Gretton, beside him, nodded reverently . . . a student observing a specialist's decision.

Then both men fell silent; until Doc remarked, a little wistfully: "It is not every day that one sees an event like this."

For to him, as mess wine caterer, had fallen the responsibility of deciding to open *Electra*'s last precious bottle of Drambuie.

Despite his keen sense of humour, and his capacity to be as irreverent as the next man, there were certain social occasions when Seymour could be as solemn as if he were presiding over a major operation; an affair where levity would not only jeopardise the patient's recovery but also be remiss, and out of place. This, then, was one such occasion, and when he made his announcement even we received it with dignity—sensing it possessed a ritualistic significance, and that whoops and shouts would be inapposite.

But, just as the glasses were filled, there came from the doorway a murmur of voices. Two Russian officers had arrived, and we had to postpone our celebration until they joined us; after which, the introductions done, we thought it suitable to propose a toast . . .

"Our brave allies of the Red Fleet, and the heroic Soviet Union . . ." Alas, even as we touched the precious liquid with our lips—taking the merest sip—our Russian guests, beaming with pleasure, grabbed hold of their glasses and knocked back that Drambuie in a single gulp, as careless of its savour as if they were drinking vodka!

Poor Doc . . . for five minutes after this impressive flourish he was incapable of speech, and sat at his place as though paralysed; a man appalled by sacrilege.

*   *   *

The party continued, our guests stayed on. The Drambuie was long since exhausted, but the vodka and the gin still flowed, and much though we loved our allies we—who had an anti-submarine patrol in the morning—were wishing them heartily home.

Suddenly an officer from *Anthony* arrived, wanting to see the Captain. *Anthony*, too, had been holding a party, but a

Russian sub-lieutenant had taken a drop too much, and was brandishing a loaded revolver. So what to do?

George danced up and down, spoke tersely to his chums, who disappeared at speed. Then he went over to *Anthony*, with May.

The problem had, however, already been resolved, and they found the wretched subbie being severely sat upon. He'd fired two rounds before they'd got him down, but he hadn't meant to hurt anyone said his hosts; he was only venting his high spirits. "So sorry that we had to treat him rough."

"*Rough!*" choked George. "I'm taking charge of him, the Bastudd! I'll give him bloody what for, yes?"

And promptly there arrived an armed escort, to hustle his compatriot off the ship.

We heard later that the unfortunate sub-lieutenant had been court-martialled, but we did not learn his fate. George, it was obvious, was very very angry with him, and although we tried to put in the odd word of excuse we just got a shrug, and the freezing reply: "He has disgraced the Red Navy, and has been punished for it. He will never disgrace our Navy again, the Bastudd!"

*   *   *

Our stay lasted a little longer than we had first expected, for the Russians wanted to send some of their ships back with us but seemingly could not make up their minds as to the numbers involved, or what speed they would be capable of producing. Discussions dragged on, but without tangible result, until eventually the British Liaison Officer came up from Moscow. After a long confab May and he stated emphatically that, whilst we were willing to help all we could, we must not saddle ourselves with vessels that could not make a minimum of twelve knots. Time was slipping fast; the weather was worsening; our own ships were needed back at home. So please could we have a prompt decision?

This note of urgency appeared to jog our allies into action, and soon we were joined by eleven Red merchantmen. There followed a convoy conference. Things were beginning to move.

*　　　*　　　*

A small Russian store vessel came alongside and we hoisted inboard a forty-gallon drum of lubricating oil for the trawlers. But when the operation was completed and I had signed the stores' note I realised that the Russian was far from happy, and wanted something else before he would take his ship away again. I turned to George to ask the reason why, and it transpired that a rubber stamp was needed: the Russian skipper would not regard a receipt as "official" unless it was rubber-stamped!

The Q.M. came to the rescue. "Why not the stamp you use on our mail, Sir?"

"Wonderful . . . top marks!"

A few minutes later the Russian was on his way home, with his documents certified throughout as "Passed By Censor" and, beneath my signature, the additional and heavily stamped inscription of "Attendance List" . . . the latter the result of our raiding Doc's medicine chest.

With the convoy ready to sail, George's liaison job was ended. He went ashore after many protestations of regret which—I am convinced—came from the heart; and our own regrets were equally sincere. A few more Georges in Russia and the post-war world would be a far less troubled place . . .

Our friend took some souvenirs with him, although I don't think his choice pleased Castle very much. For the fact of the matter was that George, a foreigner, had dared to develop a passion for his, Castle's, precious property. And Castle didn't like it. That Russian had always been hanging around *his* gun, had always been wanting to try it out. Worst of all, he had actually been aided and abetted by the ship's own officers, who had allowed him to fire the Oerlikon during a White Sea patrol. And now they had given him some shells, for keep-sakes!

Oerlikon shells are attractive things, and the bands that denote whether they are solid, tracer or high explosive, are gaily coloured. But, gay though the colours were, they could not compare in brilliancy with the green of Castle's eyes—not on the occasion of George's "presentation".

* * *

British planes flew over us as we passed through the White Sea, and then we were on our own—blessed by reasonable weather but moving much more slowly than anticipated. For it was soon apparent that the Russians had been over-opti-mistic in their assessment of the knots that could be sustained by their ships; and especially was this so in the case of an ancient freighter whose funnel smoke, infuriatingly prominent, earned her the title of Dirty Joe.

When Joe first dropped astern, we reduced speed from eleven knots to ten. But even though, by a supreme effort, she managed to catch us up, she was behind once more a couple of hours later. Night came, and we reduced to nine knots; but even this was too fast for the Russian steamer. When morning broke we could trace her only as a black smudge on the far horizon: and when *Electra* raced back to see what was the matter we found the old tub's black gang were hard-put to produce eight knots.

May turned to the Russian naval captain who had joined us, as passenger, at Archangel. "I suggest you tell her to go back; for everyone's sake—and especially her own."

But the Russian merely shrugged his shoulders; then, having bawled at his compatriots through the loud-hailer, he growled: "Oh, no. She can't go back, I have told the captain so. She can't go back, and we can't wait for her. She must carry on, and find her own way over. The captain knows the course and must take his chance."

It sounded rather terrible, put as bluntly as that. And we felt extremely guilty as we abandoned the freighter to her fate.

Our Russian passenger was a source of wonder to us. Each morning he would report on the bridge, and stop there while *Electra* ran around the convoy, counting noses and rounding up the strays. But as soon as this ritual was over he'd retire to the wardroom, settle himself in an armchair, and soberly commence to read.

It so happened that although the ship had a fairly catholic library, pride of place was taken by a very extensive collection of the works of P. G. Wodehouse. And it was to Wodehouse that the Russian now diligently applied himself, reading no one but P. G. This trait of the captain's struck us as peculiar; because never once did we detect him smile, or show the slightest appreciation that the author had intended to be funny. And Davies was particularly intrigued, conjecturing endlessly on the deductions that our guest might be drawing from his reading.

"Guns, he's got *another* from the shelf! I wonder if he expects to find a Jeeves in England?"

"Well, why not?" This from Jenner-Fust. "There's many a Bertie Wooster in Admiralty Intelligence!"

Davies and I held diametrically opposed opinions regarding Wodehouse. Both of us had enjoyed his works, but I argued that as P. G. was apparently quite reconciled to being housed in comfort as the guest of our enemies his books should be banned the Navy, while Harry, with his wider viewpoint, asserted that they were works of art, and that art belonged not to a man, or a country, but to the world at large.

"You're an incorrigible Blimp" had long been his favourite taunt, to which, since the arrival of the Russian, he was able to add: "Even the 'bolshevik hordes' are more tolerant than you!"

As the voyage continued, we grew more and more perplexed at our passenger's absorption. Maybe he thought that the characters created by Wodehouse were typical of the "decadent upper classes"? If so he was in for a shock. Or maybe he was swotting up the book's colloquialisms? This, on reflection, seemed improbable. For a chap likes to air the knowledge he acquires; and never once did we get an "I say, old Bean" from our studious guest, who remained, to the last, impenetrable.

* * *

After a fair start the weather turned dirty on us, with low-lying clouds and driving rain and a mass of stinging hail. But it was by no means as bad as it might have been, and on our third night out, there came a temporary lull, in which I saw for the first and only time in my life that rare phenomenon, St. Elmo's fire. Our topmasts and yards glowed with light, almost as if outlined by strips of neon tubing; and the reflection was so bright that we could pick out quite clearly the ship next to us. The captain came up from the chartroom to watch the spectacle, and Doc said that many of the early explorers held that it was a sign of good luck—a pleasing superstition, which in our case was justified. For although the weather again turned rough, this only made the task of the enemy's planes more difficult, and we made Pentland Firth without a single hostile incident.

When about to leave the ship the Russian captain said, rather hesitantly: "I wish we had been another two days at sea; there are still two books that I would like to have read."

We gave them to him as a farewell present . . . Wodehouse of course!

Only one thing still marred our satisfaction, the thought of the straggler we had had to leave behind. Ships and aircraft were sent out to search for her, but, try though they might, they could achieve no result. And then, several days after the rest of the convoy had been dispersed, a long column of smoke was observed off Leith. Slow but sure, Dirty Joe had made the grade.

*　　　*　　　*

Three days of unexpected leave had ended; the time had come to part. Now, as my wife walked the long country mile with me—through the soft moist early winter's day to the little station at Elstead—we were both very silent, as though not knowing what to say.

Never before had I allowed Belles to come to the station with me; I had a completely unreasoning hatred of goodbyes; I have it still. But this time I was desperately anxious to prolong our time together; and draw out even the sad moment of farewell.

We had to wait quite a while before the little local pulled in, and my sense of unease grew greater every minute. All our previous partings had, naturally, been tinged with sadness; but I was a sailor, and Belles was a sailor's wife, and tomorrow, we used to say, would bring us a day nearer to seeing each other again. Yet on this occasion our philosophy failed to give us much support, for each of us had the feeling that there was something out of the ordinary about *this* goodbye; try though each of us might to keep it in the heart.

The train chuffed fussily to a stop, and I got into the compartment, feeling faintly sick. I wanted to say to my wife: "Be brave, for there are bad days ahead for you and the boys."

But I didn't say it.

I wanted to say to my wife: "It will be a long, long time before I see you again, but, oh God, I WILL see you again!"

But I didn't say it.

I wanted at once both to warn her, and reassure her. But of

course I did neither. We just said the usual things—and *felt* the words that still remained unspoken.

The whistle blew, doors slammed. I left my wife, a lonely figure, waving . . . waving. I saw her dwindle from sight, and the station vanish too. And then I sat back, self-conscious.

It was not until I crossed London and boarded the train for the north that my depression eased. It was good to see one's fellow sufferers crowding the corridors; a relief to realise that one was not the only chap with a problem . . . an escape to feel oneself part of the pattern once again, the familiar pattern of navy blue. From now on there would be little time to brood, and self-pity would be "out". As the express roared through the night a bunch of inebriated matelots began to sing . . .

*   *   *

Back in Rosyth there were many chores to do—some of them quite rewarding, if you knew the ropes.

While snooping around the naval stores, to "acquire" various items of equipment that had been on order for months but had never been delivered, I uncovered a consignment of heavy sheepskin coats, designed to protect the wearer against the rigours of the Arctic. *Electra* "won" the lot!

Never one to split hairs about the legality of actions designed to further the ship's welfare, Jenner-Fust was delighted by the manœuvre. After all, we'd have sailed for Scapa before an inquest could begin . . .

But May said next morning, apropos nothing at all: "One day, Guns, you will get me made an Admiral. Or else—what is more probable—you will have me court-martialled!"

At the time I merely grinned. Yet my conscience was not left long untroubled. For scarcely had *Electra* reached Scapa and settled at the buoy than May was tersely ordered to report to Rear-Admiral Destroyers. Something was up!

When the Captain returned all the officers were mustered on the quarterdeck, intensely curious. But ignoring them he called me over to him.

He was wearing that "ice-cold" look that he usually reserved for moments of extreme displeasure. "Mr. Cain, I wish to speak with you."

I wilted, that "Mister" sounded ominous. The Old Man had hitherto never called me anything but Guns.

"Sir . . .?"

"Those Arctic coats that you *procured* at Rosyth, parcel them up, and send them to Rear-Admiral Destroyers—it's immediate."

"Yes, Sir!"

The Yeoman approached. "From Commander-in-Chief, Sir. You are to report on board—barge will be sent."

The Captain again left the ship, with a parting word for me. "And *don't* forget those 'rabbitted' stores!"

Miserably I superintended the return of our erstwhile winnings, watching the coats being dumped into the boat while my "friends" regaled me with stories of other officers whose initiative and enterprise had led them into hot water, mostly with fatal results. But as time went by, and as May continued to remain on the Flagship, even Harry's perverted sense of humour began to falter. We were a well-knit crowd, and even though the idea of a disciplinary enquiry might be too silly for words, we knew of so many "silly" incidents that had cost officers their careers that my queasiness communicated itself to the others, who ceased to joke.

May came back, still looking very serious.

"Those stores away?"

"Yes, Sir . . . returned intact. Anything up, Sir?"

He gave me a not unkindly glance, and shrugged. "I'll have a word with you later on."

"Hell," said Harry, who'd overheard, "but who'd have

thought the silly asses would have taken it so seriously!"

At lunch the Captain appeared to be his usual friendly self, but that meant little or nothing: for it is the tradition of the Navy to leave its problems outside the mess, and May was a great traditionalist. But late afternoon, following more comings and goings between our ship and the others, the atmosphere was pretty tense. *Electra* and *Express* had each received a signal ordering them to sea to act as targets for some of the cruisers, but this sort of thing was a purely routine job and certainly did not require a series of conferences to settle its arrangement. Then, just after we slipped, the Captain broke his silence.

"Gentlemen, you have probably been wondering about my activities today, and why I have been so long away."

My face went red.

"Well, first let me assure all those concerned"—there was a twinkle in his eye—"that certain items of equipment owe their return from this ship to the simple fact that we won't need them any more."

"For we are going east, gentlemen, to a warmer climate, to a place where the sun is shining . . . we will be escorting the *Prince of Wales*, and probably to Singapore!"

*　　*　　*

"So *that* was the reason for the conferences, the solemnity, the return of the loot—what a wonderful smoke screen you provided for the planners," said Harry, as the ship got under way.

"Singapore . . . I feel so relieved," I said, "that it could be the South Pole, for all I care."

"Poor old Guns. But every cause must have its martyr, some chaps are destined for the role . . ."

Slowly *Electra* curtsied in the gathering swell, turning past the old Man of Hoy around whose head the seagulls screamed, and I viewed the tall straight pillar with some affection, remembering how often it had been a navigational landmark to our ship, and recalling its peculiar fascination for Harry. He'd often talked about landing on Hoy, and we had planned to walk around the Old Man, if it were possible; but somehow we had never had the opportunity, and now I said, unthinkingly: "Take a good look at your friend of stone, it's the last time you will see him."

But Harry jerked round on me, suddenly grim. "What's biting you, Guns? And why so morbid?"

"Morbid?" I tried to pass it off with a laugh. It was not like Harry to be jumpy . . .

"I'm not *morbid*, I'm optimistic! It'll be a couple of years at least before we return, and by then the war will be over and Scapa will no longer interest you."

"Why shouldn't it interest me?" He was still a bit tense.

"Well, you surely won't want to bring your lady friend up here . . . to impress her with the beauties of the Flow!"

Harry smiled, but made no answering jest, and for several minutes we were silent, watching the Old Man diminish in stature, and the foam-frothed water dividing it from the cliffs blend into the darkening sky. Then cocoa came up to the bridge, and we were ourselves again.

*　　　*　　　*

Our "target" exercise never materialised: for once clear of Scapa we parted from the cruisers and set course at speed for Greenock, where everything was on top line. We came alongside the wall to find several railway waggons waiting there, and soon fuel, provisions, and cases of tropical clothing were being loaded into the ship. Only once was there a hitch in this smooth operation, when *Express* got caught up by the tide and for a few frightening seconds seemed likely to plough right through us. Then by using full engine power she managed to pull up, and, apart from a few bent stanchions, all was well.

So far the troops had been told we were going "foreign", but that was all they knew. "Foreign" could cover a multitude of places and they didn't know the purpose of the journey, or what company we would keep. Only when we left Greenock behind, and found ourselves near our point of rendezvous with the battlewaggon, could May inform them. The general reaction was one of interest: a change would be as good as a rest . . .

"What's it like out East, Sir?" asked one of the torpedomen.

"Fine," I replied, "just fine. Bags of sunshine, plenty of things to see, and something of interest happening every moment . . ."

"Be a bit peculiar, us being out of the way though, Sir? Seems strange to leave it all behind, and at a time like this . . ."

"Well, you never know—there's always Japan."

"The Japs? *They'll* never fight, Sir. Or at least I don't see how they can. They haven't got the oil, and besides there's Singapore, Sir!"

"Anyway," chimed in Bill Braley, "if Hitler can't get us down I don't see what chance the Mikado has. Horrible little yellow men, the Japs . . . but the Yanks, I think, Sir, could knock them to Kingdom Come."

Such was the substance of our conversation, as Scotland became a blur upon the sea, and then dropped out of sight . . . as *Electra* bade farewell to the Battle of the Atlantic, and turned her bows towards the south.

10

Eastwards to Singapore

CONSIDERING the tragic consequences of the move, it is impossible to reflect without irony on the smooth manner in which the arrangements for the transfer of Tom Phillips' squadron to the Far East were carried out. Seldom can a fleet organisation have worked with greater efficiency; everything went like clockwork.

Once south of Ireland *Electra* and *Express*, refuelling from the *Prince of Wales*, were screened by two fleet destroyers, which returned to base when the operation was concluded. Then, off the Azores, another escort force took over, and screened the battlewaggon while we went into harbour to top-up with fuel for the second lap.

We were very light of heart during the voyage out, and quickly engaged in a good-natured duel with our betters, the officers of the Flagship. We knew very little about Tom Phillips, although it was whispered that he was a bag of brains, a Churchill man, and had all the confidence of the powers-that-be. But Phillips had brought his own staff with him from the Admiralty, and as the "staffies" could not be expected to keep up-to-date with every routine order affecting the day-to-day running of the Fleet, their instructions to us sometimes went awry, and gave us the opportunity—so dear to every seaman's heart—of scoring against the Flagship.

*　　　*　　　*

"Escort will carry out a practice sub-calibre throw-off shoot, using *P.O.W.* as a target at 0900 tomorrow. *Electra* to engage . . ."

The signal came from *Prince of Wales*, when we were clear of the main submarine zone, and approaching Freetown.

May sent for me. "Guns, see this signal? We had better get everything on top line."

"Can't do it, Sir."

The black brows snapped together and two words exploded. "Why not?"

"You remember, Sir, that when we were in London there was a Fleet Order . . ."

"Well?"

"All sub-calibre tubes were to be returned, and ships were only to draw them on loan, when actually detailed for practice. I did tell you at the time, Sir . . .", I added virtuously.

Memory came back; "But of course you did! Have you the number of the order?"

"Give me five minutes, Sir . . ."

Every naval officer likes to get in a dig at his superior if he can, and soon we were signalling happily: "Attention is drawn to Fleet Order 726."

The practice was abandoned!

Later in the day May handed me another signal. "Just laugh *this* off."

This time the staffies were ordering us to fire two torpedoes fitted with practice heads, but I'd already been warned, and had prepared accordingly.

"What an extraordinary coincidence, Sir! Strangely enough I was checking through Fleet Orders when you called, and the one in my pocket affects the matter vitally. You will remember the order, Sir, the one that instructed us to return all practice heads to a common pool, and to fill the space gained with extra depth charges."

May smiled and turned to the Yeoman, to dictate another signal. And Tingle smiled, too, as he morsed its contents.

Round Two for *Electra*.

Next day, anchored at Freetown, we were visited by a party of officers from *Prince of Wales*.

"Where's that well-informed Gunner of yours?" they said. "We want his ears for a necktie . . ."

*   *   *

Midway between Freetown and the Cape we again refuelled, and then Tom Phillips, anxious to get in as much time as possible with the South African authorities, left us to follow at the highest speed compatible with our fuel supplies while he cracked on at top speed to Capetown. There was much heart-burning among the company at this decision—which meant that our big sister would have a longer spell in harbour—and *Electra* lifted her skirts extensively in order to shorten the disparity in privilege. We were also a bit put out because the *P.O.W.*'s destination was Capetown, while we were sent to the naval base at Simonstown; but all grouses were forgotten in our pleasure at South Africa.

The hospitality of our friends there was overwhelming, but even to see the lights of Capetown, after being used for over two years to the blackout of wartime Europe, was in itself a big experience. On our first evening ashore we were content just to stand on the side of a hill, and gaze for nearly an hour on the well-lit streets below. The shops, in particular, fascinated us . . . the shops that, freshly painted, and unstained by fire, were crammed with all the good things that we had almost forgotten. Not a blitzed site anywhere, not a warden in view, not a hint of a ration card . . . as we looked around us, like a bunch of children, it seemed too wonderful to be true.

*   *   *

We went to dinner in one of the best hotels, and the waiter

brought each of us a menu, a bound book of about the size of the postwar *Times*.

Running his eyes down the list, Davies made helpful suggestions. "What about this . . .?" and "We'll try that."

After a while, I got rather irked at such confident proprietorship. "It's all very well for you, but I can't understand a damned word . . ."

"But surely they taught you to *read*?" said Harry.

I glanced over his shoulder, and suddenly cottoned on. The menu was divided into three sections, printed in French, English and Afrikaans. Trust Harry to have bagged the English version!

We settled for a comparatively modest meal, quite forgetting that South Africans are normally big eaters, and that we had grown used to wartime helpings. The platefuls set before us seemed enormous, and I don't think we could possibly have done justice to them had it not been for the encouragement we received from the waiter, who obviously felt that we were in desperate need of nourishment. "There you are, chums, it will do you good . . ." and similar exhortations accompanied his triumphant delivery of each piled plateful, and then he'd stand back and beam upon us; benevolent, almost paternal in his determination to see that every available vitamin and calorie found its way into our "under-nourished" bodies.

His colleague, at the next table but one, had an equally unorthodox approach towards his duties. Some senior officers were seated there, and when one of them complained affectedly that the wine was "corked" the waiter merely grabbed the glass, poured himself a drink, tossed it back in a single gulp, then said informally: "Seems all right to me, chum, but don't you worry, I'll fix another bottle."

The S.O.'s looked so put out by this retort that we almost choked ourselves with the strawberries . . .

As we wandered into the lounge, intending to sit down

quietly and digest our meal in peace, we were joined by a young South African Air Force officer and his wife. "Good evening, fellow sufferers. This is Joan . . . and I'm called Rob. Care for a drink?"

We cared.

"This joint will be closing soon," he said, "but there's a dance on at McGinty's for you types, and as Joan and I are going there we can show you both the way."

Harry accepted gracefully, but I asked pertinently: "Will there be a bar?"

"Plenty of liquor," he laughed, "but nothing you can buy."

The dance was a great success, so also were the drinks. But at first we were a little perplexed as to what to use for glasses.

"Oh, that's easily solved," said the Air Force, demonstrating. "First open a bottle of ginger ale and drink half the contents, next top up with brandy and carry on drinking. After that?" He reached for another bottle. "You refill smartly with a mixture of ginger ale and brandy!"

By three in the morning there was a chronic shortage of ginger ale. But somehow, by then, it didn't seem to matter.

*   *   *

Our stay in South Africa was brief but memorable, and I don't think there is a single survivor of *Electra* who does not recall the South Africans with kindness, whatever his political viewpoint and whatever the sad differences that may exist today between our two countries, and between the "English" element and the Afrikaner. For this was a happy and momentous interlude in our lives . . . the last real chance to celebrate before our comradeship was split; the last brief relaxation for our ship before she faced the supreme issue, the ultimate agony.

In Tokio, at the Navy Ministry, a group of modern barbarians were already deciding on our fate; but though the shadow would soon be upon us, we could not sense its approach. Our hearts were light, the ship was well equipped, and while Capetown, with its generous hospitality, looked after our off-duty hours, Simonstown catered for *Electra*'s military needs—promptly, efficiently, and very willingly.

*   *   *

The standard Royal Navy depth charge is filled either with T.N.T. or a mixture of T.N.T. and amatol. But whereas the former explosive is extremely stable and can stand up to any degree of heat or cold, amatol is inclined to be a little temperamental. Although cheap to produce, and although—when mixed with T.N.T.—it can create a greater explosive effect than that produced by T.N.T. alone, it is rather vulnerable to the extreme heat of the tropics, and exudes a sort of crystal, the effect of which can be dangerous. Greater safety precautions had therefore to be taken with regard to amatol and T.N.T. combined than with pure T.N.T., but I did not want to be overburdened by such precautions. Should we have to go into action in a hurry I wanted our depth charges ready for immediate use, and wished, therefore, to return our "mixed" charges to Simonstown and get pure T.N.T. in exchange.

The Supply Officer—a civilian—was sympathetic enough, and promised to see what he could do. Then, on the day before we sailed, he came aboard again; the bearer of good news.

"I have just received airmailed instructions from London," he told me, "and although a copy will reach you in due course you can have a sort of preview.

"In brief, new regulations have been drawn up, and it has been decided that if a depth charge doesn't contain more than forty per cent amatol, and is of fairly recent issue, you can cut the extra precautions and treat as pure T.N.T."

I checked up—to find that, as from that day, all of our

charges were "pure T.N.T". And I took a copy of the Depot's letter—which saved a lot of work and worry later on.

*   *   *

"From *Prince of Wales*. Report number of depth charges carried, with number filled T.N.T., with number T.N.T. and amatol, with number filled amatol."

Once clear of Capetown the staffies had got to work on us again.

"What about it, Guns?" queried May.

"T.G.M. has the list," I answered.

"Then better ask him for it!"

Picking up the phone I asked Mash to bring the list to the bridge, and a few seconds later passed on the requested details.

Back came the anticipated triumphant signal: "Attention is called to Explosives Regulations, Chapter X, paras. etc., etc. . . . HAVE YOU COMPLIED?"

The Old Man looked thoughtful. "Got your copy of E.R.'s handy?"

"No, Sir, but I can pop down to my cabin and get it."

"No need for you to bother, send the messenger instead."

Davies shot me a wicked glance. "If he goes by himself, Sir, he will have cooked up an alibi by the time he gets back."

The book arrived on the bridge, and the Captain looked up the relevant passages.

"Dammit. It seems pretty definite in here. We haven't slipped up, Guns? We've left nothing undone I trust."

Behind his back, Harry was doing a pantomime throat cutting act, but I ignored my friend, and concentrated on the book. "Cover with canvas, wash down with hoses, etc., etc. . . ."

"Haven't done a thing about complying with this little lot!"

May smiled.

"It's old stuff, Sir." I dismissed the regulations with a shrug. "It's been superseded by the A.D.1. we got at Simonstown—there's a copy of it in the back of the book."

The Captain's gratification was intense. He had seen the letter before, but had wanted to make doubly sure of its purport. He turned to Tingle. "Yeoman, make the following signal." His tone was silky. "Attention is called to Armament Depot Instruction 999 stroke eleven, stroke four one . . ."

It was a long, long time before the Flagship sent a reply, together with the humble request that we proceed alongside, to pass by line immediately a copy of the mysterious 999!

But we did at least receive a letter in exchange. Addressed to me, it read: "I will yet catch you with your trousers down, you villain. So good luck to you, for you will be ruddy well needing it. Your inveterate enemy, Staffie."

It was our biggest moment.

*   *   *

An albatross had joined us as we left Capetown and had followed the squadron for hundreds of miles. Graceful, seemingly effortless, it appeared to glide through the still air behind the ship and we could scarcely detect a movement from its massive wings, which, rigidly outspread, reached like a cross, in virginal white relief, above the sparkling green of the tepid sea. But now, as we prepared to cross the line once more, our escort abruptly left us, as if unwilling to venture into the northern latitudes, and apart from our sister ships there was no sign of life in the vast expanse of the Indian Ocean. Not even the sharp triangle of a shark's fin disturbed the glassy flatness, and the hot wind, when it stirred, did so half furtively; conversing in a whisper, quickly dead.

After so many days and nights of storm and strain, so many

recollections of the blustering, bullying rollers of the north, *Electra*, at this stage of her journey, was possessed by a strange sort of enchantment in which, free of the menace of submarine or mine or the bite of winter weather, we saw many things to admire and wonder at; succumbing to the fascination of the phenomena around us, rather like tourists, determined to have their money's worth.

In the region of the equator the sun sets with a jerk, and legend has it that at sunset a great flash of green light spreads across the horizon. On *Electra* opinion was divided as to whether or not this was merely a fairy tale, and as the ship was due to cross the line almost precisely at sunset the bridge became packed with officers, inquisitive and eager to resolve the argument. Yet, as the sun went down, the triumphant shout of the believers, all of whom swore they'd seen the flash—"as fast as lightning"—was followed by a derisive jeer from the infidels who said they hadn't. So in the end the test was disappointing, except that it proved maybe that a man will only see as much—or as little—as he has a mind to believe in.

The following night, while sharing the middle watch with Davies, I was privileged however to witness a spectacle that, as regards its authenticity, was quite unimpeachable.

There was no moon, no sign of cloud. The stars burned more brightly than ever and the Southern Cross, hanging low in the sky, glittered like an ornament against a black velvet gown. It was one of those nights that make a man feel that sea-going is worth while, and that the ha'pence are more plentiful than the kicks. Then slowly, as we yarned, a great rich glow began to spread across the far horizon, a glow like that of the dawn but rising from the north. Puzzled, we gazed at it, as it became brighter and broader, until finally we realised what it was—a glowing belt of phosphorescence stretching ahead of our course. It must have been every bit of four miles wide, and as the ship moved through it her bow wave gleamed and scintillated with exquisite flashes of blue and greenish light. A moving and wonderful sight . . .

Said Davies: "This trip makes me feel a little guilty, the war seems so far away."

"Suits me!" I said.

And then, in the morning, we came to our secret refuelling base—a blue lagoon encircled by silver sand and screened by green palm trees, but with its present purpose betrayed by the smoke of the lurking oiler which was visible up to twenty miles away. Then followed a quick top-up with fuel and we travelled at speed to Colombo.

* * *

Tom Phillips was under pressure; so much was obvious. He had rushed ahead of us to South Africa, and scarcely had we caught up with him and entered the Indian Ocean than he had again left us to our own devices and had pushed on in the *Prince of Wales*, arriving unescorted in Ceylon. We wondered what all the rush was in aid of, and wondered even more when we saw in Colombo Harbour the familiar silhouette of H.M.S. *Repulse*. The battle-cruiser had also arrived in haste from Europe, and with her were two destroyers, the *Jupiter*, and our sister ship, *Encounter*. But we had little time to exchange greetings, for only a few hours later the order came to put to sea again, and the combined force, weighing rapidly, made straight for Singapore. But this time even the *Prince of Wales* was not fast enough for the Admiral. He had gone ahead of us by plane.

Our voyage looked like becoming something other than a pleasure cruise. Things were warming up.

Yeoman Tingle slid alongside me. "Wonder why the Admiral's gone by air, Sir?"

"Oh, I daresay he wants to use the extra time to get a complete picture of what's happening in the Far East, and the sort of situation we may expect."

Tingle: "H'm . . . Seems funny to me, Sir."

I glanced at him, warily. "Out with it, Yeoman. Just say what's on your mind."

"Nothing much, Sir." His eyes were innocent. "It just struck me that the Admiral might have sat down and begun to think to himself . . . the *Prince of Wales* and a battle-cruiser and four destroyers too, now this has happened before. The *Prince of Wales*, a battle-cruiser . . . what an unfortunate combination . . . I think it may be safer by air!" Then chuckling at his own grim joke our Yeoman moved off to other business.

As for me? Quite suddenly I felt depressed, recalling a night of darkness and rain when we'd waited to escort the battle-waggon from the builders to the Fleet. "An unlucky ship, Sir," that's what the lad on the bridge had said, "they should never have called her the *Prince of Wales*."

And then I remembered something else. The bric-a-brac floating on the ocean after the passing of the mighty *Hood*.

*   *   *

The situation in the Far East had worsened, and worsened considerably. We had been sent there as a deterrent but our bluff was being called. We had been used in a gamble, and the chips were going down. Thus Tom Phillips' dash to Singapore. Thus yet another flying visit—this time to the Phillipines, and a conference with MacArthur and the U.S. Admiral Hart.

Washington, as we now know, already appreciated that the Japanese were heading towards a conflict. But the domestic politics of the United States made it almost impossible, in the short space of time available, for the U.S. forces to join with ours in order to anticipate the attack. Consequently, for Phillips and his American opposite numbers, this hasty meeting (which their respective governments had urged with considerable enthusiasm) must have seemed a little quaint. Each of those three able men wished earnestly to concert a common plan of action. Each of them was desperately anxious to act in alliance, and to act at once. And yet, there they were—all obliged in the ultimate to confine their ambitions to a discussion of what steps they considered to be desirable, and the preparation of a report thereon.

This situation—thoroughly fantastic—was concealed from us at the time, which was perhaps as well for our peace of mind. The fate of the Far East was in the balance—but the Yanks must not act with us at Singapore, and we must not go to Manilla. The fate of one half of the population of the world was at stake—but the reactions of Congress had to be considered, a consideration that was to prove near-fatal for the West.

We mustn't provoke the Japs? There was still, ostensibly, a peace on? What nonsense such arguments make today to those who suffered as a result of them, and what nonsense they would have made at the time, to even the humblest rating . . . had he known of course, what our leading American friends already knew . . . had he, like them, had access to the latest top-secret signals sent by Tokio to its "negotiators" in the States.

*   *   *

It was on December 2nd that the Eastern Fleet reached its destination. But, though the testing time was nigh, Singapore was unaware of it, and the *Prince of Wales* and *Repulse*, making a triumphant entry into crowded Keppel Harbour, were greeted as though they were the main attractions of a seaside carnival. The destroyers, however, proceeded unpublicised to the naval base itself, on the north-east shore of the island. And there, incognito, as it were, we had time for a little hard thinking.

Quite candidly the frivolous attitude of the wealthy, social-conscious city, crammed with every luxury, and sure of itself to the point of arrogance, came as a shock to us. There seemed to be little awareness among the people we met of the possibility that the disputes between Japan and the West might lead to something worse than a war of words. From the way in which some of the local folk reacted one would have thought the squadron had been despatched from the western theatre for no more than a social call.

Said a highly-placed civilian official, on the night following our arrival: "This must be a wonderful change for you. A regular holiday!"

And then, waving a cigarette holder that must have been a foot long, he exclaimed, astonished by a query from Jenner-Fust: "*War* . . . will there be War you ask? My dear old boy, there isn't a chance of it. You fellows just don't know the queer habits of these little yellow blighters, *they are bluffing up to the hilt!*"

Yet, even among the few who did go so far as to consider that the Japs might mean business, there was a ghastly complacency—a complacency that seemed far worse than anything we had encountered in Britain in the era of the "phoney" war, and even less excusable. For in Britain complacency arose from a certain native truculence, a feeling on the part of the average man that, should the Forces fail him, he could always take off his coat and thrash Hitler by himself. In Singapore, however, we had the feeling that the majority sentiment could best be expressed as: "Relax, maintain aplomb, and leave the Forces to do their job. It's what we pay them for!"

Thus, on registering surprise that the northern part of the "island fortress"—the part which faced the peninsula—was virtually undefended, one of our number received this retort from a local businessman. "Good heavens . . . Haven't you Service chaps burned up enough money already without wanting to burn up any more?

"Singapore," he added, "lives by *trade*, and not by guns."

Later I raised the vexed subject of the apparent weakness of the island's north, and was told: "You just don't understand the geography. There are hundreds of miles of jungle between here and Siam. An enemy would have to keep to the roads, and even a handful of troops could hold him for months.

"An attack from the north? Just take a look at the map, old chap . . . if you said such a thing in company you'd be the laughing stock of the Club!"

But, if a sense of apprehension was conspicuous by its absence, so too—I speak in general terms—was a sense of service. And although I hate to be unkind about it, especially in view of the valiant way in which so many of the European community were to rise to the occasion later on, there is no doubt in my mind that the "business as usual" attitude of the majority, and the manner in which they preserved their precious shibboleths, had a disheartening effect upon the Services and contributed to the subsequent disaster.

Taking tea in "Raffles", we hardly knew whether to be amused or saddened when a "lady" at the next table eyed us up and down, and then declaimed: "Yes, they may very well be officers, my dear, but if so they must be terribly, terribly junior officers. And temporary too, of course!"

*　　　*　　　*

From the banner headlines in the press, and the way in which the arrival of the squadron had been "written up", you'd have thought, as Ted Mash said, that the entire naval might of the Empire was mustered at Singapore. It was almost as if we were trying to impress somebody—and he could give one guess as to who that Somebody might be! But would the Nip be fool enough to fall for it? And—if he didn't—what came next?

Mash was not alone in his puzzlement. In the wardroom we too attempted to find an answer. One battleship, one elderly and ill-protected battle-cruiser, and four destroyers—three of them ageing—would not mean very much in a showdown with the Imperial Japanese Navy. Together we formed a force that was strong enough to be missed by the battle-line at home, but we could scarcely be regarded as strong enough to intimidate Britain's foes abroad. Yet, on the other hand, ours not to reason why too closely; and it was probable, we concluded, that our presence formed part of some secret master-plan, whereby should the balloon go up we would be fighting side by side with the massive Pacific Fleet of the United States. In this respect our intervention might serve to be decisive.

We were not to know that although Great Britain had been pledged to declare war on Japan should America be attacked, the pledge was not reciprocal. We were not to know that there was no positive guarantee that America would not stay neutral in the event of an attack upon British power alone— odious though the role would be to the U.S. Navy, and however short might be its duration.

But equally were we ignorant of the fact that something was under way that, in the next few hours, would make such considerations as guarantees, pacts, pledges, and the rest of it, appear about as meaningless as bits of paper, blazing in a fire.

Already Nagumo's carriers were bearing down upon Hawaii; already three hundred Japanese naval pilots were toasting tomorrow's dawn.

11

End of a Myth

IT was December 7th, 1941. Even by Singapore standards the night was hot. Wandering up from the wardroom before turning in I tried to fathom the reason for the strange uneasiness that had come over me a few hours earlier and still persisted; this untoward restlessness that I could not shake off. The air was so heavy that it was as though an invisible curtain had spread itself around the ship. It weighed on me, and yet I was sure that my fidgetiness had little to do with the weather.

I nodded to the Quartermaster: "Looks as though we're in for a storm."

"Won't be for the first time, Sir," he answered, unconcerned.

I glanced at the land; a lighter shade than the night, and framed by a great glow to the south—the reflection of the gay lights of Singapore City. Yes, everything was in order, everything was under control; yet even the extent of the silence struck me as peculiarly ominous, like the calm that presages the weather's breaking. The mud of the Johore Strait, between the island and the mainland, stank to heaven; the tide against *Electra*'s side ran sluggishly, and lapped but limpidly the mangrove roots of the shore: my restlessness continued.

The cabin was like an oven. I was sweating when I reached my bunk, and found difficulty in breathing. The port was wide open, but made little difference in terms of comfort: and sleep came all too slowly, although I was very tired.

I awoke—to a crescendo of sound, and a flash that lit up the bulkhead. So my guess had been correct, I surmised sleepily—a tropical storm. I reached up, to close the port and keep out the expected rain. And then I awoke in earnest; for the "thunder" was the clamour of the guns, and the lightning too was theirs. Great sheets of dazzling white were shooting angrily over the cone-shaped hills, and the tracers were stretching like rows of beads among the shellbursts . . . those bright new stars that winked in the crackling sky. Grabbing a tin hat I raced to my action station. The war had caught up with us again!

The Japs flew high. Clearly illuminated by the searchlights they scudded like tiny silver flies across the island, in perfect formation and impervious to our fire. They were far above the reach of the snub-nosed Buffalo fighters that formed Singapore's air support. And they were also above the reach of the guns, or so it appeared. They did not stay for long; they were to stay far longer on subsequent occasions. They did not create much damage; the worst raids were to come when the defence, scant though it was, had been weakened still further and the bombers could operate from captured bases, nearer to the target. But, all the same, the attack had come to Singapore as a terrible shock. The first cracks had begun to appear in the "impregnable" fortress.

When daylight came we heard that there were some two hundred casualties. And we gathered that, although the local civil defence forces had worked with great efficiency and devotion, native nerves had been badly rattled. Disturbing rumours were getting around, the start of a legion. And the Jap-inspired Fifth Column was setting about its dirty work with relish.

*   *   *

The news of Pearl Harbour reached us—like a blow between the teeth. Then anger succeeded our initial stupefaction, and confidence came too. So the Yanks had been caught like a row of sitting ducks—we might have expected it! They were raw, they were unprepared, they had had things far too easy. But with us it would be a different story. We were warned, we were waiting, we were "rarin' to go".

The radio commentator did not tell us that the entire Pacific Fleet had been almost eliminated. But we could guess that things must be bad, to say the least of it. The Nips wouldn't have risked a blow against America without packing a lot behind their fist . . . sufficient, at any rate, to send their adversary reeling. Yet, on the other side of the picture was the hope that the enemy's concentration of his main forces against Hawaii might give us—in South-East Asia—a better chance to meet him on equal terms. We hadn't held the ring against Germany for two years and a quarter without learning something of the art of war. And we were confident, absolutely so, of beating the Jap—should we meet him in battle at sea, and at anything approaching his strength. Then, in the early afternoon, fresh tidings reached us. Hongkong was being attacked, and was resisting savagely—though hopelessly—a three-dimensional assault. The Nips were pouring into Siam, coming by sea and land from their bases in Indo-China. And now Malaya was facing an invasion threat.

Enemy transports were said to be unloading troops at Singora, to the Federation's north.

We sailed at 17.30.

*　　　*　　　*

Unbeknown to us, those most directly concerned, the Admiralty had originally opposed the despatch of the *Prince of Wales* and the *Repulse* to the Far East. Then, giving ground reluctantly, it had urged that the "deterrent" be based in a less forward position than Singapore, which was an ideal base for a strong striking force, but was too far exposed for a weak one.

The Admiralty view appears to have been that any hope of "tying up" a superior force of Japanese warships by the threat of what our small squadron might do was dependent on our possessing a refuge, or jumping-off point, which was well screened from enemy observation or surprise attack. Against this view prevailing, however, were many other considerations, political and diplomatic. And the deference paid to these —which doubtless appeared formidable enough—were, in the end, to result in tragedy.

We now know that, shortly before the Japanese attack began, Admiral Phillips had made plans to disengage from Singapore. Furthermore, he had actually received Churchill's belated blessing for the move. We also know that, immediately *after* the Japanese attack, the former arguments of the War Cabinet were reversed, and that it was decided (to quote Sir Winston) that "the big ships must go to sea and vanish among the innumerable islands".

But by then it was too late. The deterrent having failed to deter, we were in it—up to the neck!

*   *   *

Once clear of Singapore we steered north-east and a rumour spread that we were going to the Philippines. Only four destroyers, *Electra*, *Express*, *Vampire* and *Tenedos*, were available to escort the battlewaggons and we had the idea that we were joining up with the American Asiatic Fleet, which, though not possessing capital ships or carriers, had about a dozen destroyers and three heavy cruisers. But all misconceptions were quickly corrected . . . We were to intervene at Singora.

Broadly speaking, the Admiral planned to keep to the existing course for the next twenty-four hours and then, on the 9th, he would turn towards the north as soon as darkness fell. After that, if we had still succeeded in evading Japanese reconnaissance he would make a high-speed dash past Cape Cambodia—

the nearest point of Indo-China—and go straight for Singora.
The Fleet, he planned, would arrive at dawn, beat up the convoy, attempt to bring the Japanese battle-cruiser *Kongo* into
action, then start a quick run back to base, protected by shore-
based fighters against air reprisals.

It was a bold scheme, and its details were clear cut. It looked
pretty good to us. If it had come off as planned it might have
changed the face of human history: that it didn't come off was
one of the saddest tragedies of our time.

* * *

The night was quiet, but with the dawn the Admiral learned
that air support off Singora could not be given. This was a
major blow. Originally he had made adequate air cover a pre-
requisite for the operation's attempt, so how far dare he risk
continuing without it?

Yet, though the hazards were high, so too was the prize.
The Japanese had not yet observed the squadron's move: they
might well continue in their ignorance. There was a chance of
catching the enemy off balance: that chance would have gone
once his troops were installed ashore. Thus Phillips decided to
press on, despite the new development. For the time being at
any rate he would continue on his original course. But if
spotted during the day he would immediately turn for home.

The rest of the morning passed peacefully enough. Noon
came, and still we remained completely undetected. By tea-
time the scene continued to be tranquil, and we were full of
bounce and hopeful expectation. We had steamed over five
hundred miles since leaving Singapore. The ships were on top-
line as regards discipline and training. Now only twelve hours
remained before we had our chance. Our ignorance was
remarkable . . .

We knew nothing of the ghastly coincidence that had caused
a Japanese submarine to blunder into our path. We knew

nothing of the fact that it had surfaced shortly after 2 p.m. and—quick to profit by the accident of the meeting—had called up the enemy air bases in Indo-China. Nor did we know that on distant Saigon airfield nearly one hundred aircraft were now preparing for battle. One of the Nip Navy's best air formations was loading rapidly its torpedoes and its bombs. And we were to be the target.

*   *   *

"Aircraft Red! Close up at Action Stations . . ."

It was just after 6 p.m. when we went to the guns. A Japanese recce plane had been sighted, hovering on the horizon like a bird of ill omen before turning away and disappearing towards the east.

"Think he's seen us, Sir?"

May shrugged. "I don't suppose he's missed much."

Two other planes appeared. And then, dejected, we altered course, turning back for home.

Armchair critics have since frequently condemned Admiral Phillips' decision to venture into the Gulf of Siam. He should never have done so, they say. It was ill-contrived and rash. Yet we—at the time—were critical only of his retreat from this decision . . . *we* felt that the Admiral was being far too cautious. We were absolutely convinced that we could cope with air attacks, and there were many grumbles from the troops when the operation was called off.

The reasons for this astonishing over-confidence were rather complex, and had their roots in peculiar soil. To start off with, our intelligence services had made the most extraordinary miscalculations regarding the fighting efficiency and equipment of the Japanese. And especially did this apply to the so-called smaller details, the things that, paradoxically enough, mattered the most. We had been told—to quote a notorious example— that the standard Japanese navy torpedo bomber was "a somewhat inferior edition of the early Swordfish". And certainly we would have had little to fear from anything so archaic as an inferior edition of the Swordfish. We had also been told that the Jap was physically handicapped as a flier; that he was short-sighted—myopic was the favourite word—and shaky under stress. His prospects of becoming an accurate bomb-aimer did not, therefore, seem bright.

But it was not only what they'd *told* us that made us optimistic: it was also what we had *observed*. Since 1939 we had been obliged to develop a keen and intelligent interest in aeronautical progress, and thus, on our way to the Far East, we had lost no opportunity of mugging up the silhouettes and performance of all known types of Japanese aircraft. But the conclusions we had drawn from the data at our disposal were reassuring, invariably so. For we did not know, until it was far too late, that the venerable planes portrayed on the aircraft recognition charts bore little or no resemblance to the article we would have to combat.

*　　*　　*

It is 1 a.m. on the morning of December 10th. The squadron, pulsing through the dark, is well on the way to Singapore and safety. The Japanese have not attacked, they must have missed us in the night. Every minute that passes brings us half a mile nearer home.

But, suddenly—a change of plan! It follows the receipt of a message from Singapore. It causes the *Prince of Wales* to abruptly change her course. *Repulse* and the destroyers immediately follow suit; and, slightly bewildered, we get the order "Prepare for Surface Action".

The enemy is reported to be landing at Kuantan, nearly three hundred miles south of our original objective, and only a hundred miles from Singapore. If correct, this means that the Jap is coming in *behind* the main body of the defenders, now engaged upon the frontier. If successful, he will be able to cut the Peninsula in two.

So we head, at speed, for Kuantan—but look in vain for the enemy.

*   *   *

The sea was empty—empty of anything more formidable than a local tug, which was heading for the river leading to the port, with a string of barges in tow. It was just after 8 a.m. or thereabouts. The estuary glittered in the rays of the sun, the mist rose like steam from the warming shore. The rollers moaned softly over the roots of leaning trees, dark green against the silver of the sand. In the mess at Kuantan airfield, only thirty miles away, they would be thinking, we said, of breakfast.

Express, who had entered the river to check up at close range, began to signal by lamp. And as we read her report— "All's as quiet as a wet Sunday afternoon"—we shared a wry laugh. She seemed to have summed things up with admirable accuracy. True that Jap spotter planes had been reported a couple of hours before, but we had not been alarmed, or even very much interested. We were now nearly five hundred miles away from the nearest enemy base, and no torpedo-carrying aircraft could operate at such a range, or so we thought. Furthermore, according to the map, our position was covered by the R.A.F. base at Kluang, as well as by the aircraft which waited—or which we thought were waiting—only five minutes' flying-time away, on the outskirts of Kuantan.

So once more we set course for Singapore. Having travelled a thousand miles, and achieved precisely nothing, at least— we consoled ourselves—we'd be back in time for tea . . .

*   *   *

"Air Raid Warning!"

The troops were narked as they went to tneir stations; trust the Nip to start something before they were piped to dinner!

I went to the Bofors, to select targets for our short-range armament.

"*You* won't be needed," said Cruden, hastening to the three-inch H/L. "They won't be venturing into *pop-gun* range."

The first flight of Japanese bombers came up from the south. There were nine of them, and they were flying very high. Although rather surprised that none of our own aircraft were around we were still not greatly bothered, for high-level bombing was usually more frightening than dangerous. Even when delivered by the Germans, it had proved to be singularly ineffectual against ships moving at speed: so that we felt we would not be impressed by the onslaught of the Nip—especially in view of his "myopic" tendencies.

Repulse was the enemy's first objective, and she was by no means an easy one. Captain Tennant had plenty of sea-room, and knew how to make the most of it. Weaving a crazy zigzag across the ocean, he drove the battle-cruiser flat out, until she was travelling at over thirty knots and raising with every twist and turn a crackling ceiling of high explosive. We watched for a moment or two, in admiration; and then the Nips released their bombs.

It was the most impressive pattern we had ever seen. It horrified us, destroying all misconceptions in its thunder, for in that brief instant *Repulse* had disappeared, had disappeared completely, in a "forest" of cascading bomb-bursts which, merging together, were replaced in seconds by a giant wall of water. It was a fantastic, near-incredible spectacle, and then, after a shocked silence, a spontaneous cheer went up. For out of the chaos charged the "lost" *Repulse*, with black smoke pouring from a hole in her deck; but otherwise seemingly intact, and with the bright orange flashes flaring angrily from her side as she hurled yet another defiant salvo at the enemy.

"One hit . . . some damage . . . but under control. Fighting efficiency unimpaired."

Her lamp blinked at us, and as Tingle translated word by word we cheered again. Then four more formations of bombers came into sight. High level stuff . . .? We were quickly disillusioned. The naval aircraft shown in our pretty pictures may have looked like "string-bags" but these did not. Sleek-bellied, twin-engined jobs, they were travelling fast and we didn't realise their purpose until, peeling off, they swooped like swallows to skim across the waters.

"Torpedo bombers . . .!"

Cruden's gun went off with a crack that almost split my eardrums; then Bofors, Oerlikons, and point-five machine guns joined in the symphony as *Electra* opened fire.

Two grey shadows almost wave-hopping swept up from the south, and May hurled our ship between them and *Repulse*. One of the Japs got a knock on the nose from Cruden's three-incher and to our raving delight crashed into the sea; the other, temporarily jolted, released his missile and missed by half a mile. But our jamboree was premature . . . the Japs seemed to come at us from twenty different directions, and we couldn't be everywhere at once.

From the low-level attack—although it was estimated that seventeen torpedoes had been fired at her—*Repulse* emerged intact. But not so the *Prince of Wales*. She was hit on the port side, her speed fell to seven knots. And then she was hit again, and further crippled.

Yet scarcely had we a chance to reload than the next wave was upon us, and this time the Nips were doubly fortunate. They came at *Repulse* in a scissor-like movement; cutting at her from port and starboard and scoring a hit. Then they switched back to the Flagship, and placed three torpedoes in her.

The minutes went by: the guns still slammed away, the

planes still screamed at us . . . but we were fighting now in a sort of desperation, and no longer with hope: for there could only be one ending to this terribly unequal battle and we knew it. How many bombers had attacked? And how many were attacking? . . . fifty, sixty, seventy? One lost all count!

Soon after midday I saw a torpedo race towards the *Repulse*. Exploding close to her bows, it sent a column of water towering high above her upper deck, and, while it was still climbing, a second column began to rise, a few yards further on. The ship's steering went, and she veered round blindly; staggering, tormented and powerless to evade her punishment. A third, a fourth and a fifth explosion registered on the battle-cruiser's side, and her decks became alive with men. Slowly she began to roll, and then to sink . . . her smaller guns firing until the moment when she plunged.

In the brief lull that followed—I don't know how long it lasted—we looked round for the *Prince of Wales*. But she, too, had been stopped and was in a critical condition, listing into the water and belching smoke and steam. A melancholy spectacle, she lay there helpless until the moment when the last flight of bombers, high-level bombers, gave her her quittance. Only one bomb hit her but that one was more than sufficient. Slowly she settled lower in the water, her doom upon her.

Silence reigned across the ocean. And then the R.A.F. arrived . . . in time to watch the rescue work.

*   *   *

Though calm and self-controlled as usual in his conduct, May was taut-faced, and a certain harshness was evident in his voice. Once more had *Electra* become senior ship in a force that had suffered major disaster. And once more had the mantle of responsibility descended upon him only as the direct result of tragedy. His first move had been to pass the news to Singapore: it was still a complete mystery to him as to why air support had not been called for earlier. We'd been sighted in the early morning. So why wasn't wireless silence broken at the time? But then he dismissed his thoughts. First need was to concentrate on the work of rescue.

"The *Prince of Wales* and a battle-cruiser . . . what an unfortunate combination!"

As we drove through the cloying oil and the tangled wreckage I thought of Tingle's wisecrack and was fool enough to remind him of it. But Tingle's retort was strained: "Oh God, Sir . . . don't talk about that *now*!"

Express had gone alongside the *Prince of Wales* and some hundreds of survivors had been able to walk on to the destroyer without even getting their feet wet. But we, meanwhile, were dealing with the survivors of *Repulse*, who had had no chance at all to launch a boat, although a few Carley rafts had been slipped when the ship had begun to heel. Hundreds of men were in the water, and as the oil, spreading rapidly, pursued them, enveloping the stragglers in a hideous sticky stream, we were soon as black and oily as those we dragged to safety: but at least we were still O.K. internally, which was more than could be said for some of the swimmers. For a strange and terrible phenomenon had begun to make itself apparent; men would come inboard, apparently fighting fit, and then, for no obvious reason, would collapse and die. There was no sign of any wounds upon these fellows, and all attempts at artificial respiration were made in vain. We lost twelve in this fashion— men who died quietly and without fuss, and with none of the horrors that accompanied the passing of other victims. The delayed action of blast? A form of shell shock? Or the effect of the fuel oil? We had no time to find out. And, in the meanwhile, tragedy was nearly piled on tragedy.

Express had shown great pluck in staying so close to the sinking Flagship, and now, as the battlewaggon rolled over on her side, she almost shared her fate. For the massive bilge keel slid beneath the destroyer's belly, then, rising swiftly, threatened to capsize her. Only by the engine-room's prompt reaction to her Captain's "Full Astern Both" was our sister able to get out of danger. Had she tarried seconds longer her end would have been certain, and cruel. Less fortunate, however, were the men who had jumped from the battleship's tilting deck. When *Prince of Wales*—the companion of *Hood* and the "home" of the Atlantic Charter—took her plunge, a whirlpool, spreading over the water in brief fierce testimony of the violence of her passing, wiped some of the swimmers from the sea like chalk figures from a slate.

On *Electra*, meanwhile, the wardroom and the cabins were filling rapidly with injured, and the upper deck was crowded with the able-bodied—squatting, or standing, for there was no space for them to relax. Supplies of hot tea, in fannies and mess kettles, were brought up in relays from the galleys; and the seriously wounded were taken to the mess deck, where Doc had set up his H.Q. Yet despite all the horror they had endured, and despite the horror that some of them were continuing to endure, not once did I witness a case of panic.

Doc said, and he was not one to hand out unearned bouquets, that the uncomplaining wounded were probably the bravest patients he had ever tended. But I, for my part, would like to record that those who had escaped injury were abundantly full of fight. For discipline was excellent, with the first batch of survivors gravitating almost by instinct towards the action stations they knew best. It was a moving experience to see these men—who only a few seconds earlier had been struggling in the water—stand by the guns to give our ship cover against the enemy's intervention; and thus free our own chaps to carry on with the work of rescue. Captain Tennant had every reason to be proud of his company: they were "knit-together" well, and were an example to us all.

*　　　*　　　*

We hauled aboard the ship's dentist, so soaked with sea-water and oil that his shorts clung to him like part of his skin.

"But *my* job's with the casualties," he said. And shrugging aside all suggestions that he should rest, he went at once to Seymour, bent among the wounded.

Later, I saw him again, at work in the hospital. The deck was as slippery as a skating rink: no freshness came from the hot unstirring air. The place reeked of blood, and chloroform, and fuel oil. Even the briefest visit there was enough to turn the stomach. And yet he moved among the men—this dentist-turned-doctor—with a sort of desperate devotion, refusing even to change his clothes, or interrupt his ministry by pausing to swallow a mouthful of tea. When we had first picked him up all sun-tan had vanished from his face; he was pallid with strain and shock. But now he was a man transformed, a fellow full of confidence and vigour. He did tell me his name— Draper, or Roper, or something like that. But, though I have forgotten it, the wounded would remember. And with him was a young R.N.V.R. doctor, a mere boy in years, but equally preoccupied with the responsibilities of his calling. For this pair no praise could be too high. They worked with Seymour as though they had been in partnership for years; and they helped him solve many problems, not all of them anticipated.

For one thing most of the survivors had kicked off their shoes before plunging into the water, but this "precaution" turned out to have serious disadvantages. In the tropics the upper deck of a destroyer gets as hot as a baking sheet, and only an Indian fire-walker could have remained immune to the blistering heat that was concentrated over *Electra*'s engine-room. Some of the earlier arrivals were hopping around in agony until we could get them clear, and, as the S.B.A. gave treatment to their burns, I resolved that—come what may—I would always retain my footwear.

Another problem arose from the fact that some of the men

we saved were so coated with oil that the location of their
wounds could not immediately be ascertained. A special party
was therefore detailed to strip the survivors of their clothing.
Then they were washed down, with handfuls of cotton waste
soaked in the shale oil we used for the torpedoes.

And lastly there was the task of "classifying" the wounded,
for Doc insisted that each man must have a card attached to
him; a sort of case-history detailing his injuries and the treatment given, so that the shore, if we ever reached it, would not
waste precious time in wondering what to do. For Seymour
and his staff there was never a dull moment.

At the end of our rescue work we had nearly 1,000 men stuck
cheek by jowl together on board a ship that had been designed
to house less than 150. And had the Japanese attacked again, and
hit us with even the smallest of their bombs, there would have
been a shocking massacre. But the Nips kept out of the sky—
and that was the way we liked it.

*　　　*　　　*

Darkness had fallen when we got back to Singapore, but
a long queue of ambulances and lorries was waiting on the
quayside, ready to deal with the wounded and remove unhurt
survivors to the naval barracks. The Armament Supply Depart-
ment was also quick off the mark and, as soon as each ship
secured, a barge loaded with ammunition was ferried alongside
so that we could top-up with a fresh supply of shells and return
the empties. On *Electra* there was little scope for indulging in
melancholy reflection. The job of re-ammunitioning, refuelling, and clearing the decks of the worst of the oil, took hours
to complete, and when at long last I managed to escape to the
mess to get a drink I found Doc slumped in an armchair, and fast
asleep. His teacup was still in his hand and its contents had spilled
over his chest without his noticing. He was worn to a frazzle.

*　　　*　　　*

No doubt about it, the Nips had won a great victory. British prestige and power had taken a terrible tumble, and worse tumbles were to come.

By two decisive blows the Japanese had attained freedom of movement across one-fifth of the earth's surface. With over eighty million square miles of ocean theirs to command they could move their crowded invasion fleets with comparative impunity against the Philippines, Borneo and the Dutch East Indies. They barred Hongkong and its valiant garrison from aid; they probed through the misty Aleutians; they threatened Australia.

In Malaya the tactical by-products of this strategic supremacy were particularly noticeable as the hard-pressed Empire forces, reeling back from the frontiers of Siam, had to prepare for amphibious attacks against their line of march. The sea was no longer a barrier to the enemy, and the long east coast of the peninsula, with its shaded creeks and anchorages, had become an open door. Yet, while the tattered, embittered soldiers endured the nightmare environment of ambush and treachery in the green silence of the jungle, life in Singapore City, the fortress refuge to which they endeavoured to fight their way, continued to be almost indecently "normal". Nor did we at the naval base, have to sacrifice much in terms of human comfort; not for the first three weeks or so. A game of tennis, a long drink in the afternoon, a plate of chips at the club, the occasional dance—all these were ours when the sea-going stint was over. Sleep was available to us. So too were freshly laundered clothes. By comparison with the Pongoes we were incredibly, unjustly, fortunate.

Even our operations followed a reasonable routine. Take out a convoy, and bring one in—it was Scapa all over again, with only minor differences. We sweated instead of froze; and we worked stripped to the waist, or in vest and shorts. Another distinction was that—with Singapore only ninety miles or so from the Equator—we passed from the northern hemisphere into the south, and back again, practically every time we went to sea. Normally this "crossing the line" is a milestone in a sailor's life, and he is only too ready to blow about the number of times he has achieved it; but our tally was soon so impressive that we gave up counting—yet lacked the necessary conceit to "blow". Too many more important things were happening, and they were happening to others, not to us.

Meanwhile, whatever the march of world events, such apparently prosaic details as the training of our young seamen in seamanship, gunnery and torpedo work, had still to be attended to. And attend to them we did, sometimes with surprising results.

One day, having examined Ordinary Seaman H. Smith, and having congratulated him on his ready grasp of basic electrical knowledge, I received the reply: "Thank you, Sir. But actually I have a slightly unfair advantage. I have a degree in the subject, Sir . . . Cambridge."

Confusion of examiner.

* * *

The war situation became even more depressing. At first, thanks to the local censorship, we had believed that our troops were holding their own. Now it was clear that they were not. Each paper "victory" had been followed by fresh evidence of disaster. And slowly we had begun to appreciate that the authorities in the Far East were less truthful, as regards their war reporting, than the authorities back home. The realisation was not pleasant.

A place which we had imagined, from the tone of the communiqués, to be at least a hundred miles behind the lines would suddenly fall to the enemy. And yet—a week later— we would get the information that it was being "fiercely defended". A battalion of British or Australian troops, which we knew for a fact had been forced to retreat—reluctantly and under orders—without a shot being fired, would be eulogised in the Singapore press, regaling us with the account of a battle that had never been fought. "Heavy losses" of Nip aircraft would be announced, after a raid which, due to our lack of planes, had been almost unopposed. Soon, as the truth dawned, and the refugees began to come over the Causeway, their numbers increasing daily, even the complacent island began to get the jitters. For what went on? In England we had been able to trust official statements, but in Singapore we dare not.

It was, as Number One confided, when pondering on some particularly fatuous gaff, "a little like Meader's animals, you know. Only somehow his animals seem more *real*."

For it was about this time, as Christmas passed, and January came, and the Jap raids became heavier and more concentrated, that *Electra* experienced the "animal craze", a fantastic notion that was to populate her with imaginary "pets", who stayed with her until the moment of her sinking.

It began with A.B. Meader appearing on the upper deck— and making coaxing noises to something that was completely invisible to the rest of the ship.

Standing alongside a stanchion he crooked his finger at the air, and began to wheedle: "Now come along, old girl . . . No, *this* side my darling, there's plenty of room."

Perturbed, I intervened: "What's to do?"

"Please, Sir, it's *Phyllis*," he replied, "Phyllis the elephant, and I'm having some trouble with her. She just won't listen to what I've got to say. I keep telling her there's more room this side of the stanchion, Sir, but she just pays no attention. She's very obstinate, is Phyllis . . . Just like all the ladies . . ."

It *could* be the sun; I decided to humour him. "An elephant . . .? Have you put in a request to keep your pet on board?"

"Oh no, Sir. Not yet, Sir. But I'm sure the Captain won't mind. After all she is only a *little* elephant . . ."

Pause. Then as two of Meader's chums arrived, I realised with relief that his hallucinations were more apparent than real.

"We're getting her stern round now, Bill," bawled Boysden, pushing at the imaginary Phyllis with a convincing appearance of effort.

"O.K., we got her on the path at last," breathed Boys, wiping the perspiration from the brow.

"Well for Cripe's sake mind her feet," warned Meader irritably, "for she'll crush the life out of you if you don't keep clear of her feet."

Yes, Phyllis was a great success; as were the other "pets" that joined *Electra*. Among them was an imaginary dog, attached to a very real lead, and that imaginary dog just couldn't keep out of trouble. It kept getting its lead caught up in the most inconvenient places, tangling it around the legs of the passer-by, or securing it to the stanchions, the guys, or anything else that offered. And similarly a favourite was a sinister "Siamese", who spat defiance and fury at the other pets until—becoming heavily enamoured by an Australian "tom"—she settled down to motherhood, and became the object of the solicitude of everyone, from the Captain down.

Though doubtless the psychologist would probe for some deep motive in *Electra*'s "silly season", there is no doubt that the menagerie did much to enliven the daily routine and give us all a talking point or two. For many were the discussions, some of them frivolous, some passionate, and some astonishingly learned, that arose concerning the pets, their qualities, and the best ways of looking after them. Whether penguin or parrot, each had its following; and each was allotted its Action Station . . .

Air Raid Warning! And I was first on the platform. Then the gun crew arrived, one of them gravely indicating a (non-existent) glass bowl.

"Alphonse, the Goldfish . . . I like to have him near me when the sirens go. Gives him a chance to swim, Sir!"

A lone plane aimed a solitary bomb at us, and, after a brief exchange of fire, went on its way.

"Please, Sir, do you think a goldfish is prone to sea-sickness?"

"Doubt it," I answered, inspecting the spot where Alphonse was supposed to be. "But you ought to protect that bowl. If the gunfire cracks the glass the poor little beast will be left to flounder on the deck."

"Good idea, Sir. I'll see to it immediately. Anyway, I'm glad to hear that you don't think a goldfish can be sea-sick!"

"With respect, Sir," interrupted a studious Leading Hand, "I would say that, although Alphonse is in his natural element, in a manner of speaking, he is as likely to be as sick as any one of us.

"For," he explained, "a goldfish bowl is normally stationary, and the fish revolves around the bowl. . ."

"*Inside* the bowl, not *around* the bowl . . ."

The Leading Hand ignored his mate's correction. "But when the ship rolls," he persevered, "Alphonse will be in the centre of the disturbance, so that the little perisher will see everything revolving around *him*, and the effect may be upsetting. If you see what I mean, Sir!"

Poor Alphonse. The argument concerning his well-being continued to spark intermittently for nearly six weeks, and his bowl was placed in all sorts of peculiar sites, so that his behaviour could be studied under every type of stress. The last time he "appeared" on the gun platform was as we cleared for action in the Java Sea, when they placed his "bowl" in the centre of a stack of lifebelts. He accompanied *Electra*—and his "master"—to the grave . . .

*   *   *

Time was running short. Following the death of Admiral

Phillips, Admiral Geoffrey Layton, hitherto C.-in-C. of the China Station, had taken over as C.-in-C. of the Eastern Fleet. But, although the title sounded impressive, Layton's means were very limited. One of the very few men to foresee that Singapore would soon become a beleaguered city, and thus be quite unsuitable as a base for a major naval force, he decided—very wisely—to adopt the Admiralty's original plan and set up H.Q. in Colombo.

But this move, although approved by London, was most unpopular locally. It was shrewd, it was inevitable, but it showed how the wind blew; and to many the revelation was uncomfortably abrupt. Nor was the change made any happier by Layton's method of announcing it; though whether he wrote his own farewell message, or whether others wrote it for him, is still, to me, an intriguing mystery. For the message, as we got it, was somewhat as follows: "With your heads held high, and your hearts beating proudly, I leave the defence of Singapore in your strong and capable hands. *I am off to Colombo, to collect a new fleet!*"

Well, doubtless the Admiral had only meant to be encouraging; but the report of the messdecks was inevitable . . . "Up ladder, Jack—I'm inboard!"

Yet if *Electra*, knowing Layton as an energetic, forceful, and very gallant leader, was critical, the Shore was ten times more so. We of the Fleet were merely criticising the Admiral's choice of *phrase*, for his *decision*, we conceded in our hearts, was quite unavoidable. But to the Shore it was the *decision* that hurt the most, for it was felt, quite erroneously, that the Navy was running out on its commitments.

Dire indeed are the penalties paid by the best of fighting men for making the right move at an unpopular time, and trying to make the move popular by the use of the wrong language. For while Layton incurred much high-pitched recrimination, especially from the ostriches of yesterday, the change-over

made very little difference to our working routine. Singapore
was still, of course, "impregnable", provided that it was reinforced. Soldiers were needed for the "fortress", and we must
see that the fortress got them. True that the new Fleet units,
posted from Europe, would be organised in Ceylon; but back
we must go to the convoys—and the task, the incredible task,
of delivering to Malaya yet more human raw material, to face
death or wounds in battle, or else endure a vile lingering in the
barbarous prisons of the Japs . . .

*   *   *

Strange days they were, and possessed of a kind of unreality.
We brought in the *Empress of Asia* and other liners . . . tall
ships crammed with men who had never been trained for jungle
warfare, and yet, stiff-jointed after three months spent at sea,
were to be hurled into battle as soon as they stepped off the gangplank. We brought out the ships with the pitiful refugees . . .
the women, the children, the old and the sick . . . the civilians
who we passed on to others for transit to the safety of Australia,
or else watched debark in the Dutch East Indies, which were to
fall to the Japanese only a month or so later.

Each voyage led us through a fairyland of lush green isles,
and sparkling seas. Each voyage presented problems of naviga-
tion that would have made a less resolute soul than Davies
give up the ghost. First we had to pass through the narrow lane
in the minefields to the south of Singapore; a lane over which
Jap bombers were constantly on the prowl. And next we had
to proceed through the tricky Rhio Strait—renamed Bomb
Alley—before threading our way through the channel that lay
between tree-swathed Banka Island and the Sumatran shore.
After this, we would either steam for Batavia, along a coastline
directly exposed to Japanese sea attack; or else, when escorting
a Ceylon-bound convoy, we would negotiate the Sunda

Strait, where at last we were free to turn to the west, and comparative safety.

Each time we cleared the Sunda, so soon to witness the last fight of H.M.S. *Exeter*, I was conscious of an immense relief. The seas of the East Indies were so landlocked, so enclosed, that they gave one a sense of claustrophobia: it was good to make a temporary escape. And yet, once we had achieved the sea-room for which we craved, and had emerged into the Indian Ocean, there would come a strange reaction—a crazy desire to get back.

For Singapore, reaching from its death-bed, was laying its claim upon us. And our consciences were touched by its grisly fingers, however much our reason was repelled. We dreaded the moment of encounter, and yet were nostalgic for the sight of its pale white face . . . seen dimly through the veil of the smoke by day, or raised above a necklace of fire by night. In the fate of the Fortress all would be involved, ourselves included. Its fall would send a tremor through the earth, and millions would follow it—as victims to the tomb.

12

The Fall of a Bastion

THE Japs were now less than ninety miles away and as *Electra*, back from Java, dropped her hook in the waters of the naval base, the Peninsula's last defence line—meandering through the cinders of once luxurious bungalows and the dark green silence of deserted plantations—was slowly beginning to crack. It was a thin line, a very thin line indeed, and to make matters worse the enemy had landed behind it.

Two or three British and Australian destroyers of the old "S" and "W" classes and a flotilla of M.T.B.'s manned by New Zealanders had done some excellent work in inflicting losses on the invading forces and we were hopeful, for a while, that *Electra*'s assistance might also be invoked. But no word came, and when it became clear that we would not be needed May was able to send some of the troops on shore leave.

With the environment of Singapore daily becoming less attractive, and with all libertymen having to return to their ships by 6 p.m. it might have been expected that the Captain's concession would have had a somewhat limited appeal. And yet, perversely, this was not so. The magic word "leave" had always exerted an almost hypnotic influence upon the company, however poor the facilities that the shore might offer. In the Andrew, they agreed, you never refused a thing: you took what you could, before it was taken from you. Again there was beer, in quantity, still to be found ashore, and the Far East could produce a very exacting thirst.

The afternoon passed uneventfully enough for we of the duty watch, and then, at five minutes to six, the sirens gave forth their familiar wail—a strong enemy formation was approaching from the north. Almost simultaneously I saw the liberty-boat, travelling at speed, and crammed with matelots. They were singing happily as they came alongside, and were a bit unsteady as they came inboard. Singapore had been kind!

Only one of the party seemed at all concerned about the Nip attack. But in him, Fred Castle, it had aroused a sense of personal grievance. For, while he'd gone ashore, the Oerlikon —his precious Oerlikon—had been placed in the care of Another, and now that the perishing Nips had arrived it was still in the hands of Another. Fred, scowling, lurched towards the platform.

"Wotcher doing with *my* cannon? You gimme my cannon right away."

The second layer protested, but protested in vain.

"'Op it," said Fred, with a menacing jerk of the thumb. "Scarper . . . I got the right to man this flippin' thing, and no one will perishin' well stop me!"

I hastened from my perch among the point-fives. "All right, enough of that!"

I had Fred lashed to the mounting, more to keep him upright than anything else. It was a high-level attack, I reflected, so he couldn't do much good however sober, and he couldn't do much harm however tight. But, in the meanwhile, I wanted him to shut up . . . for the Old Man's eyes were upon us.

The first flights came over at such a height that not even the shore artillery was of much use. And then, quite unexpectedly . . . Low Level Attack!

The single-engined plane with the Red Sun markings roared down over the naval base, machine-gunning as it came, then swept over our masthead and flew on towards the Straits. My machine-guns missed. So too did the three-inch. Then Fred let fly. He got that Nip in the sights of his "cannon", and unleashed a wonderful pan. Every shell went home, hitting the yellow man where it hurt the mostest.

From the second boatload of libertymen, now riding alongside the ship, came a chorus of bucolic applause.

"Come on, Fred. You do the bloody bastard!"

From the cheers and handwaves you'd have thought it a local derby or Millwall on a Saturday afternoon. Then Fred loosed another burst and as the wing of the plane burst suddenly into smoke and flame the yell that went up was a rival to the Hampden roar. The Jap spilled sideways, like a scorched moth, then plunged into the sea.

As the white steam rose from the swirling water Fred Castle smacked his beloved on her bottom, struck a pose, and said thickly to the delighted ship: "Alone . . . alone we done it!"

* * *

Since Admiral Layton's departure the shore organisation had inevitably deteriorated. Many of the regular officers had been withdrawn in order to meet the needs of the new base in Colombo, and we found that H.Q. was being occupied by a galaxy of locally entered R.N.V.R. officers—some of them untrained and with little or no knowledge of the Navy or the sea.

This transformation could not have been effected at a worse time, a time when even the most experienced might have boggled a bit at the load that the shore was expected to shoulder. In addition to arranging escorts for the convoys, synchronising their rendezvous, and providing for the prompt unloading of valuable cargoes under constant air attack and during the rapid approach of an invading army, there was the need to organise transport for the refugees and initiate offensive raids against Japanese amphibious forces. A vast mass of administrative detail had to be attended to in pursuing these objectives, and no mistakes could be afforded; no margin for error remained.

Unfortunately this latter fact did not seem to be appreciated at H.Q. Many "locals" did excellent work, but—I hate to say it— there were too many cases where an excusable ignorance was unconfessed, and covered up by individual arrogance.

*   *   *

A hotch-potch of former civilian craft, ranging from launches to river steamers, had been pressed into naval service. Many of them were highly successful, thanks to the skill of the R.N. and R.N.V.R. skippers who commanded them, but others were completely wasted. And almost invariably—as in the following example—this was "Admin's" fault.

*   *   *

The elderly destroyer *Scout* had made her way from Hong-kong, commanded by a very experienced Lieutenant Commander R.N.R. One day, having been called upon to take a small river steamer down to the Rhio Straits, he came storming in to May to ask his support for a protest.

"I have just been up to Operations to tell them I can't take that old tub to sea . . ."

"What's the trouble?"

"She hasn't even got a compass!"

May sighed. He'd heard worse stories before. "But perhaps they didn't know?"

At which *Scout*'s captain really blew his top: "*Didn't know*! I told 'em what had happened and immediately some super-cilious little twerp of a two-striper swivelled round in his chair, waved his cigarette holder at me and said: 'Oh, don't worry about that, old boy. You don't *need* a compass . . . we have routed you where to go, so all that you have to do is to follow the routing laid down for you!'"

Electra's turn came a couple of days later. It was just before lunch and Commander May was standing in the gangway talking to me when the Captain of the *Express* came aboard. Although somewhat surprised by the visit May was his usual hospitable self: "How very nice to see you. Have you joined us for a drink?"

"Thank you, Sir." It was our visitor's turn to show surprise. "But I really came along to know what time we're sailing!"

"*Sailing?*" The Old Man turned to me. "I have seen no sailing orders. Have any come to the ship?"

"As Officer of the Day, Sir, I have seen none . . . The Postman called at Central Office this morning, but reported there were no signals."

"Then you'd better send for him!"

Express broke in: "So sorry, Sir, but I quite thought that you would know. I received a copy of the signal early this morning . . . and we were both to escort the S.S. *Nellor* to Java . . ."

May gave me one of his "frozen" looks betokening trouble; and Macready came aboard a moment or so later with one or two bits and pieces of mail, but still no sailing signal.

"Are you *sure* you called at the office?" . . . I had always considered our "post" to be thoroughly reliable, but this was peculiar, to say the least.

"Yes, Sir. The officer told me there was nothing for *Electra*."

The Captain took a hand. "Then go back to the office and ask again. Take note of what is said and report back to me."

A rather worried Macready mounted his bike again, then returned with the missing signal—and a story to go with it.

"The officer was just going to lunch, Sir, and when I asked him he almost went up the pole."

"Well, what did he say?"

Macready grinned. "He said, 'You were here ten minutes ago, and I told you No . . . and now you come bothering me again. When I say No I mean No. You understand? Or don't you speak the King's English? Don't you appreciate a No when you hear one?'"

"And then?"

"And then, Sir, a Wren piped up. '*Electra*,' she says. 'But I'm sure there was a signal for *Electra* this morning. Perhaps its been overlooked, Sir? Maybe it's in your basket, Sir?' So the officer looked in his basket, and sure enough there it was. He never said a word more—just picked up the signal and flung it at me!"

May murmured something under his breath. The affair could have tragic consequences. *Nellor* was filled with women and children, and the signal instructed him to collect her at two o'clock. It was already past noon. *Electra* had no steam. The rendezvous was ninety minutes away. Promptly he sent *Express* ahead, then called McLeod to the bridge stressing the urgencies.

Mac did his best: and did it so well that *Electra* met up with her charge just fifteen minutes after the appointed time. But then arose another snag, for the *Nellor* was lying peaceably alongside the quay, and with no sign at all of being ready for a voyage.

"Just when do you intend to go to sea?" asked May, with heavy sarcasm.

"Am sailing, as ordered in the signal," came the reproachful reply, "*at* 1400 *hours tomorrow*."

Well, someone had boobed—and boobed in more respects than one. For on closing with *Nellor*, and comparing our respective briefings, we discovered that the refugee ship had been instructed to avoid the Rhio Straits while we, her escorts, had been ordered to pass through them!

Next day, after Commander May had put on his very best uniform and paid a call ashore, there was a new officer in the mail room, and when you mentioned the name *Electra* you got a top-line service.

* * *

Few idle moments now. The *Nellor*'s voyage concluded we stood out into the Indian Ocean, escorted some troopers to Singapore and then, while waiting for the convoy to unload and turn round again, got the job of towing an "I" class destroyer down to Java. The destroyer had been undergoing a major refit at the time of the Jap attack and was a sorry spectacle. Holes drilled in her bottom, and designed to take her new propeller shafts, had to be sealed up; her stripped-down machinery had to be stacked in her mess deck.

Apart from a small party sent from *Electra* to attend the tow, the ship was completely "dead". But we weren't worried about that. The journey was a short one, by our standards, and most of it was to be made in daylight. Again, a "dead" tow was a far easier responsibility than a crowded liner, it weighed more lightly on one's conscience. Yet one very minor problem did puzzle us a bit—our electrical distance recorder had broken down. Normally we wouldn't have given this a thought, for we could plot our position fairly accurately, and we knew of course the capacity of our engines. But how were we to estimate our own speed through the water when we were dragging another ship behind us?

It was Doc who supplied the answer. "As she's roughly the same displacement as ourselves," he said, "then we'll make two-thirds of our engine speed." His theory was correct.

This incident, recalling as it did Doc's mathematical dissertation on the planing speed of *Rodney*, amused the Captain, so much so that he decided to "promote" our dogmatic friend to the Honorary Officer of the Watch and present him with an "Honorary Watchkeeping Certificate". Unfortunately, however, our little ceremony went adrift for a Nip plane picked us up and, as the alarm bells rang, the party dissolved in disorder.

He was a cautious type that Nip, or else he believed on playing on our nerves, for he followed us for at least an hour before attacking, and when he did decide to have a go it was from a high level, and out of range of Cruden's gun. From our point of view it was a picturesque performance and unattended by unpleasant consequences; the bombs merely straddling the tow rope, and the troops jeering loudly at the retreating plane. "Get your specs on, Johnny . . . if you can't do better than that then you'd better stay away." And yet as Jenner-Fust suggested gravely, there could have been a scientific explanation for the bomber's failure.

"A slight miscalculation on the airman's part of the drag imposed upon us by the tow, Sir. Had Doc been his observer he'd just about have hit the "I" class in the stern . . . provided of course that he was aiming the bombs at *us*!"

*   *   *

The Japs were reported on the Causeway when *Electra* took her last look at Singapore. The airfields were abandoned, all bar one: the naval base was under fire; Keppel Harbour was smoking from a bombing raid. Yet at headquarters they still talked of victory; the fortress was still a fortress although beleaguered; the island could hold out like other islands . . . Malta for example. And then, so ran the argument, would come the turning point when, reinforced, the defenders would go over to the attack. Few of us, hearing such optimistic views, could really believe them to be held sincerely. Much though we might admire the brave pretence inspiring them.

Singapore a Malta? A more accurate comparison would have been the Isle of Sheppey! The Johore Straits were 5,000 yards across at their widest point, and narrowed less than to the length of Southend Pier. Singapore a fortress? Yes, but the defences were facing the wrong way round, and such of the big guns as could be brought to bear (at a pinch) on to the Strait, were equipped with armour-piercing shells, lethal against warships but hopelessly ineffective against widely spaced-out infantry, moving invisibly through a massive jungle.

Singapore a Stalingrad? This invidious comparison, made in the "inquest" period when Stalingrad had been fought and won, and Singapore had been ten months dead, was the most far-fetched of all. For Stalingrad was accessible to massive relieving forces, and Singapore was not. Again, with Singapore's population swollen to over a million by an influx of defenceless refugees, the prospect of a house-to-house carnage, however militarily attractive to Russian generals and others unencumbered by the responsibilities of humanity, was not likely to be hailed with much enthusiasm by the more squeamish British. What hope then remained for the fortress island? The hope that the defenders could hold the enemy on its fringes? And continue to hold him until the Navy (in a year or so maybe) was able to gather sufficient strength to battle its way through to Singapore's relief? That hope seemed pretty slim. For even to maintain and supply the existing garrison, and the million civilians behind them, would require a monumental effort, beset by complications unparalleled elsewhere.

Every ounce of food required by the defenders would have to be brought in by sea: in convoys threading their way through treacherous narrow waterways, studded by enemy-held isles and islets; in convoys that would be under constant attack from sea and air and, at their terminal, from shore batteries as well. Large numbers of merchant ships would be required for each and every voyage, and heavy escorts would have to be provided for their protection. But where were the merchant ships, the escorts, the reinforcements and the supplies to come from? The nearest base was Australia, and she, threatened by invasion, had none to spare. The Middle East? Even the limited numbers of troops withdrawn so far had dangerously weakened the strength of the Eighth Army— facing a near-disaster. Then Britain perhaps? But even presuming that Britain could spare the vast resources that were now needed, and even presuming that by some stroke of luck or planning the relieving convoys were loaded and ready and waiting to go, it would be at least three months before the first of them could appear in Eastern waters, and under escort of the Navy begin to fight its way through the Japanese-held approaches. Three months! The defenders were not machines but men.

One did not need to be a professional strategist to appreciate the disabilities inherent in a situation where five divisions, supported and reinforced by overwhelming sea and air power, faced the remnants of three divisions supported only by a hotch-potch of non-combatant troops, a sort of armed mob spread thinly around a wide perimeter, and never knowing where the blow would fall. Nor did one need to be a student of psychology in order to appreciate that the regular troops, who must face the main force of the attack, were desperately weary; and dejected by the persistent reverses that had followed their bloody and hard-fought encounters with the Nips on the Peninsula. They had always been short of material equipment, now, after so many demands had been made on it, their morale was running low. They needed time to rest and regroup before taking up the fight again, and time was a commodity denied them.

Once, when the seaways were open and before the Japanese had captured the airfields, the addition of a couple of divisions or so might have enabled these bitter veterans to hold their own. But, as so often happens to Britain's distant garrisons, aid from home had come tardily, and in piecemeal . . . too little and too late.

*   *   *

As *Electra* and her sisters, shepherding a motley collection of merchant ships, manœuvred cautiously through the minefields before proceeding south-eastwards to the temporary sanctuary of Java, the battle of Singapore had not yet begun. And yet,

to all intents and purposes, it was already lost. Perhaps it had
been lost at the very beginning, lost when the Jap bombs
smashed the American fleet at Pearl Harbour, and our own
squadron off Kuantan? Or perhaps it had been lost even
earlier, when, back in Westminster, a Parliament, anxious to
economise, ignored the warnings of the military and reduced
the sum available for Britain's imperial defences? Or perhaps
. . . but one way or another we were all of us, in some respects,
to blame. Singapore was finished, and struggle though we
might to kid ourselves, we knew that it was so.

13

"Sacrifice is Necessary"

"WHAT do they call it?"

"Tanyong Pree-okk."

"Sounds like a brand of pickles! Sure you got the spelling right?"

"How'n Hell ud I know? It's the way the Dutchies say it!"

The port for Batavia, Java's capital, Tanjong Priok was a new one on *Electra*'s company when they'd first arrived out East . . . weeks, months, or was it years ago? Since then, with the ship on convoy work, the name had become a trifle more familiar. Now it had assumed considerable importance, as the base for our operations following the withdrawal from Singapore.

For the first day or so the contrast between the Javan scene and the siege on which we'd turned our backs was almost bewildering. Batavia, only eight or nine miles inland, was literally bursting with prosperity. The clubs, the hotels and the dance-halls were full; the shops were doing a bumper business; the food was plentiful. To hell, we argued, didn't they know there was a war on? Weren't they aware that the Singapore shield was breaking above their heads?

"Things seem to be running pretty smoothly here," I said, with heavy innuendo.

May, back from a conference ashore, smiled chidingly. "Steady there, Guns, don't perpetrate injustice. Our allies,

believe me, have few illusions—despite the apparent jamboree."

Jenner-Fust backed him. "A pretty tough breed these Dutchmen. They regard the Nip's coming as inevitable, but they're
not putting on their mourning clothes in advance. Don't forget,
you old traditionalist, that even Drake allowed himself a game
of bowls before beating the Armada."

"*Armada*! But that was a piece of cake!"

May was right about the Dutch, so too was Number One.
In Batavia they were fully aware that their island empire
would be the enemy's next objective, and even their resolution
to adhere to their daily routine had a certain defiance in it.
For, while the saxophones wailed the latest jazz hits into the
sticky oriental night, Dutch phlegm was by no means unsup-
ported by warlike activity. They were coldly determined that,
should they be overrun, the Nips would find nothing of value.
Already, in neighbouring Sumatra, the black smoke rose like
a mountain over the burning oil-fields; in Java, too, a scorched-
earth policy was under way.

In the weeks to come I was to regret my hasty and uncharitable initial impressions of the Dutch; but, all the same, I was
right about the Armada. For Drake had it the easy way, in
comparison with us; although, like our allies, we tried to
make the best of things.

*   *   *

Shortly after *Electra*'s arrival in Java I was placed in charge
of eight sailors and went ashore as Officer of the Patrol. Each
ship took its turn in providing this force and, though a policing
job is seldom popular, we found compensations for the role
that would have been lacking in, say, the more prosaic surroundings of Pompey or Chatham. First, there was always the
possibility of the enemy staging a surprise attack, and therefore
the men felt that they were fulfilling a fairly useful purpose . . .

by helping the recipients of Java's lavish hospitality to maintain their legs we were probably enabling them to save their necks. Next there was the fact that patrol duty enabled us to indulge our curiosity, plus our insatiable desire for a change of scene. The Dutch, who were always very helpful, had placed a wagon at our disposal, and the pleasure of seeing new places, new faces, and sampling civilisation once again was by no means to be sneezed at. But the location of Patrol H.Q. also helped to make the job congenial. Set in the former German Embassy, the Allied Servicemen's Club was as comfortable a venue as any poor seaman could hope for.

*　　　*　　　*

The club was quite crowded but its clientele, I observed with relief, seemed remarkably well behaved. British and Australian, Dutch and American . . . a handful of Indians from their fine little fighting frigate, *Sutlej* . . . a group of Javanese from the local infantry . . . all were jogging along quite happily, and with no symptoms of friction. I hoped it stayed like that. Drawn from six different nations, speaking as many languages, and attired in every shade and shape of uniform, from shorts to bell-bottoms, from crisp-white to crumpled jungle-green, these fellows, together with the Dutch girls, who acted as voluntary hostesses, made a picture of allied unity that would have sweetened even the sourest cynic. It looked like being a nice uneventful evening.

A few minutes later I despatched the bulk of the patrol, under Petty Officer Dilley, to have a snoop around the town; then, retaining A.B. Boys and Telegraphist Binner as personal escort, I installed myself in the committee room, in unaccustomed and agreeable splendour. For Hitler, whatever his faults, never grudged his diplomats an attractive décor . . .

*　　　*　　　*

"Call from the hall, Sir."

Our tranquillity had lasted precisely twenty minutes.

It was a relatively trivial matter, and concerned an Australian who, not content with too-freely partaking of the local beer, had helped himself to a note-book. It was a very ordinary shorthand note-book, and of no use to him at all: it was a thing worth sixpence at the most, and his pocket was stuffed with money. But there was a point of principle involved. *He* wanted the book as a "souvenir", whereas the young lady behind the reception desk wanted him to surrender it to her: it happened to be her note-book.

Settle this? Mere child's play! Taking the Aussie aside I had a bit of a yarn with him, and then, after he'd returned the loot and had apologised profusely to his victim, I wandered back to my armchair, feeling reasonably content. Tact, that was all that one needed as O.C. Patrol.

Five minutes went by, then ten, then came another S.O.S., this time from the billiards room. "Someone's going to get his block knocked off if the patrol don't get 'ere quick!"

We arrived at the double, to find that our friend the Aussie was again the centre of intensive argument. He had breezed in on a game of billiards, and had started to break it up. Dutch seamen had been the sufferers, it seemed . . . "Effry time vee shape for a shot Mister, he swings off der end of der cue!"

I weighed up the situation. The Aussie was bellicose about the "square-headed barstards". And the Dutchmen were nearing the end of their patience. "Vee don't vant him to get in trouble, Mister, but vee vant to finish our game."

"Barstards! I'll clean up the lot of them . . ."

"Belay that!" I said, and my advice was sound. For although the Aussie was a very large Aussie the Dutch were even larger. And there were four of them; each of them stone-cold sober.

I called to my bodyguards, with pretended nonchalance. "Just take this lad outside, and give him a chance to cool off."

"Now come on, Chum," said Bonner and Boys, "we're going for a walk."

But Aussie had different ideas. He allowed himself to be escorted only as far as the door, then suddenly broke free. A terrific punch landed high on Boys' face, and with lightning rapidity the blow was returned. A vicious hook to the jaw caught the Australian off balance, and sent him reeling against the wall.

Things brewed up. Australia straightened himself, and growled: "I don't take that from a bloody Pommie policeman."

At which the "policeman", whipping off his cap and silk, promptly dropped into a fighting attitude and announced in a most unpolicemanlike manner . . . *Then come on . . . let's have it out!*"

I intervened, quite scandalised. "No violence there. Arrest him properly."

"Aye, aye, Sir!" Boys jumped to attention, turned towards me, then whipped round again to meet his antagonist, in the middle of a charge. A quick side-step was followed by one of the finest right hooks I had ever seen. There was a dull forbidding thud that made us wince. And then the Aussie dropped as if pole-axed.

"That's that, Sir," said the "policeman", calmly. "And what do we do now?"

Theatrically the effect had been most impressive, and there was silence among the audience, the silence of respect.

I looked at the seamen crowded by the door. "Any of you Aussies belong to the same ship as this chap?"

Two of them stepped forward. "Can we look after him, Sir?"

"All right, but he's your responsibility. Get him back to the jetty—if he makes any more trouble I'll put him in the cooler."

As Jack the world over knows how to look after his pals the

cause of the excitement was revived, lifted to his feet, and forth-
with poured into a taxi and taken away: but this was not the
last we saw of him. For after two hours he was back in the club
again, demanding audience.

"What's it this time?"

But Australia had sobered up. "I thought I'd tell you how
sorry I am for the rumpus, Sir. I'm a bit of a puncher myself,
but that so-and-so of yours most certainly packs a wallop!"

"Very well then," I said. "It's finished and done with. But
remember—no further trouble."

"*Trouble*? If anyone starts any trouble, Sir, then just you call
on me . . . *for me and that bloke of yours could rip this joint
apart!*"

A little later I saw Boys, Binner, and the Aussie in amicable
conversation. They were all sitting at the same table, and
although patrols on duty are not supposed to drink, three large
beers rested in front of them. Said Aussie smartly, as I wandered
over: "I'm waiting for two of my pals, Sir. These drinks are
theirs."

Well, Nelson's blind eye never harmed the Navy . . .

*   *   *

At eleven o'clock the bar closed, and we began to ensure
that the libertymen reached their ships. Many of them were
tottering, but were good-humoured enough, save one.

He, with his back turned to me, made a rude retort. In a flash
Boys had swooped on him, and spun him smartly round.
"That's my Gunner you're talking to! Stand to attention and
say you're sorry."

The culprit took one look at Boys, whose fame had spread,
then meekly said: "I'm sorry, Sir, I didn't realise . . ."

"You seem to know quite a bit about fisticuffs," I commented to Boys. He merely grinned. I didn't know that my
policeman was a former middleweight champion . . .

The club shut, we jumped into the wagon and toured Batavia, to clear the lads out of the dance-halls. In general the operation went off fairly smoothly, but there was the occasional exception: and in the last hall to be visited a fracas between a British sailor and a Dutch soldier had developed into a glorious free-for-all, with chairs flying, girls screaming, and the blood flowing like claret. As we paused on the threshold Petty Officer Dilley blew a long blast on his whistle. Then, in the momentary lull that followed, I ordered: "All seamen outside, and around the truck!"

But even when the British reluctantly responded the trouble was not over, for the Dutch were none too keen to let things end with their adversaries' retirement. Regrouping rapidly they advanced menacingly upon the patrol, who had spread out across the exit.

Pacifically I held up my hand. "Now, lads, let's forget the argument. We all have a bigger enemy to deal with; there's no sense in fighting among ourselves."

But allied unity had been strained to breaking point.

A Dutch corporal came forward, very excited. "We wanted to be friendly, but your men started a fight. Okay," he added. "You start a fight, and we damn well fight! All right?"

And the looks I got from the blackened eyes behind him were more eloquent than a volley of hear, hears. Then inspiration came.

"Steady on," I pleaded. "It's your beer that must take the blame. It's too strong, too good, for quiet chaps like us."

The Corporal hesitated: I quickly followed up ". . . So by all means break the bottle, but not your allies' necks!"

A grin, a quick translation—and all tension vanished. We left the hall to the accompaniment of much back-slapping, many protestations of friendship, and loud cries of "Good beer, eh? You come back for some more!"

The Java night was clear, and bright with stars. The air was cool. It was early a.m. when we marched through the yard at Tanjong Priok, but Number One was waiting up for my report on the night's proceedings, and as we were talking the duty Signalman arrived. I glanced at the form. There were no absentees . . . the stray sheep had found their fold.

I was glad to get my head down.

* * *

"Guns, how did the Patrol go?" It was the Captain asking.

"A very quiet evening. But you've probably seen my Nil Report?"

May nodded. "I have not only *seen* your Nil Report; I have taken the dreadful responsibility of countersigning and forwarding it. But just gratify my curiosity if you please, and tell me what *really happened*?"

I told him.

There was a thoughtful silence. Then a smile.

"Very good, Guns, and so nice to know there were no absentees. But I hope the Patrol never gets involved on a really lively night! . . . if it did it might find itself in trouble!"

* * *

Singapore had fallen. In silence we listened to the sombre and candid words of Winston Churchill, relayed from London half a world away, and braced ourselves to meet the future. The general mood was grim, but morale was good. The worst had been said, the inevitable had come to pass. All that remained was to fight as best one could.

There was now no real hope left of maintaining Java. The central link in the island chain that reached from Malaya to Port Darwin in Australia, it presented to the enemy's frontal attack over five hundred miles of coastline. Its left flank had been turned by the invasion of Sumatra; its right by the Japanese landings in Bali and New Guinea. The air was dominated by the Nips, there was a formidable fifth column. The army, though its morale seemed high, was less than 30,000 strong. The area to be defended was about as large as England.

Even had the allies possessed naval superiority they would have found it difficult to have parried an attack that could be launched, with the attacker's choice of place and date, from bases as far apart as Indo-China, Sumatra, and South Borneo. But, as it was, we did not possess superiority. We were hopelessly outnumbered in ships, and woefully weak in gun-power. For the defence of what remained of the grandiloquently-styled A.B.D.A. area the Dutch Admiral Helfrich had but eight cruisers, three of them obsolete: about a dozen destroyers, of which six were modern; a handful of submarines. Furthermore, while the Japanese force was homogeneous the Dutchman had to operate a fleet which, drawn from several nations, differed widely in its traditions, practices and warlike equipment. And yet the worst handicap of all was that Helfrich had to dissipate even the meagre resources he possessed, dividing them into so-called Western Striking Force based on Tanjong Priok, and an Eastern Striking Force at Sourabaya.

Victory, under such conditions as these? And when the enemy, whatever he might lose in one battle, could always bring up reinforcements for the next? The prospects were not bright. For Helfrich, placed in the saddle only when the great powers had withdrawn their senior officers from Java—thus emphasising, rather tactlessly we felt, exactly what they thought about its chances—we had considerable sympathy. If he placed his trust in a combined force concentrated in one place, then the Japs might strike in another and our ships would arrive too late to interfere. So now he was trying with a divided force, not strong enough to intervene decisively, but determined in any case to intervene . . .

Yet, if an effective defence was quite impossible, why then was a hopeless defiance still attempted? Today, strangely enough, the answer seems far less clear-cut than it did at the time; for the publication of official documents and so forth has actually confused the issue, or so I think. One sees merely the helplessness of Java, and the issue of whether to fight or not become, on the printed page, a problem of simple mathematics with only one solution. But at the time when one's neck depended on the deliberations of Bandoeng—the Javan town that had become supreme H.Q.—the situation seemed to have its moral aspect, and this could not be ignored.

Looking back, I think that very few of us were unaware of the extent of the hazards to which the island was exposed. For even the youngest and most recently joined members of *Electra*'s company were hardened by adversity and, on the surface, fairly cynical as well. They didn't really love a set-up in which Royal Navy ships were placed under the command of a foreigner, a man whose name, until now, had been completely unfamiliar to them. Nor were they particularly cheered by the reflection that, owing to Holland's long history of neutrality, this man, and the Dutch officers who served him, had had little experience of handling a naval force in battle.

For guts, as *Electra* had learned the hard way, were no substitute for guns. And a noble determination was vain, if one lacked the material strength to back it. We were committed to fight in the worst possible conditions; to manœuvre against a superior enemy in what was practically a land-locked sea. The shores were his, with the exception of Java. And the skies were his, completely so.

And yet, despite such considerations, which look formidable enough when put down on paper, and detached, as it were, from their context—the long day's routine in which one had little time to "consider" and far less time to brood—I don't think there was a man among us who would have opted for the sensible way out, which would, of course, have entailed our abandonment of Java.

We knew that we couldn't win; not in the ultimate. But at least we could fight, and fulfil our obligations. We knew that we couldn't stop an invasion, but we were still pretty confident that we'd take our toll of the invaders. We knew that the Nip was formidable, but we were sick of being chivvied around by him . . . British, Australian, American and Dutch, we were all in it together.

* * *

One raid was over. Another was beginning. The go-downs and the derricks on the quays of Tanjong Priok stood in pale silhouette against the pitch-black smoke. The crackle of the flames spread over the greasy river; the reek of the burning savaged our nostrils.

Now, as *Electra*'s gun crews closed up, a corpse bumped gently against the destroyer's side, then drifted out into the stream again. Entangled in the pulped matchwood which was all that remained of a native fishing boat, it rode high, and with a grotesque dignity, as if reviewing us while sitting bolt upright in a chair.

Said Charlie, querulously: "It's enough to make you spew."

"You won't have the guts to spew with, mate, if you don't man that flickin' gun!"

The Japs were regular visitors nowadays, travelling in silver shoals above the sea and shore, aloof, untroubled and serene in a cloudless sky. There was something almost unearthly about their visitations which, unopposed, assumed a rare beauty of appearance. And, as they rained their bombs upon the earth beneath, it was difficult to reconcile this majestic, intimidating approach to war with one's mental picture of the men inside the smooth skins of the bombers, the little men with the dirt-yellow faces and the goggles hiding slanting eyes; the little men in loin-cloths and oxygen masks who sweltered beneath the cockpit covers, and bared their bad teeth in their eternal grin.

"High-altitude stuff, AS usual," said Cruden, wearily resigned beside the three-inch H/L.

"But why not go up after them, if they won't come down to you?"

"You have the quaintest sense of humour, Guns. No wake would be complete without you."

The Nips droned piteously towards us, but were out of reach of course. It seemed extraordinarily unfair, this one-way traffic in explosives; a traffic whereby, through "capitalising on the accident of gravity", as Harry once described it, the enemy could send things down so much further than we could throw them up!

"'Orrible little bastards," grumbled Castle to his Oerlikon. "If only they'd come low enough to give a feller a chance."

Small hope of that, I thought, for despite his reputation for fanaticism the Nip never made a false step. He would risk his neck willingly, but not unnecessarily.

"Maybe the cruisers will have a go, Sir? Maybe their guns will carry the distance?"

"Maybe, but one thing you can be certain of . . . *Exeter* and *Perth* won't miss any chances."

We were in distinguished company. H.M.S. *Exeter*, heroine of the River Plate, and the Australian cruiser *Perth*, as pretty a pair of fighters as ever you'd wish to seek, were moored in midstream; but I doubted if even they could do much against this type of air attack, for they carried only the four-inch gun as their main A.A. weapon.

And then an extraordinary thing occurred . . . by a chance in a thousand the Japanese formation, wheeling leisurely into position, came into the area covered by the big guns of *Exeter* and *Perth*. It could only have been for a fragment of time, a few seconds at the most, but, for the disciplined men in the cruisers, it was more than sufficient. The eight-inch guns of *Exeter* and the six-inch guns of *Perth* opened up, with a roar like a thunderclap; and the effect was devastating. The shell-bursts landed right in the middle of the Japanese, and blasted their neat array to ribbons. Three of the planes tumbled like falling leaves. A fourth, damaged, tried hard to maintain height but failed; receiving the pent-up fury of the fleet's light armament in the course of its way down. And then the formation broke.

It was the first time we had seen an enemy bomber group shattered, and the sight was a tonic for us all. A spontaneous cheer went up from every ship in the squadron, and on *Electra* the troops were dancing with excitement.

"That's the hammer, that's the hammer. Come on and give us some more!"

But the Nips were so stupefied that they flew off without dropping a single bomb.

* * *

"Invasion forces believed to be at sea."

It was February 25th—the day after *Exeter* and *Perth* had so cheered us by their fancy shooting—that the news broke; the news that we had been anticipating every day, the news that was to mean so much to each and every one of us and the ships in which we served.

Large convoys of troop transports, heavily escorted, were said to be heading for Java, and the fleet was being deployed to intercept.

As the ships prepared for sea the general sensation among the men—hearing the buzz, which was not yet officially confirmed—was one of intense relief. For many weeks they had endured the frustrations of a period in which, with few exceptions, they had never met their enemy face to face, and yet had been involved unwillingly in an unbroken sequence of retreat.

Now, at long last, the time had come to make a stand, and, they were glad that it was so. In the course of an unprecedented and confusing onslaught they had complied without question or complaint to every demand that had been made upon them; yet all their efforts had been fruitless and the sacrifice of their fellows had been made in vain. The Eastern Fleet had attempted to seek battle upon the sea, and had been massacred from the air: troops had been brought unscathed to Singapore, merely to be engulfed by its collapse: planes had been taken to Sumatra, to be destroyed upon the ground: refugees had been carried to "safety", to fall captive to the enemy as each new refuge failed.

And for most of this despairing and tragic period the surface ships of the Japanese Navy, the instrument whose supremacy had made such disasters possible, had remained remote, inviolate. A threatening shadow on the minds of men and paralysing every physical reaction, its influence unchallenged extended from the open shores of Alaska to the Bay of Bengal, from the Gulf of Siam—the grave of the *Prince of Wales* and *Repulse* —to the coasts of California, where the survivors of Pearl Harbour were building up strength again.

For never before had the flexibility of sea-power been so remarkably demonstrated. The carriers that had struck against Hawaii in December were to menace, in March, Calcutta and Ceylon. In February they had ravaged Port Darwin, destroying the only advance base from which Australia could send us aid, and now they might swing their weight against us; we who were waiting in Tanjong Priok. But so much success on the part of the enemy served only to goad the men of our little fleet into a desperate desire for action. No one would ever again dare to despise the Jap's capacity to wage scientific war, but, given at last the opportunity of close action, we still hoped to give him a very bloody nose.

*   *   *

Half a chance of achieving a surprise, half a chance of getting at the laden transports . . . just half a chance, that was all Helfrich wanted. But he doubted if he'd get it.

For, as seen from his Batavian H.Q. the scene was complex, confused, and acutely unsatisfactory. He sensed that the decisive hour was approaching, and deduced on such slender clues as had come to hand that the main effort of the enemy would be directed against the eastern part of the Island; but the exact point at which the invaders would disgorge was still a mystery. The allies' tragic lack of reconnaissance planes, or rather their lack of the fighters necessary to protect those planes, prevented any accurate plot of the enemy's movements, or any positive forecast of his intentions. Furthermore, while the scanty naval forces available to the defence must seek their foe blindfold, the Japanese air forces would be keeping the convoys well informed of every allied movement, and would be ready to whistle up the maximum support, both by sea and air, to help them.

And yet, such factors notwithstanding, the allies could not stay in harbour to await the outcome; retreat having been ruled out they must advance as best they could. But advance to where? Feeling as he did that the Island's eastern end would bear the brunt of the first attack, Helfrich decided that the Sourabaya force, hitherto a Dutch and American formation, should be reinforced. At the same time, any such reinforcement could come only from the Western Striking Force; and as a withdrawal of this force from Tanjong Priok would leave Java's western shores completely unprotected, he had to think twice, about how far he could back his hunch.

*　　　*　　　*

On the afternoon of the 25th *Electra* sailed for Sourabaya in the company of *Exeter* and *Perth* and the destroyers *Jupiter* and *Encounter*.

But the remainder of the Western Striking Force, consisting of the elderly cruisers *Dauntless* and *Danae* and the Australian cruiser *Hobart*, remained behind.

In the nature of this compromise was reflected the dilemma in which the fighting Dutchman found himself. And his final signal to us was grimly prophetic.

"Sacrifice is necessary for the defence of Java."

14

Forward through the Smoke!

IT was noon on the 26th when we arrived at Sourabaya. And time for a temporary respite, we thought. After several days and nights of strain and having spent the past twenty-four hours continually on the alert, while probing without result for enemy forces reported off the coastline, we hoped to get our heads down, if only for a few hours. But Sourabaya, stinking from an air raid, was no sailors' rest. It took *Electra* three hours to negotiate the minefields, and no sooner had she arrived at the end of the winding solent and dropped her hook than Doorman, commanding the combined force, ordered her to prepare for sea again. We had arrived at 3.30. We must be ready to sail by seven.

Blast!

All the same, despite their surface grumbles, the troops were in good heart, although extremely tired. For we gathered that Doorman had at last got firm intimation of the whereabouts of our will-o'-the-wisp opponents and aimed at a night action. Which suited us. An attack by night against the invasion fleet would mean plenty of scope for the destroyers. And with May an exponent of night destroyer tactics we fancied our chances.

The squadron weighed on time.

* * *

It was good to meet up with one's allies. Together we looked more imposing than we'd thought. The Sourabaya force consisted of the U.S. heavy cruiser *Houston*, the Dutch light cruisers *Java* and *De Ruyter*, and eight destroyers, five of them American and three Dutch. Practically all these ships had seen action against the Japanese. And though their efforts had been fruitless it was not for want of trying. The Dutch had served bravely off Borneo and Bali, Sumatra and Timor, while the *Houston* had suffered, three weeks previously, nearly a hundred casualties as the result of Nip air attack in the Macassar Strait. But she was still as bouncy as ever; full of fight and eager to get fighting.

Nor was our own contribution negligible. *Exeter's* reputation was deservedly worldwide, and both she and the *Perth*—a veteran of Matapan, the evacuation of Crete and other triumphs and reverses of the Mediterranean Fleet—had captains of first-class calibre. Gordon, of *Exeter*, was a cool, tenacious officer, as clever as they come. "Hec" Waller, the Australian, was full of dash and impudence and skill—a destroyerman whose fame had become almost legendary when commanding in the Med. the flotilla leader *Stuart*. The remaining ships of the British force—*Encounter* and *Jupiter*—were both old friends of ours, the latter having recently achieved the distinction of flushing a Japanese "cruiser" submarine, and the pair of them being fellow survivors with us of Tom Phillips' fated force. The destroyer partnership was firm, well tested.*

So by and large it didn't look bad at all and when Harry and I came off the dog-watch and sat down to dinner, we had no misgivings, no premonition that things were not as good as they looked. The flaws in the perfection of the picture afforded by the combined allied squadrons were to be more obvious later on, but in the meanwhile we were more concerned about

---

* *Express*, having sailed with us from Europe, was temporarily out of commission. She was refitting in Colombo after a fire had raged through her boiler-room.

the menu. Something special had been arranged by Gretton and we might as well make the most of it.

True that, as Harry said, this might be the last meal we would share together, but neither of us really believed it. For such things happened to others, not to us.

*   *   *

Gretton was in some dismay. He'd gone shopping just before the old tub slipped from Tanjong Priok and bought two geese from a Chinese trader . . . a couple of geese which, alive when he'd first seen them, had looked quite big and yet, since their decease, had seemed to shrink. In fact, now that he'd plucked them they looked no more than two small chickens! The Chinks, he swore, had done him, his "bargains" were nothing but a handful of skin and bone.

But that wasn't the worst of it. To be swindled was one thing, an Englishman's prerogative you might say, but to forget one's position was quite another. And now the terrible lapse had occurred, a lapse that he would never live down. For Gretton had done the best he could with those wretched geese, the very best. He had supervised their cooking, and he had carved with great economy. He had succeeded in eliminating the leather from their goose skins, he had miraculously succeeded in making the portions go round. He had quartered the birds, he had served one portion to each of the eight officers, he had Achieved The Impossible . . . And then, on confiding to the wardroom just how difficult his task had been, he had found that he had forgotten the Captain. The Captain would be without His Goose! The shame of it momentarily shook Gretton rigid. For never before had he perpetrated anything even remotely resembling such a social solecism.

"But fancy forgetting the Captain."

Number One's words, uttered in amusement, really hurt.

And then, with a stupendous effort Gretton recovered his balance.

"The Captain," he replied with cold dignity, "is particularly partial to an omelette when we are at sea, Sir. He has almost a passion for omelettes, Sir. We must do our best to cater for the Captain's tastes."

*   *   *

The night had come down when Gretton retired to the pantry, the night that was violet-hued and carried the scents of the shore to the shadowy file of ships, fourteen of them, as they nosed their way swiftly through the Java Sea. This night was to be the last night of all for five of them, the last night but one for another five. And meanwhile the men who occupied them spent the brief period of grace remaining in their usual prosaic way. Most of the time they were closed up at action stations, for the rest they told broad stories, jested, dreamed of home, or groused; their grousing becoming more and more frequent.

"Sacrifice is necessary for the defence of Java . . ."

As the hours went by, and it became increasingly evident that the operation to which we had so keenly looked forward was conforming to the usual pattern of frustration, Helfrich's signal became a major topic of the mess decks. The resolute Dutchman had enjoined us to fight to the last ship and the last man . . . which was fair enough. But as Bandoeng was so obviously in ignorance of the enemy's whereabouts and intent, the message had been received with some degree of irritation, which now increased.

"We'll have a bash all right," said Mash, "but for Pete's sake let him tell us *where* to have it! Just let him tell us where to find the Nips, he can save himself the rest!"

In this my T.G.M. spoke for the entire ship's company. They were keen enough to fight, but they were desperately tired and strained. They didn't need exhortations to "sacrifice", they *did* need some reassurance that H.Q. knew what it was doing. And this they did not get.

Wearily the squadron beat up and down the coast; finding nothing at the point where the Japs were said to be, then extending its search to other areas, equally empty. Dawn came, and with it a recce aircraft, but otherwise there was no sign of the enemy. Save for the allied ships the sea seemed clear. Air reconnaissance from the shore was undertaken. It too failed to get results. Further caustic comments arose from the jaded troops, none of them blaming the allied airmen—possessing only a handful of slow and highly vulnerable aircraft—all of them speculating just why our numerical and qualitative inferiority in the air had always to be accepted. Daily London regaled us with fresh communiqués of the giant bomber offensive against Germany. Couldn't they have spared a few planes for us, their poor relations out East? And where else, apart from the handicapped air patrols, lay the fault . . . the fault in the allied intelligence network that persistently mis-forecast the enemy's intentions? Just where did H.Q. get its information . . . ? This information that had sent us on three abortive sweeps within the week, looking for a foe who had failed to materialise?

Such were our criticisms—unfair and uncharitable perhaps— as morning broke, and still we searched in vain. And Doorman seemed aware of them. Indeed he appeared to have exaggerated them. For turning back to Sourabaya with the obvious intention of refuelling the ships and resting their companies before setting out on yet another night patrol, he reported that: "The men have reached the limit of their endurance. Soon they will be past it!"

*   *   *

We entered the long approach to Sourabaya in the early

afternoon, *Electra* leading. And then, when we were almost at the base . . .

"*De Ruyter* making signal, Sir."

The cruiser, in which Doorman flew his flag, was preparing to turn seawards once again.

"FOLLOW ME. THE ENEMY IS NINETY MILES AWAY."

Tingle, translating, looked at us and grinned. "Looks like the real McCoy. . ."

"The real McCoy!" assented Number One.

And all of us felt a lot more cheerful.

*   *   *

A slight breeze stirred the Ensign at *Electra*'s gaff, as clear of harbour, she took up her position ahead of the Fleet. The troops eyed the rustling flag with subconscious approval; it was the ship's best White Ensign, unstained by funnel smoke, untorn by weather.

"Seems strange though," interrupted Castle, "us serving under a foreigner, I mean; doesn't seem right somehow."

"Forget it," brusquely retorted Mash, "with the Owner as S.O. destroyers—our British destroyers—*you've* nothing to worry about. Just leave the Nip to do the worrying."

I glanced at the bridge. May had had little sleep since the 23rd. It was now the 27th. Yet just to look at him was to be reassured. His tall slim figure moved with its customary quiet command, his face showed no sign of strain. Yes, *he'd* do all right, I thought, unconsciously echoing Mash; but all the same there was no doubt that the mixed composition of Doorman's command posed quite a few problems.

Every man of us knew that the ships of the four national groups represented in the so-called "Combined Force" differed widely in their individual armaments, their sizes and their speeds. We had no common standard of training, no common method of fire control, no common signal code; and each message from the flagship would have to be translated by resident liaison officers before being retransmitted to the Fleet. For a naval battle, where events have a habit of moving fast, and where one's reflexes must move fast to cope with them, this method of communication between hand and brain was, to say the least, unsatisfactory.

"*Don't* they look *well*, Sir!"

Roused from my reverie I glanced at the ships astern.

And then, it being seven bells, or 3.30 in the afternoon, we conformed to Navy custom and wet the tea.

* * *

Four o'clock—and *Electra* was well ahead of the fleet. Five miles in advance of the cruisers, she had *Jupiter* and *Encounter* in company.

Presumably because he felt that the shortcomings of his signalling system would preclude complicated individual manœuvre, Doorman had chosen to handle his cruisers in close formation: *De Ruyter* being followed in single file by *Exeter*, *Houston*, *Perth* and *Java*. The destroyers had been concentrated according to their national groupings, with the British forming an Ahead Screen and *Kortenaer* and *De Witte* acting as close escorts to the cruisers. The Americans—weaker in gun-power but stronger in torpedo armament—brought up the rear. Visibility was at maximum: the sea was calm. On board *Electra*, and every other ship of the fleet, there was a keen sense of expectancy. All were on their toes.

At three minutes past four our lookouts detected against the prevailing powder-blue of the sky a faintly darker streak; well over to the north-east, on our starboard bow.

By five minutes past four the streak had widened, revealing itself as smoke.

And then *Electra* commenced to tell the Admiral about it. ENEMY FLEET IN SIGHT!

*   *   *

One Nip cruiser, followed by six destroyers . . . another Nip cruiser, followed by eight destroyers . . . two Nip heavy cruisers looming up behind.

So this is the start of it, I thought, the start of the thing that you've been trained to face all your life, battle at sea. And it's all so damn casual, the overtures at any rate. It's all so much like the text-books have told you it's going to be, so far as they go. One line of ships meets another line of ships, orange flashes flicker from grey hulls, shells raise blasted great splashes in the water . . . then the range is corrected, adjusted, and the new salvo spotted. And so it goes on, until one or the other of you brews up and someone's got a victory, maybe you, maybe him, and then the newspapers explain it all.

"A near one!" says Ted Mash.

And the latest Nip brick hurls several gallons of ocean across the upper deck.

At the time of *Electra*'s enemy report the Japanese had been proceeding in a south-westerly direction while the allied force had been proceeding north. And for several minutes the opposing squadrons had continued this approach; converging slightly until Doorman, apprehensive that the Japanese might succeed in passing across the head of the single column and thus—"crossing his T"—bring all their broadsides to bear upon targets which could retaliate with only part of their armament, turned to port. Thus, owing to the distance between the two forces which were now pursuing parallel courses, the smaller ships had not as yet been able to participate in the action. With one exception . . . And we were the exception.

Commander May, disposing the British destroyers for battle, had given *Electra* the job of flank marker to aid the cruisers' fire.

So positioned—way over to the starboard of Doorman's line—we were much nearer to the Nips than were the rest, and had become a veritable Aunt Sally.

The first shells had fallen around us at 4.16. They were being followed by many more. A Jsintu class light cruiser—the first ship we had sighted—had started the ball rolling with a salvo of five-point-five's. Now she was hurling the stuff at us thick and fast, and some of the Japanese destroyers were also joining in. Their shooting was good—extremely good—but in May they met their match.

The Captain was handling the ship very skilfully and coolly, and so far we had escaped unscathed. In fact, to judge by the way he was interpreting the thinking processes of the Japanese control officer he would have made an excellent mind reader: he seemed to anticipate the enemy's every move. Time after time had he brought *Electra*, twisting like a hare, into the spot where the last salvo had dropped, thus causing confusion among the Nips as they adjusted their ranges in accordance with the previous fall of shot. And time after time had he changed this tactic, and driven the ship straight on as though not caring a damn until—while we winced and waited for it—the Nip unloaded his bricks on the very spot where a repetition of our previous evasive action would have carried us! It was quite uncanny, this clairvoyant performance, and after the first few minutes of it we had begun to relax and admire the view. Those of us who weren't with the gun crews.

For *Electra* was not only being shot at; she was also shooting back, and shooting fast. And the gun crews had plenty to do. The routine of the tubes crew, however, was infinitely less laborious. With the range at 15,000 yards, there was no chance of *Electra* using torpedoes, and during the opening stages of the battle—while our comrades sweated to feed the smoking breeches—we found ourselves in the role of mere spectators, though doubtless our chance would come. But, we couldn't complain of boredom, there was far too much to see.

The Japanese, using H.E. shells that burst on impact, had mixed some sort of colouring agent with their explosive. This experiment, designed presumably to aid their spotting, produced a fantastically weird effect—with the shells bursting in brilliant greens, yellows and reds, and the splashes, rising high, emitting a sort of yellow smoke. Aircraft were extremely active, but made no attack: so we guessed that they too were assisting the Nip gunnery.

In the meanwhile things were extremely noisy. And, with the shells whistling over the masthead, shrapnel whirring on to the deck, and our four-point-seven's cracking away like whips, I found myself possessed by a sort of undefined excitement, an excitement in which, strangely enough, fear played but little part. Nor was I unique in this respect, for most of the others felt the same. We were exhilarated rather than intimidated, though I don't know why this was so. Bombing had often given us the most terrific jitters, however much concealed. And I can't explain why the shelling shouldn't have had a similar or even worse effect. All that I can say was that it did not. *Electra*, at the start of her last fight, was almost in holiday mood. It was quite extraordinary.

*   *   *

Straddled . . .! The water rose like angry geysers on both sides of the ship at once, then smacked against the hull as *Electra* shook to the blast. And Jasper, Paddy Reilly's pal and the sharer with him of the penalties imposed for the "gunman" episode, came ambling along the deck to bring the torpedomen a fannyful of tea.

He was taking his time about it—Jasper always took his time when it suited him—and was seemingly oblivious to the bits of metal that were singing around his ears. Instead, standing bolt upright on the side of the ship nearest to the enemy, he paused to peer at the Nip line, and then, after dawdling another few yards, gaped up at the shell bursts with an interested and pleased expression on his face that I (concerned about his neck) found quite insufferable.

As soon as he got to us, intact, I rounded on him: "Why the hell didn't you use the disengaged side, away from the fall of shot?"

He looked at me, quite hurt. "But, Sir, you have always told us to walk on the lee side, the side that's away from the wind, Sir!"

*   *   *

In every battle there is said to be a moment of decision, a moment when, at a single stroke, the issue is resolved, however much the fighting may be prolonged. In the battle of the Java Sea, a fierce encounter which was to last until midnight, and which was to be renewed by its survivors in the Sunda Strait the following night, this moment of decision came rather early—less than an hour after the first exchange of shots.

By 5 p.m. the action appeared to be going tolerably well—from all that we, squatting on the tubes of our small destroyer, could grasp of it. *Exeter*, intervening decisively against our own tormentors, had hit one of the Nip light cruisers, which had turned away making smoke. The Japanese, launching a destroyer attack, had again encountered a reverse; being beaten back with one of their ships severely damaged. The allied line—meanwhile—was quite unscathed, and only one thing puzzled us now, as the opposing fleets steamed westwards. Just why was Doorman still maintaining his parallel course? Why didn't he *close* the enemy? Only two of his cruisers, *Exeter* and *Houston*, could effectively use their guns at the existing range. The remaining three cruisers had been silent, except when in brief action with the Nip destroyers. Why could he not get nearer?

Yet apart from this criticism, which arose more from impatience than a genuine apprehension, we were happy enough about the way in which things were shaping. Happy, that is to say, until the moment of decision. Happy until 5.8 p.m.

*   *   *

"Torpedo tracks!"

Quite suddenly the sea was alive with them, and four of the torpedoes passed close by *Electra*'s stern. They came as a complete surprise. The Japanese destroyers were 15,000 yards away, and well out of torpedo range—*our* torpedo range. So how the hell . . . ?

"A submarine," I hazarded. "A submarine has taken a crack at us! And other submarines have loosed their salvoes too."

"But God knows what they hope to hit," puzzled Mash. "For apart from the spread near us they must have loosed 'em into the blue!"

Well, it was nice to know that the Nips had their quota of B.F.'s too, we thought—watching the white shadows flit towards the fleet. For they'd peter out, those mouldies, however lively they looked; then came the pay-off.

It came five minutes after our own escape. It came with a dull explosion in the far distance, as the Dutch destroyer *Kortenaer* began to sink. Not that we realised it was the pay-off; not at the time. We never guessed—not for one moment—that the torpedoes had come from a surface ship; still less that they'd register at twice the range that our own torpedoes could carry. We had a lot to learn, and too little time to learn it. For, in the brief passage that had elapsed between our sighting the torpedoes and the *Kortenaer*'s sinking, we had been worrying about *Exeter*. For *Exeter* had copped it.

This—with the launching of the Japanese "secret weapon", the long-range torpedo, and the crippling by an unlucky shell of the allies' most formidable ship—was the moment of decision.

*   *   *

For maintaining a distance between the fleets which precluded his six-inch gun cruisers from joining the action, Doorman probably had excellent reasons, none of them known to us at the time, but only guessed at. He may well have considered that the inadequacy of the liaison set-up, and the enemy's numerical (and individual) superiority in destroyers, left him with no recourse but to allow time to elapse, in order to get his force working together. He may have suspected that Japanese forces additional to those encountered were in the offing, and may therefore have decided to wait until he could obtain fuller information. It is conceivable that he may have had some scheme in mind whereby he might be able to preserve his main force for the main purpose, and get at the convoys, whose location was obscure. It is equally conceivable that he may have felt that any move to close with the enemy squadron might lead him even further away from the elusive invasion forces. But whatever the reasons for Doorman's apparent policy—and even today, some seventeen years after his losing his ship and his life in gallant action, we know little that is concrete about those reasons—the results were catastrophic.

*   *   *

When *Exeter* steamed into battle she was regarded as the king-pin of the fleet. Her reputation was formidable, her marksmanship excellent, her morale superb. But there was a reverse side to the picture. *Exeter*, although a most useful ship, was of less than 9,000 tons displacement, and, as a result of the familiar peacetime requirement of "economy", she was smaller than the County class, carrying only six eight-inch guns instead of the latter's eight. Both in armour and in armament she was comparatively a lightweight.

Nor was her comrade-in-battle, the American cruiser *Houston*, the ideal choice for a ship *v.* ship slugging match—not when the enemy was represented by the *Nachi* and *Naguro*, each of them, at 13,000 tons, having a displacement that was a third over that permitted by treaty, each of them having made use of this illegal "surplus" to heap steel belts around their bellies, and strengthen, at the same time, their punch to the maximum. *Houston*, as first designed, was heavier than *Exeter* and better armed; but the Nip air attack that had exacted such a heavy toll of life, had destroyed one of her treble turrets. Now she, like *Exeter*, could command only six big guns. And the Nips each carried ten . . .

Such odds as these were heavy indeed and yet, despite them, the British veteran and her American partner—one bearing the scars of an old battle, the other marked by a more recent wound—had acquitted themselves well. Strangers to each other whereas the Nips—units of the Fifth Cruiser Squadron—had trained together for years, each of them had been so little acquainted with the other's methods that at one stage *Houston* had fired on *Exeter*'s target, and *Exeter*, rather than waste time by correcting matters through the allies' complicated communications system, had crossed fire with her to engage the rearmost enemy. And yet, despite such temporary confusion, each of them had handed out more punishment than they took.

So caught up in the rush of events that their captains had had no chance of making even the most cursory of joint tactical arrangements before the battle opened, but had put to sea within two hours of their meeting, these undergunned and underprotected ships had actually come within an ace of tilting the scales decisively in favour of an allied victory. And then had come 5.8 p.m. . . . and that ill-omened shell.

Only the second to hit the *Exeter* in over forty minutes' shooting, it passed through a gun shield. It spread death and destruction around the mounting . . . but did not detonate. It tore through the cruiser's decks . . . and still remained intact. Then it entered a boiler-room . . . and there exploded!

So in a moment did the whole balance of the battle change, and allied fortunes slide . . . towards the bottom. The Jap cruisers, having had so much reason to hate *Exeter*'s sting that they had recently concentrated all their fire upon her, now switched to *Houston*. And as *Exeter*, her speed reduced and her boiler-room a shambles, turned slowly out of line, the American turned too, to avoid collision, and *Perth*, believing that Doorman had ordered a change of course because of the torpedo threat (it could not have come at a worse moment), turned after *Houston*. Next *Java*, at the end of the line, and confused by the smoke, followed *Perth* round. And then the *Kortenaer*, struck by the torpedo, collapsed in two. All was confusion . . . with the flagship still maintaining course, alone against the enemy fleet, the cruisers blindly following *Exeter*, one destroyer sinking fast, the others, Dutch and American, weaving a trifle bewilderedly among the shell-bursts to see where to help, and how.

The allies' lack of liaison had come home to roost with a vengeance.

*   *   *

To *Electra* only one thing was clear about this unhappy incident, which occurred so quickly that we had only the vaguest idea as to what it was all about—*Exeter* must be protected; given time to get under way again. For the crippled cruiser now lay stopped, pouring out thick funnel smoke to act as a shield while her engineers laboured to shut off the scalding steam, and the destroyers, including the American destroyers, commenced to lay the thickest smoke screen we had ever seen.

For some minutes *Perth*, seemingly reluctant to leave her comrade as Doorman recalled his errant squadron, remained on the scene, banging away at the spot from which the "submarine" attack was believed to have come; then even *Perth* conformed to the prevailing pattern and, the allied cruisers, again in line, pressed on towards the north, following *De Ruyter*. The three British destroyers were now on their own again.

*   *   *

We were on our own, and knew what to expect. The Nips would not be content with merely damaging *Exeter*, they would come and come again; be anxious only to make sure of her by sinking her. And we, being destroyer-men, had no doubt at all as to the nature of their chosen instrument . . . torpedo attack. Between us and the enemy the smoke screen lay like a wall upon the sea, protecting the cruiser from the guns of the "heavies", but also providing the Japanese destroyer force with security while they mustered for attack; giving them their chance of approaching unobserved. And the Nips had fourteen destroyers, all of them bigger than ours.

Thus we on the tubes anticipated that our chance was coming; and waited for it quietly. The peculiar excitement experienced earlier had passed, and had been replaced by a certain grimness; but still there was no feeling of apprehension. I remember thinking for a moment that if "it" had to happen to me then I hoped that God would spare my eyes; but even this thought was rather detached; for the idea of anything personal happening seemed unreal. The ship, the torpedo tubes, the ammunition trays, the company of one's fellows, the reek of the smoke—all *these* were solid and substantial things; things that were not of the imagination, but alive; things that could be detected by the senses . . . things that reassured.

For as the anxious moments passed, and *Exeter* by some miracle or other got slowly under way, we were all of us, I think, sustained by the subconscious illusion, said to be common to men facing the moment that menaces their existence, that our surroundings were permanent, untouchable . . . that other ships sank, and that other men died, but that we were immortal, not destined for the accident of death. But this feeling was as I've said, subconscious and our surface meditations—I speak for myself—were neither morbid nor profound. It was good to be with *Electra*; not one of us would have swapped our berth.

The minutes passed, the smoke hung broodingly; intact save here and there, where it dissolved only partially, forming vague avenues of shifting misty grey. And then, as Doorman led his cruisers round with the intention of steaming between the enemy line and *Exeter*—now preparing to retire but with her main armament again in action—the flagship made a signal . . .

It was 5.25, and as *Electra*'s nose swung to starboard a calm voice came over the phones, to inform the ship: "The Japanese are mounting a strong torpedo attack against the *Exeter*. So we are going through the smoke to counter-attack."

Electra's hour had come.

*　　　*　　　*

May on the bridge, with Harry close beside him . . . Number One with the gun armament, and me with the tubes . . . 173 of us, officers and men together, deck crew, engine crew, all of us together . . . we came to the barrier of the smoke, and then passed through it, emerging near-blinded into a dazzling and alien world.

All our friends had vanished. We were naked to our enemy. We were beyond the smoke.

The sun, soon to die, glared down upon the ship, and the rhythm of the turbines and the sea accompanied her. The bow wave reared sheer on either side, well for'ard of my perch, and seemingly as metallic. We were very silent, each man a citadel.

Was *Electra*, so far from her northern hunting ground, destined, I wondered, to die alone? Was this, our home through the blustering months of the western war, to sink without trace in this tepid and sluggish ocean?

But introspection was out of place, and could not last. For, in a moment, the guns—raging at the sight of the line of black destroyers—put paid to it, tearing the quiet asunder. So too did the favourite oath—ripped from a score of throats, projected in half a dozen dialects. From the cockney of Fred Castle, harnessed to the Oerlikon, to the Ulster twang of the doctor, his instruments spilling on the tilting deck, we cussed the Nip down to the most unmentionable depths, then jumped to our duties as the party opened, and the salvoes tossed the waters into storm.

15

Beyond the Smoke

ONE light cruiser, with bulbous funnel tops and pagoda foremast, six heavy destroyers with steep trawler bows and lumpy upperworks . . . *Electra*, all alone, had met her enemies at close range, as they charged for the smoke Opening fire immediately she drew first blood and then in a split second, in less than the time it took for the result of her marksmanship to manifest itself in the dirt-grey blossom that shot from the leading destroyer's superstructure, she received the unleashed fury of the Nips' reply.

No doubt—no doubt at all—as to what the end must be Not in May's mind, not in the minds of any of us: not now! May, on receiving Doorman's order, knew that it took no account of the existing circumstances, knew that his three ships were far too dispersed to deploy for concentrated counter-attack. And yet, although divisional action was therefore impossible, and individual attack near-suicide, he had accepted his mission, made his decision, would abide by it until the bitter finish. *Electra*'s life, his own life, meant nothing now. His to attack—to create as much a diversion as he could; then pay the penalty.

It was a fierce encounter, tooth and claw. And it was conducted with lightning speed, with scant regard for science, for neither side had the time for science, only the time it took for the voice of the director-layer to reach through the head phones to the sweating gun crews, only the time it took for the loaded guns to fire. Five-five's and five-one's . . . the bricks flew at *Electra*, bricks flung by the entire Japanese line and falling on all sides of her. Near misses rocked her, and the stench of the Nip explosives swept down on her with the falling spray. But her guns were still firing furiously, still aiming at the leading enemy; their crews, by habit, undistracted by the tumult that raged around them. The pedals snapped down, the guns recoiled, brass cylinders smoking, empty, rolled from the mounts to end up on the deck. Splashes rose around the Nips, corrections were made and breeches clanged shut again. Then two more hits sparked along the enemy's hull; two hits that were followed by a ragged yell from the men around me; a yell of primitive pleasure dying abruptly; drowned by the explosion that registered below the bridge . . . *our* bridge . . . a blow that hit home like a hammer, sent the ship reeling, and was followed by yet another, and then another.

"That's torn it!"

The first shell had cut off all communication from the bridge to the rest of the ship, and from the director to the guns. The next had landed in the forward switchboard, wrecking the electric system for'ard. But the third was the most serious of all. Escaping steam roared from *Electra*'s bowels; she had suffered a direct hit, on the after boiler-room! Disabled, the ship lost way, shuddered, came to a stop . . . and the enemy disappeared at an angle into the smoke, slinging over one last vindictive salvo as he went.

I bumped into McLeod, his white overalls stained with oil, as he came up from the engine-room to report.

"What's it like?"

"Pretty sticky . . . I've lost a lot of bodies."

"Can my chaps help you, Chief?"

A flash of spirit. "Thanks, Guns—but no. It's a job for the experts. Given half an hour though and I think I can get her moving."

"Half an hour, *hell*. They're likely to give us half an hour!"

He shrugged, grinned briefly, and was on his way down again, to fight through an inferno of scalding steam.

He never got his half-hour.

A sitting duck we lay there, awaiting the enemy's attention. And the waiting didn't last for long.

A heavy Jap destroyer came back out of the smoke, six long-barrelled guns blazing away at us. Cursing, I took pot luck with a salvo of torpedoes, but, stopped as we were, we had neither swing nor spread, and against our fast target the effort was in vain.

The gun crews hit back; but with each gunlayer having to judge his own range and fall of shot, and the Jap making rings round us the battle was hopelessly unequal. "A" gun was the first to go; a direct hit. A fire broke out under "B" gun, and the ship began to sink. The searchlight platform went and a fire started aft, stopping the supply of ammunition. "X" gun and "Y" gun still continued firing: then one of them was blown sky high, and the other ran out of shells.

A message came from the bridge: "Prepare to abandon ship."

*   *   *

Gretton came up from the flames. In charge of the ammunition supply parties he had refused to leave his post, despite the blaze, until ordered to close down the magazine and shell rooms. And he had done this reluctantly, as though it went against the grain.

Doc came up to the side, to superintend the loading of some of the wounded into our one remaining whaler, our other whaler and the motor-boat having been smashed to pulp.

"You going, Doc?"

"Don't be crazy, I've got work to do."

Frank McLeod arrived from the engine-room, his eyes blinking at the unaccustomed light, his face as lined and black as that of a miner—a miner emerging from the shaft, a miner who has seen his comrades die.

"Anything I can do?"

"Your job's done, Chief. You'd better join the whaler. It needs an officer . . . Good luck . . . and see you later."

"Thanks." He hesitated. "But *should* I go?"

"Yes. It's your duty."

"She's been a grand ship, good luck to you, Guns." And with that he moved away.

The whaler had pulled clear of *Electra* a minute before, and was lying some yards off; so Frank had to swim for it. Seconds later a shell scored a direct hit on the boat throwing her into the air, then hurling her back into the sea.

So died one friend—and many with him.

*   *   *

Number One was as cool and unruffled as ever, directing here, helping there, and generally behaving with the greatest good humour, as though the whole episode was a social event, and not to be taken too seriously. Strolling along the upper deck he stopped for a moment. "Can you manage to free that float, Guns?"

"We'll do it, Sir."

"Good . . . *Rather* looks as though we've had it, Guns."

With that he moved away for'ard; and almost simultaneously another salvo struck.

A first-class officer, Jenner-Fust had been, to the last, urbane.

*   *   *

All this time the Japanese shelling had never let up, and our loss was heavy. A large Carley raft was stowed across the lips

of the tubes and some torpedomen and engine-room ratings
were struggling to lower it to the upper deck and get it from
there into the water. The tubes were trained to starboard to
assist them, and I called to the men on the outboard side to lift
their end of the raft and slide it down. But none of them moved.
They just looked up at me, then one of them said, tears running
down his face: "We can't, Sir, there are dead men below us."

"Then *move them*."

"Sir . . . they're our pals, Sir!"

They couldn't, just couldn't touch them.

Eventually it was tough Ted Mash who helped me shift the
bodies. It was a shambles down there, and as we did our horrible job he was growling like an animal in pain.

The ship had developed a steep list. No time must be lost.

"Lift and shift, men," and the raft started to move. It was
then that I was wounded. I felt suddenly as if a red-hot poker
had been thrust straight into the top of my leg, and that for
good measure a dozen red-hot needles had been plunged into
my thigh. Then my back went numb. Subconsciously, the wail
of the shell still in my ears, I thought: "They say you never
hear the one that gets you, and as usual THEY, the bloody
knowalls, are wrong!" And I found myself giggling, at my
excellent repartee. But the float . . .? My brain cleared—the
float was the thing. Nothing was so important as the float,
nothing else seemed to matter but to get it into the water. And
eventually we got it there.

*   *   *

"You *bought* one, Sir! Better get inside."

It was Mash speaking. He and the rest of the troops had been
helping push all the wounded they could find into the float,
and now he had seen the blood, running down from beneath
my trousers.

"Sorry," I said. "But I'll join you later."

His rugged jaw set. "I'm not leaving you here, Sir."

"Thanks T.I. But it's an order. Take charge of the float, get clear of the ship. I won't stay longer than I have to."

He growled something, shook hands, and went.

The Nip destroyer had now partly switched her fire. She was still playing on *Electra* with part of her armament but, evidently for diversion's sake, she was also amusing herself with the floats.

Our hard-won raft received a direct hit. I never saw Tiger Mash again.

*   *   *

After parting from Tiger I had moved over to the other side of the ship where some more of our people were joining a raft. Leading Seaman Fred Castle, flanked by Petty Officer Big Bill Brayley and Polly Perkins were holding it alongside. Then, even as I went over to them, a hail of shrapnel ripped inboard and Castle, straightening up, said: "Leave me, chaps. I've had it!"

"Come on, you silly old blighter. Over you go," they said, and they lowered him into the raft; they, gentle as women, he uncomplaining, stoical, resigned.

"Coming with us, Sir?"

"I'll catch up as quick as I can."

Leading Seaman Barrett arrived and, in spite of the chaos, pulled off a smart salute before reporting: "Depth charges rendered safe, Sir."

I looked at him with some admiration, wondering not for the first time at the manner in which men face with discipline their accustomed chores, even when life itself is at stake. This Leading Seaman had a far more vital job than any of us— at the moment, and in the existing circumstances. Had he neglected it, then one of the depth charges might explode when the ship's turn came, and many more men would die.

"Thank you, Barrett."

Then I remembered something. "Got your young brother with you?"

"Yes, Sir. I'm keeping my eye on him."

"Very well, then, away you go."

The ship's list to port was now so pronounced that I crossed to starboard. Things did not seem to be quite real. My earlier sense of urgency had been lost, and I seemed to have all the time in the world. I could feel the blood running down my leg and into my shoe, and found it vaguely irritating, as though I was walking in a puddle with a leak in my sole. The rafts were drifting away from the ship in the failing light of the sunset, silver splashes dancing around them from the Japanese shrapnel. The heat of the day was past, it was as soft as an English summer's evening. Then Gretton came scurrying along, with a practical problem. ". . . two wounded men aft, Sir. What are we going to do with them?"

I went with him to the quarterdeck. The men were not badly wounded, but victims of smoke and shock, so we lashed one to an empty ammunition box and the other to a grating and lowered them over the side. There was nothing else we could do except to tell them not to despair; they'd be bound to be picked up in the morning. And then, as they drifted off, I shivered slightly and turned away, making for my cabin.

The last post had brought some photos of my wife and our sons and somewhere at the back of my mind was the thought that I must pick up those photos; they would keep me company should I be captured by the Nips. But having got what I wanted I was suddenly seized with panic. It was, I think, the look of the walls that did it, the way they tilted, and tilted more alarmingly for every fleeting moment. I was quite terrified . . . of dying there, of being trapped like a rat. I made the deck in double time.

Gretton too had been below, though apparently for a purpose less pious than my own. "Sorry about the shortage of glasses, Sir," he was brandishing a half bottle of whisky, "but I thought you'd care to join me in a drink!"

I refused, with thanks. I could have used that Scotch, but was doubtful about its effects. We might be in the water for a long, long time, and it might only add to our thirst. Gretton hesitated, looked sadly at the bottle, shrugged temptation aside. "Just as you wish, Sir."

A pause. Then perking up again, and with a swift shrewd look at my leg he said: "Doesn't seem much else left to do, Sir. Don't you think it's time we left?"

I agreed.

*   *   *

There was no sign of life in our part of the ship, and when we released the newly discovered "tadpole" and ditched it over the side the upper deck was deserted, except for the dead. *Electra*'s list to port continued. She was well down by the bows, and her starboard propeller was so far out of the water that as we dived I thought for a moment I was going to hit the shaft. But this didn't happen and we reached our new refuge intact, Gretton balancing on one side-float and me on the other, and both of us gazing at a very melancholy spectacle.

The sun had set, but a bright moon rode the sky, bathing *Electra* in a soft, cool light. The Nip destroyer had ceased firing, and, sheering off, had left us to the tender mercy of the sea. Now, apart from the sound of men's voices and the noise of the swimmers splashing about in the water, it was very silent. From somewhere or other, far away, we heard the guns but their music was much muted, like the sound of muffled drums, and growing ever fainter as the battle pressed steadily on. I was worrying about absent friends. Had Harry got away? But somehow I knew he hadn't . . . without any proof I knew it. Harry, with his high spirits, his keen brain, his ardent questing mind . . . Harry was dead. And the Captain? Where was the Captain?

A second later a shout went up from some of the men, a shout which resolved into a cheer, a cheer in which we, sitting astride our restless perch, most fervently joined. For framed in the brilliant moonlight, May's tall figure had appeared on the near side of the bridge, and now, leaning over the bridge rail, he was waving to us, his Company. More shouts, and then a note of urgency . . . a note of desperate urgency—with us yelling to him to waste no time, to jump for it while the going was good.

"Come on, Sir. Jump! Jump while there's time . . ."

The death-rattle sounded in *Electra*'s throat, a violent convulsion coursed through her slim, much injured body.

"She's going . . . she's going! For God's sake, *jump!*"

Still showing the apparent casualness befitting the proud but very sad tradition of such occasions, May gave us one last wave, then turned away.

"He's going to leave from the port side," I hazarded.

"*But he's left it too bloody late!*" snapped Gretton.

And I realised I was crying.

A swirl of water spread from *Electra*'s bows: she began to plunge. For a moment, as her stern rose steeply she seemed to hang before our eyes, with her nose buried deep in the ocean and her propellers, stopped for ever, silhouetted against the stars. And then she died.

Only one gentle sigh came from our ship as she plunged below, her torments ended. She went very swiftly; and owing to the angle of her descent the last we saw of her was the main-mast, with the White Ensign still flying bravely from her gaff.

*　　　*　　　*

An hour went by. On *Electra*'s departure the troops, regardless

of their plight, had raised a lusty cheer; a cheer of farewell
that was completely spontaneous and welled up from the heart.
I had often heard of similar incidents accompanying the last
moments of other ships, but I had never understood just why
sailors, preoccupied with their own problems of survival,
should react in such a way. Nor am I sure that I am much the
wiser now . . . except that it just seems to "happen". When
saying goodbye to a ship you love you just can't help your
emotion getting the better of you.

But after our demonstration—this unleashing of a primitive
urge which could no more be stopped than a sneeze—an
extraordinary lassitude had descended on me. Gretton and I,
paddling the float clear of the film of oil fuel, had spotted the
dark shape of a Carley raft ahead of us, with what appeared
to be another raft some distance beyond. My legs were at last
beginning to throb and I felt terribly tired. Would I live?
Would I die? Suddenly, neither course was terribly important.
I was content to drift on, with my legs in the water where I
couldn't see the blood, and my mind winging across thousands
of miles, travelling way back across the ocean to Belles and
our sons; my thoughts dwelling on them fondly and yet leaving my body still unspurred by effort on their behalf. I was
sorry for them, and sorry for myself, but my will had ceased
to fight against our apparent fate, and in addition—it may have
been because I had lost too much blood, or it may have been
just as a reaction to the shock of events—I must have become
a little lightheaded. At least, probably that's what the doctors
would have said . . .

For gradually I lost all awareness of the sea around us and
found myself watching a whole crowd of my old shipmates,
drawn up in rank before a massive gate. Among them were
some who I knew for a fact had been killed, yet I was not
surprised to see them. And among them were others whose fate,
until then, was still obscure. They were tired and battle-stained,

those friends of mine, and marked with their wounds.
And yet as they stood there in dazzling but heatless light there
was a great contentment about them and I was not at all
worried about encountering them. In fact, from first to last,
I had no sense of fear in our uncanny meeting, but tried to
approach, eager to speak to them . . . and yet I could not; for
try though I might the words just would not come. I was
divorced from those men I realised, with a shock that was
almost painful, separated by some barrier I could not feel or
see. They seemed to know that I was there, and smiled at me:
but their lips moved soundlessly and I could have wept because
I could not hear them. And then, as the Gates of Heaven opened
to them, I heard, more as the echo of a voice than the voice
itself, the two words that contain the highest praise the Navy
has to offer: "Well done!"

Dream? Vision? Delirium? I wouldn't know. Except that
I can remember its every detail. But what of the triteness of
those words of welcome? Hadn't Paradise a more eloquent
greeting to command? Again, I wouldn't know. Maybe I
didn't hear aright, maybe the whole thing was the figment of a
temporarily disordered brain, but, don't forget, St. Peter was
a fisherman.

I came to myself, with the water under my chin. Either
Gretton or I, or both of us, had fallen from the raft and caused
it to overbalance. With some difficulty we righted it, and on
regaining our perches resolved that we must keep ourselves
awake, and to this end we talked about our families, our homes,
and our life before the war. Then Gretton, right out of the
blue, said: "Sir, you know that bloke wot sold me them geese?
Blimey, just you wait until I see him next time. I'll do the
perisher . . . I tell you I'll really *do* him."

I felt my old self again and began to laugh.

*   *   *

The night seemed endless and when I managed to get some idea of the time by the passage of the moon and the position of the Southern Cross I was surprised to find that it was only midnight. Only six hours had elapsed since *Electra*'s sinking, and I hoped most fervently that the next six hours would go a damn sight faster. Then Gretton's voice broke in upon my thoughts.

"What's that ahead of us, Sir?"

I looked up . . . to see a large conger-eel type of fish, with zebra stripes across its body, swimming lazily on the surface in the shape of a huge letter S.

"Will it hurt, Sir?"

With a confidence I was far from feeling I answered: "No. Don't worry about him. Quite a harmless type, probably frightened to death of us."

And then I remembered, very miserably, that the Java Sea was the home of some of the most vicious sea-snakes in the world. Could this be one of them? Slowly the wretched thing circled round us, taking its time. And we, acutely conscious of our dangling legs kicked and splashed frantically in order to warn it off. But despite our panic our efforts were successful and after yet another slow encirclement and a formal, speculative stare, as if weighing us up, the unwelcome visitor submerged and disappeared. We breathed again.

One query answered, Gretton piped up once more. "Any sharks around here, Sir?" He seemed quite unafraid but his curiosity was insatiable.

Sharks? Until now I hadn't given them a thought, but now I began to wonder *why* I hadn't. "The gunfire will have driven them well away . . . there isn't a shark for miles. Except for *you*."

"Yes, Sir." A pause. "It's blood that attracts them from a distance, or so it's said.

"*Blood*," he repeated, then followed an embarrassed grin.

"So sorry, Sir . . . sounds potty, but I clean forgot about your legs!"

Once again we dozed off, and once again we capsized. This time, on recovering, I decided to close one of the rafts to see who was there, and wondered why the devil I hadn't done this obvious thing before. I felt far stronger since my "vision" and my head was clear. Gretton, too, had benefited from his nap. Together, paddling with our hands and feet, we gradually managed to reduce the space between us and the raft which, owing to our inactivity, had increased considerably. It was a long job, however, and when we got within hailing distance the moon was beginning to set.

"Boat ahoy!"

Seen dimly in the fading light, three figures detached themselves from the side of the raft . . . Big Bill Brayley, Polly Perkins, and A.B. Tuffin.

"Who is it?"

I replied: "The Gunner and Gretton."

The news was yelled back to the raft, and an answering shout of "Good Old Guns" and other expressions, obscene but flatteringly friendly, floated across to us.

Tuffin, who was rather on the tubby side, was wearing a cork lifejacket and an inflatable belt. Now he stood out of the water looking as large as a house. "I AM glad to see you, Sir."

Rudely I answered: "If you're pleased to see me then the answer's *balls*."

"Fancy you using a naughty word like that, Sir." And despite our predicament he roared with laughter.

"You'll be pleased to hear we've got the Doctor with us."

Pleased was an understatement.

"How many others have you got with you?" I asked.

"Forty-one, Sir . . ."

"But the raft's only made to take twenty . . ."

"Oh yes," this with the utmost casualness. "But we've

given the wounded most of the space. We fit chaps just take it in turns to swim around."

He paused. "A funny old place this for us to be gossiping in. So we'd better lend a hand to bring the tadpole alongside, Sir—might as well be together."

And so we started for the raft—with five of us pushing together, and all of us rather excited. Then, out of the darkness came a dramatic intervention.

A submarine surfaced. Next moment, from her bridge, came the flash and report of a revolver!

*   *   *

After our recent experiences, this excitement proved bad for the nerves. Those around the raft, expecting to be machine-gunned or worse, scattered and became disorganised. But we, around the tadpole, just froze, being so close to our fate that we could see no possible escape. And then, despite the darkness, I recognised the nationality of our visitor and yelled, or maybe squeaked to the others, in a relief I can't describe: "It's all right, lads . . . It's *all right* . . . It's a *Yank*!"

Figures appeared along the submarine deck, and a voice cried: "Who are you?"

"Survivors from *Electra*," I answered.

"Then come aboard Mac, and make it snappy."

Our little tadpole was bumping against the submarine's side, but I didn't find it easy to get over the saddle tanks, and two burly Americans leaned over to help; each seizing a wrist they slung me into the air, landing me on the plates of the catwalk like a fish on the end of a rod.

"Thanks," I panted, breathless but sincere; but then another flap broke out. The men on the raft couldn't see what was happening very clearly, and believed that I'd been kidnapped. "It's a *Jap*," they yelled. "The Gunner's just gone back inboard with his hands up!"

"Back away, lads . . ." The response was enthusiastic, but though I could hardly spit a sixpence I managed to call them back. "Come alongside, and quickly," I yelled. "It's all right, I tell you. It's a Yank!"

"How come you recognised us so quickly?"

"Oh, just a bit of luck. I saw your Admiralty-type anchor.*"

"Sherlock Holmes stuff, huh?"

"Elementary!"

The S.38's Captain received me on the bridge. "Lieutenant Munson, at your service . . ."

I shook hands, warmly.

"How many you got?" he asked.

"Forty-three with me, and I hope there'll be other raftloads too."

But he didn't panic. "Don't worry, Bud; we'll pick up all we can."

And then the American added: "So sorry about the shooting; but when I saw that queer contraption you were riding in I thought that maybe a Nip suicide squad was coming my way with a mine!"

*   *   *

The rescue work proceeded smoothly and efficiently, despite an initial misunderstanding.

The Americans wanted to move the able-bodied first, so as to have elbow-room to clear the casualties more efficiently, with the minimum discomfort; but our lads had expected the wounded to go first, and, not appreciating the American motives, promptly turned round and said they wouldn't be rescued until they'd seen their pals away. Intervening, I told the troops to do what they were told, and reminded them that, as regards the best way of packing a submarine, the Yanks must

---

* The U.S.A. was the last major sea-going nation to discard the old-fashioned Admiralty pattern anchor. Hence the identification.

undoubtedly know best. But once I had resolved this dispute, the cause of which was highly creditable to both sides, a new problem arose; for no sooner did the fit ones condescend to come inboard than several of them insisted on stopping to shake hands with me. This social pleasantry caused quite a jam on the bridge, delaying things still further, and I was worried about the American's reactions until Munson, exceedingly patient and understanding, said tolerantly: "Time's short, Guns, so get them below and keep the welcome stuff for later."

Our friends now set about their task of moving the wounded, conducting it with vigour, and with gentle care as well. The transfer of badly injured men from a raft to the crammed interior of a submarine is never an easy job, but when the sub is crowded with passengers and is liable to be attacked at any moment, and when the movement is carried out in darkness, it becomes a major operation. First *Electra*'s wounded had to be negotiated over the bulging saddle tanks of the American. Next, strapped to stretchers, they had to be lowered down the narrow conning tower, Doc waiting at the bottom to receive them. And then, of course, room had to be found for them . . . room for twenty-two of them in a submarine designed for a crew of thirty-five . . . room when the submarine was already overcrowded with twenty-one of the wounded's able-bodied comrades. Yet somehow, miraculously, the job was done, and Munson, despite his cares, continued to persevere in the search for more survivors. He picked up another raft; he saved eleven more of our family. Then came the dawn, and reluctantly he dived.

*　　　*　　　*

"Still sea-sick?" joked the U.S. Captain. They'd brought me a cup of coffee, and I'd vomited all over the place.

Munson had yielded me his cabin, and when he'd called to see me the English side of the alliance was anything but dignified. I was clad in nothing but my birthday suit, having hung my shirt and trousers up to dry; although I still retained my shoes, those precious shoes; I had not forgotten the survivors of *Repulse* and *Prince of Wales*.

"No, not sea-sick," I said. "It's just that I don't appreciate good coffee. So maybe I'd better have another cup to get acclimatised . . ." This time it stayed down.

Munson told me that he intended to remain submerged during the day, then surface at night and reopen the search again before proceeding to the entrance to Sourabaya, where he hoped to transfer us to a Dutch ship. After that, he must proceed in accordance with his latest orders and sail for Australia.

As the hours went by the conditions on S.38 became progressively less hygienic; eighty-nine men made excessive inroads on her precious oxygen, and the air was pretty foul. I was pleased to see that, for all their discomfort, the troops were settling down extremely well; after being snatched from the embrace of the Java Sea they were busy counting their blessings, and did not complain. The Yanks played their part too in the development of equanimity; they couldn't do enough for us. Clothing the near-naked from their own meagre wardrobes; surrendering their bunks; bringing us endless supplies of coffee . . . they were so busy in good deeds that, had the ship been British, we couldn't have felt more at home.

Then, in the forenoon, Munson sent for me: "Sorry, Bud, but I've got some news. We've picked up a Jap escort group. They're heading our way, and if they locate us it *could* be quite unpleasant."

"I see what you mean," I said. "But what do we do about it?"

"Well, from experience, I'd say that the yellow man's asdics are not up to our standard, but his listening devices are pretty good. So I plan to emulate Brer Rabbit ... there will be no talking, no movement."

I waited, then Munson continued: "Now my chaps are used to this sort of thing, yet even for them it's bad enough. But with your chaps it's new ... I daresay that not one of them, bar yourself, has ever visited a submarine before, and it's going to be kinda hard on them, this 'silent routine'. But it's got to be carried out, or else we'll *all* be put away. So do you think you can impress the need for quiet upon them? Are you prepared to tell them that they've got to keep absolutely quiet, absolutely still? Shall I tell 'em, Bud? Or shall I leave the job to you?"

I said: "You leave the job to me, it's *my* responsibility ... and there's no need for you to worry; the men won't let you down."

But, when I went for'ard, I felt a lot less confident than I had pretended. I would have backed our lot for courage any day, when in their natural element or in their normal physical shape, but even *their* nerves must have a breaking point: and maybe we were now approaching it. For here they were—all of them recently shipwrecked, most of them possessing a surface sailor's horror of submarines, several of them wounded and in pain. Wasn't it hoping for too much to suppose that not one of them, not *one* of them, would yield? An unfamiliar routine, hopelessly cramped quarters, and above all else, the inability to hit back ... Would not these factors, added to their recent shock, and the days and nights of strain that had preceded it, prove just that bit too much for these fatigued and bereaved fellows when warned of the probability of fresh attacks and asked to help prevent them?

"You have been on the dishing-out end of a depth charge often enough." (I *hoped* I was sufficiently casual.) "But today we are likely to be at the receiving end. However, there's no need for anyone to start wetting his pants just yet, for the Yanks know all there is to know about the Nip. They have dodged him before, and will dodge him again.

"All that I insist on is that you do exactly as you're told: you must keep perfectly still, you mustn't say a word; you must stay as stiff as ruddy statues, and as dumb as Colchester oysters. I've told the Yank here that you know how to do just that; incredible though it seems. And I think he almost believes it; he seems to trust us anyway. So, silence then, and no movement, and we'll all come through all right . . ."

A reflective pause. And then, as I was wondering how my words had registered, a sepulchral Cockney voice said slowly: "Sahnds a great deal to ask, Sir, but what time do you think we'll get Up Spirits!"

16

From Java to Australia

SILENCE. All machinery was stopped: even the smallest fans had been switched off. The air was so stale that you could almost *feel* it. In the low-lit control room Munson and a little group of officers and petty officers stood motionless. The depth gauge, I noticed, registered ninety feet.

One of the wounded, who earlier had been coughing his lungs out, was gripping a rag with his teeth. Another lay there with only his eyes alive, sweat trickling down his face. Then gradually into the church-like hush obtruded the throb of propellers, growing ever louder. I grinned at the youngster next to me, with an attempt to encourage. He licked his lips nervously, but smiled faintly back. And then—you didn't have to be a submariner to discern the fact—the first of the Nip destroyers began to pass overhead. Right overhead.

Tensely we waited, with at least one of us—myself—anticipating the worst, and feeling sick about it. So *this* was what we had been preserved for—the rush of the depth charges, the roar of their explosion, the torment of the water around the fragile hull. It would be a quick death if we were lucky, and a lingering death, if we were not . . . the nastiest sort of death one could possibly imagine.

The propeller note grew fainter; seemingly less urgent. But it was followed by another. Yet still the wounded at my feet kept their silence, and their faith with the Americans. For, while the submarine tingled to the sounds of the enemy searchers, the only sound that arose from we passengers was the sound of our heartbeats which only our own ears heard.

The noise of the second destroyer lessened, and was followed by yet another. And then there was silence, the Nips were continuing on their way. Not until several minutes had elapsed, and not until the Americans around the hydroplane controls and the downed periscope had begun to stir again, did we dare to believe our luck. Not until then did I realise that, throughout the entire episode, I had been standing at attention—with my fingers crossed.

"Well, that's that," said Munson cheerfully.

I ventured. "I thought I could pick out three ships . . ."

He shot me an amused look. "That old submariner stuff again . . . but there were more than three . . ."

A moment later a distant explosion rumbled through the sea. It was followed by others, seventeen in all. The Americans treated the occasion with levity.

"That's our opposite number. Reckon those garbage cans will have given her a shaking."

*   *   *

Doc arrived, worn out. For hours he'd been working among the wounded, probing, stitching, bandaging. And now his face seemed shrunken, pressed round the cheeks with tiredness and strain and shock. "For heaven's sake take a rest," I said, but he shook his head. "No, Guns, there's still work for me to do. I'll have a look at you, now."

Munson chimed in. "Come on, Guns, hop on my bunk and let Doc do some needlework."

I obliged.

"H'mn, this one's an exit wound, don't have to bother about that much . . . but this chap's more serious. Decent lump or shrapnel in there, must be very close to the sciatic nerve." Doc paused in his running commentary. "Lucky you can still walk. I'll have to put some stitches in—it's going to hurt."

He was right, as usual ... But I couldn't complain, not when I thought of the Buffer, Petty Officer Watkins, and A.B. Meader, all of them very badly wounded and still sticking it out, none of them complaining. And then, when I'd been temporarily patched up, I asked after Castle.

"Guns, I'm sorry—but Castle has just died. There was *nothing* I could have done, not even if I'd had the resources of a hospital behind me."

I dared not look into Seymour's eyes. For I knew the frustration and defeat that I would see there. It would be like viewing one's sick image in a mirror.

"But one thing, he didn't suffer." And at this the Doc shut up, slumped forward, and just sat there, his head in his hands.

Munson, who had been listening, gently touched his shoulder: "Okay, okay ... you've dished your Gunner up. Now go and get some rest. But ... just one thing though. Can you let me have some details of the chap who has died? It'll be necessary for the record."

Doc looked up. "I have done that already, Sir."

"Have to hand it to him," said Munson a few moments later. "You've got a Doc in a million."

Half an hour after he'd been ordered to rest Seymour was on his feet again. There was nothing left in the submarine's medical box and the last shot of morphia had been exhausted; but still he placed himself among the wounded, using words to comfort them in default of drugs and dressings, and writing up their case histories, for the benefit of the Dutch.

When night came again Munson, as good as his word, once more resumed the search for survivors. The probable drift of rafts or wreckage had been very carefully worked out, but although, during the daylight, he had several times brought the submarine up to periscope depth he had seen nothing. Now we cruised on the surface but still without success. On the other hand we were not so depressed as we might have been, for the Americans had received a signal stating that a hospital ship had been sent into the area, and we were therefore hopeful that she had had better luck than we. It was not until several days later that we learned that this ship had been intercepted and taken by the Japanese. Similarly, we were cheered by the fact that all the reports so far received concerning the progress of the battle were extremely favourable to the allies but on this score too we were subsequently undeceived.

*   *   *

It was nearly daylight when we arrived off the minefields that guarded the sea approach to Sourabaya. A Dutch sweeper had been sent to meet us, but a slight difference of opinion now arose between our rescuers. For while Munson was anxious to move us immediately, the Netherlands captain had been ordered to take only me on board and transfer the rest in more sheltered waters. This led to a rather embarrassing situation— with me a passenger on the sweeper, the rest of *Electra*'s survivors following in the submarine, and the American almost going up the wall with impatience. As he had been ordered to get out of this dangerous area by dawn, and into deep water, away from air attack, Munson's feelings were understandable. Hopelessly late, and in addition committed to a long trip through the narrow swept channel, plus a compli- cated hand-over of his guests at the end of it, his lot was certainly not enviable. And neither was mine. Feeling com- pletely cut off from the troops, and fearing every moment that the S.38 although so overloaded, might suddenly decide to slip the leash and turn to sea again, I was in a considerable sweat, not cooling down until the transfer was effectively completed . . .

When eventually we waved goodbye to the Americans—

the hazardous voyage to Australia before them—our gratitude was coupled with considerable misgivings about their future, and yet, as it happened, we could have saved ourselves the bother. For despite the lateness of their start, and despite the fact that the sea and sky around them swarmed with the enemy, our friends got safely home. Furthermore, they bagged a Nip cruiser and a freighter while getting there.

*   *   *

"We're out of the flipping frying pan," said Bill Brayley, "but we're into the flipping fire!"

The "security" of the land proved rather illusory. No sooner had we come alongside than a heavy aircraft attack had obliged the ship to put out to sea again; then, when we'd returned to load our wounded into the waiting ambulances, another raid had opened and we had been sent to a shelter. This latter attack had lasted quite a while and as soon as it was over we had been told to start marching to the dockyard gates where a truck would be waiting for us. But we found the going extremely difficult. The sun had risen, the asphalt road was burning the feet of those who had no shoes, and then, just to make our joy complete, a Dutch officer rushed towards us, shouting: "Run like hell! The ammunition dump is on fire."

Run like hell! To run barefoot on a red-hot roadway is hell indeed. Sheer hell. Hopping, skipping, and jumping, the troops turned the air blue with their protests. I was lucky of course— lucky in one respect. I had my shoes! But my good fortune stopped at that, for *I* couldn't run because of the shrapnel in my legs.

It was a queer sort of journey, considering there were hundreds of tons of high explosive parked, burning, behind us, to egg us on.

First, with typical generosity, Bill Brayley and Lofty Barrett ranged alongside—offering me a chair lift.

And then when I refused they wouldn't leave me.

"For God's sake get to the shelter." But they took no notice.

And then some of the chaps ahead stopped short.

"What the devil's holding *you* up?"

"We were waiting for you to catch up, Sir!"

At which they again took up the lead, progressed another twenty yards or so, and stopped, to wait once more. As the man responsible for our safety, the Dutch escorting officer had a pretty thankless role.

Said Bill when, having reached the bunker, we whiled away our time by mulling over recent events: "You know when that Yank told me just how many flipping warships had been over us I nearly had a baby."

A voice from the back of the shelter cut in: "Don't you go having a baby, Bill. We're in trouble enough already."

Which was true enough.

*   *   *

The big bang having failed to materialise—thanks to the devoted work of the Dutch fire-fighters—we were taken to the naval base where we were temporarily separated. Everything on the admin. side seemed to be running pretty smoothly there, and the troops were taken away immediately, for a hot bath, fresh clothes and a meal. But Doc and I were not so lucky, for no sooner had we seen the rest of the party settled than we were called upon to go to headquarters for interrogation. There, with empty stomachs and quite unwashed, we gave them our version of events, then listened sombrely to the rest of the story, as far as it was known.

Of the five allied cruisers that had set out so bravely from Sourabaya not one remained afloat. All three of the British destroyers had been sunk. Both of the Dutch destroyers had been sunk. One of the four American destroyers had been sunk, and the three that remained were on voyage to Australia. It was a frightful tale of disaster—the Battle of the Java Sea—although we did not hear *all* of it at the time, for information was sketchy. Events were moving too fast for there to be an accurate record.

After being engaged by *Electra* the Nip destroyers had been warmly received on the other side of the smoke by *Encounter*, *Jupiter*, and by *Exeter* herself. Then, on Doorman bringing his cruisers round, the *Perth* had intervened with her six-inch guns and the enemy had been forced to retire. Next *Exeter* had been able to begin her withdrawal to Sourabaya, where her injuries were to be repaired. Her engineers had by then succeeded in working up her speed to fifteen knots and her main gun armament was again functioning—so effectively that, finding a Nip cruiser in her path, she actually succeeded in forcing him to turn away, and turn away for good.

At first, as I've said, the action appeared to be going rather well . . .

In the meantime, however, while *Exeter* and a Dutch destroyer were pursuing their way south, Doorman had brought the rest of his squadron on to a northerly course, presumably in an effort to take advantage of the dark in order to outflank the Japanese naval force and get at the transports. But in this he failed. Contact was lost with the enemy warships, but there was still no sign of the transports, and steadily Doorman's little fleet began to shrink. Piece by piece it was whittled away.

First the American destroyers left him. Having expended their torpedoes, and with fuel running short, they withdrew to base.

Next the *Jupiter* bought it. Mine? Torpedo? Nobody knew.

Next, with flares from Jap aircraft falling all around the five ships that now remained, Doorman turned south again, searching for the transports he had failed to find in the north and eventually finding himself back in the area where the battle had begun. And there were survivors in the water, scores of them from the *Kortenaer*, so he ordered the *Encounter*, his sole remaining destroyer, to leave the line and pick them up.

By ten o'clock the cruisers were on their own, yet still the Dutchman persevered.

It was ten-thirty when the allies sighted their foes again. Two heavy cruisers were engaged immediately by *Perth* and *Houston*, and hits were scored, but then the Japanese struck—attacked with torpedoes.

It was still not apparent that these torpedoes* were fired by surface ships.

Thus *Java*, evidently suspecting the attack was launched by submarine, turned smartly away, only to be hit and sunk by another "spread" fired by a heavy cruiser of the Nachi class.

Then Doorman in *De Ruyter* met with tragedy. His ship blew up and sunk a moment later.

The battle was lost.

Following the Dutchman's death Hec Waller, of the *Perth*, took charge of the allied ships remaining—all two of them. Australia's *Perth* and America's *Houston* could command between them six eight-inch guns and eight six-inch guns against an enemy broadside of twenty eight-inch and fourteen six-inch. Again, the allies had no destroyers while the Japanese had eight. With these facts clear to him, Waller now conducted a manœuvre that many may think should have been carried out much earlier. Skilfully succeeding in disengaging he set course for harbour, arriving at Tanjong Priok the following morning.

Well, it was bad enough, this story that we heard. And the

---

* Said to be based on a British device—rejected by the Admiralty as "too costly" and "too risky for practice shoots".

compensations were not too obvious. But it didn't appear to
be as bad as it really was, for the full facts were not yet to hand.
We still did not know of the fate that had overwhelmed the
British and American survivors; not until three weeks later
did we learn the worst. As far as we were concerned the *Exeter*
had got away: we knew nothing of the fact that, leaving
Sourabaya after conducting makeshift repairs, she had met
up with four Nip heavy cruisers and nearly a dozen fleet
destroyers, and had perished, together with *Encounter* and the
American destroyer *Pope*, in heroic battle. Nor were we aware
that *Perth* and *Houston*—sailing from Tanjong Priok—had
encountered the bulk of the enemy's invasion forces; or that
after inflicting heavy damage among the transports, they too
had been destroyed. In fact, of all the ships which had assembled
so impressively in the solent but three days earlier, only three
remained, and these the least significant—three small twenty-
year-old American destroyers. But, as I've said before, we
didn't know. News from the Java Sea was hard to come by,
and even while mourning their own extreme bereavement the
Dutch were convinced that the Nips had suffered too.

No, things didn't appear to be so bad as they really were,
except in one respect—that, whatever the toll exacted from the
Japanese, it would make little difference to the fate of the East
Indies; for the fall of Java could not long be delayed. The Nip
invasion forces were pouring ashore, and advancing at speed
with little to oppose them. They were on the outskirts of
Sourabaya; they were on the outskirts of Batavia. Their warships had rounded the Sunda Strait; they had entered the
Indian Ocean. Now only one of the island's ports remained
usable, Tjilatjap on the south-east shore.

The end was in sight, and I was to take my party and the
survivors of *Jupiter* on to Tjilatjap and get there as soon as
possible. God willing, we would go by train from Sourabaya
they said, and God willing, the train would leave at 5.30 p.m.

But one thing was certain, that train would be the last one out!

*   *   *

Our orders received there was only one thing left to do—to call at the hospital and try to reclaim our wounded. But we ran into snags, serious snags; for the Dutch Colonel-in-Chief in charge of the medical services refused to part with ten of the men on the grounds that they were too seriously hurt to move. "Your doctor has already performed miracles for them. Would you make all his good work useless?"

I agreed about Doc's good work. ". . . but we can't leave our friends behind."

The Dutchman shook his head: "You don't know what you're asking. This hospital is the most modern and best equipped in the East Indies. If you take your men away three of them will be dead by nightfall, the others will follow them within a week. So much is certain."

I hesitated. "I still don't like it."

And he answered wearily: "Then you had better ask your own doctor to give you *his* opinion.

I brought Seymour into the discussion: "Sorry, Guns. It goes against the grain, I know. But he's right. It would be fatal to move them."

"You see," said the Colonel, "and now I will take advantage of my rank. I will *forbid* you to move them!"

"But who looks after them when the Japanese arrive?"

He looked at me, as if insulted. Then replied with tremendous dignity: "Who else but my colleague and I? Your wounded are under our protection, and are our responsibility. We will stay with them whatever happens."

I told him that I thought he was a very brave man.

*   *   *

The Dutch Padre then came in to tell us that poor Fred

Castle would be buried that same evening at six o'clock. Would we form a party of mourners? I answered we had been ordered to report to the railway station at 5.30. "Had Leading Seaman Castle lived his friends would have done anything for him, but it's now my duty to try to get away so that they can fight again."

"I understand," said the Padre gently. "And you are right of course. He is in the hands of God . . . but pray for him!"

I said we would do that; and meant it.

I found the *Jupiter* survivors, forty of them. They had paddled their float for thirty hours—all through the night after the sinking of their ship, all through the blazing day, and all through the next night too. The first thing that they saw on landing was the Japanese invasion force, swarming along the coastline only a few miles away but they had made Sourabaya by "borrowing" a score of bicycles, travelling two men per bike. They were exhausted, and suffering from exposure, but there was no time for us to treat them. We'd got a train to catch.

*　　　*　　　*

It was a strange railway trip . . . on a train that was packed with naval and military personnel; with government officials; with women and children. It was menaced by land attack, air attack, and acts of sabotage. And its passengers were haunted by the fear that they would be met, at their destination, by the barbarous representatives of the enemy. But all the same, we were lucky to be on it, lucky to have the chance to fidget about what *might* happen rather than experience what was happening; happening to others. We were lucky to be free, for the moment anyway, free and not captive and objects of derision . . . clubbed and bayoneted . . . tortured and betrayed . . . men without hope.

Nor were the physical discomforts of the journey as great as I'd expected. Our chaps soon saw to *that*!

First, they discovered a kitchen car, although the kitchen staff had fled. Next, they managed to find some fuel and get the range working. And next, having mysteriously acquired some tea and sugar they plied me through the night with hot sweet tea, contained, for want of better crockery, in a salvaged bean tin. "I'm sorry about the *milk*, Sir," said Gretton . . . "But if only this blessed train would stop we'd get out and catch a cow!"

There were Dutch officers in the compartment, and although they were friendly enough to us as individuals (after all they shared our tea!) they were inclined to be very bitter about the way in which they felt they had been let down by Britain.

"You English say you are turning out such colossal numbers of Spitfires and Hurricanes . . . yet one week's output would have saved Java, and you sent us next to nothing!"

The argument was, of course, familiar. One week's output of aircraft, delivered early enough, could have saved, not only Java but also Singapore. And it was difficult to advance the official argument with conviction . . . namely that *everything* must be given to the battle against Germany.

"Ja, we admire the British fighting spirit, and agree about your world-wide responsibilities," said an elderly captain. "But all that we are asking is why *this* part of your world-wide responsibilities wasn't worth a week's supply of fighter-planes!"

It was hard not to sympathise with these valiant Dutchmen whose leaders had based all their defence strategy on the assumption that Singapore would be held, and who had sent their best squadrons to its defence. On the other hand there was the undoubted fact that if Britain herself should fall then everyone else would fall; whereas, after defeating Germany, she would be able to devote all her resources to reconquering the lost territories of the East, the Dutch territories among them. And some such thought did occur to me, and was put forward by me, though it made little impression, I am afraid, on the audience or even on myself. For it is difficult to maintain a nicely balanced assessment of the future when one is travelling as a fugitive in a ramshackle blacked-out train through the sticky, tropical night, when one is a member of a defeated, disorganised community rendered suddenly rootless, displaced . . . a man whose closest friends have just met with violent death, a man whose small world has collapsed about his ears. It is impossible to consider the niceties of world strategy in the dawn that follows the sleepless night, when one's wounds throb and the sun comes up like a blood-red orange over Tjilatjap; impossible to think of triumphs to come when, arriving in the middle of the inevitable air raid, you are pushed into the dank embrace of the lush green-foliaged jungle, to seek, on your belly, a refuge from the bombs.

*   *   *

Farquharson was tough, no doubt about that. His square jaw reminded me ominously of Sammy, and his voice was charged with aggression. A small party from the British naval base had taken over the *Verspeck*, a small inter-island steamer, and he, a Commander, was in charge of them—and us. I now had a superior officer to answer to.

"What strength's your party?"

"Forty-two *Electra*, forty *Jupiter*, and a couple of spare bods we've picked up on the way."

His heavy eyebrows lowered threateningly as he eyed me up and down—and well might he be surprised at what he saw!

I had no cap, and was very much unshaven. My white uniform jacket was stained and torn, my grey flannel trousers were covered with dust and mud, my shoes, once virginally white, were coated with oil and filth. No one could have looked less like a naval officer.

"How many engine ratings have you?"

I told him.

"Then they've got a nice job on—if they're not too bone-idle to do it. They will have to work the ship to Australia. So turn 'em to!"

I listened incredulously. "Yes, they'll do that—and all you want. But first they need a square meal, and a couple of hours' rest."

"*Rest*! Couple of hours' rest?"

And then, his face brick-red he bawled: "Good God, can't you tell them there's a war on!"

At which I blew my top. Seniority, court-martials, career—all such considerations were thrown to the winds.

"Do you expect me to tell these men there's a bloody war on! Do you think they don't know? Don't you realise they have fought a bitter action, and have seen their comrades die? Don't you realise that they've been days without sleep, have seen their ship sink, and been saved by a bloody miracle! Good God," I almost screamed. "They've left ten of their pals in the base hospital, and may never see them again! They've stuck together . . . thick and thin together, and for all that they've been through they've never belly-ached once. And you want me to tell *them* . . . men like them . . . that there's a bloody war on!"

I came to a stop, choking with anger. There was plenty more I wanted to say, but I couldn't get it out. All the accumulated strain seemed, at last, to have told. They could take my rank away, they could do what they liked with me. I just didn't care any more. And then, quite suddenly, I knew my man, and realised that I was not after all, addressing a hostile public meeting. For Farquharson was laughing. Yes, actually laughing.

"Steady on, Guns," he said. "Calm down or you'll burst a blood vessel. I'm not really such a nitwit . . ."

"Just bring 'em aboard," he added. "And put them on

normal watches, and see what you can scrounge. Only I'm going to get this ruddy ship to Australia if it costs me my life! The ship's European officers are aboard, but the crew has gone bush . . . so for all our sakes we've got to get things organised."

I simmered down. He seemed to have the situation buttoned up, I thought. And this estimate proved correct.

"You and your ruddy party!" he murmured when I complained that the Second Mate would only offer my men a meagre ration of rice and potatoes. "But just pop over to that Australian corvette, the one ahead of us; I think you'll find that they'll have something to spare."

It was a profitable visit, and we obtained from the generous Aussies a case of corned beef, a case of ship's biscuits, and many tins of fruit. But the *Verspeck*'s hospitality was still not extended to us, and what little we could get had to be extracted—by physical persuasion.

*   *   *

Barrett came along: "We've found a case of eggs, but one of the Dutchmen says they're for the first-class passengers only. So what do we do?"

"How big is this bloke?"

"About your size, Sir." Barrett, twice as big as me, looked surprised at the question.

"Then stand in the doorway of the galley. Don't let him in, and tell Cookie to get cracking!"

"Do you *really* mean that?"

"Of course . . . and if he wants to argue the point, throw him out!"

The wounded had their eggs.

Meanwhile Doc had enlisted the aid of some of our chaps and turned the boat deck into a temporary hospital. Though Heaven knows where they got the gear from. They rigged canvas screens, and a canvas awning, they discovered some garden seats, which they turned into beds, and they "won" a pile of blankets. But their prize find was an inflatable mattress, and this they hid—because this was for *our* Gunner, when *our* Doc finally put him to bed!

To be candid I was no longer adverse to treatment, despite my verbal protests. My leg had puffed up, and I was dog-tired. All in all, it was a great relief to hand over my responsibilities to Farquharson, and submit to Doc's ministrations—even though when he started on his stitchcraft, watched in silence by some of our boys, I felt rather as if I were being dealt with in the middle of the main street. Then, when it was all over, he gave me something to drink and told me to go to sleep.

*   *   *

It was a horrible awakening. For a moment I thought we had been taken by the Japs. Complete with pebble spectacles, buck teeth, slit eyes and a pistol, the native Customs official was not a pretty sight. He was quivering with rage, and as he jabbered away a few of *Electra*'s stalwarts hovered in the background, evidently hoping for permission to drop him over the side.

"What do you want?"

He accused my party of breaking into a warehouse and stealing a case of cigarettes. "I demand that they be punished and the cigarettes returned!"

The hair on the back of my neck began to bristle. "And who the hell are you to come here demanding things? Can you identify these men?"

"No, I never saw them, but I know the cigarettes are missing, so it must be your men!"

"Good God, this is the end. Do you realise there's an armed sentry on each gangway and that no one is allowed to leave the ship? Besides, who are you keeping the cigarettes for? The Japs?"

He ignored this, repeating stubbornly: "But your men must be responsible. Nobody else could do it."

"All right, then, if you're still going to be stupid about it, then you have permission to search the ship."

"But I've already searched the ship," he moaned, "and I can't find them. Yet they must be here—these cigarettes. It must be *your* men!"

That did it; and struggling to my feet I roared at this apparent lunatic. "So. Somebody pinches your wretched cigarettes. You don't know who it is. You search the ship without finding them, yet you stand there making stupid accusations against my men. Get out!"

We weighed at eight o'clock with a small Australian corvette for escort, and as soon as we were out of sight of land my cheerful batman, A.B. Freddy Fox paid me a visit.

"How are you off for fags, Sir?"

I said: "There's the best part of a packet on that shelf. You'd better leave me two and share the rest out."

Fox seemed slightly shocked. "Oh no, we couldn't think of that, Sir. We can manage."

He went away, to return a few minutes later with half a dozen fresh packets. "Here you are, Sir. Take these." I looked at the cigarettes. They were of an unusual and expensive brand.

" . . . But that Wog searched the ship. Where on earth did you hide them?"

"Under your bed on the boat deck, Sir. We knew you wouldn't let us down, but we thought you'd act more authentic if you didn't know! It did us good," he added, "to hear you ticking that bloke off!"

* * *

"Boat stations!"

And almost as soon as the order came the heavens opened

and the tropical rain enveloped the ship. A thick mist descended, visibility dropping to zero.

"Why the alarm?" I asked.

"A couple of torpedoes were loosed at us, or so they say."

Disgruntled I retorted: "I suppose some damned look-out's having double vision."

When, after an hour, the danger was judged to be past, and the passengers and crew were stood down, two of my torpedo-men arrived. "You awake, Sir?"

"Awake! Who could sleep with this racket going on? . . . just because some inexperienced clot is seeing things."

A chuckle came out of the darkness.

"But it's your fault if the look-outs can't detect a torpedo, Sir. You trained us. *We* were the look-outs!"

Which was different, of course.

"What happened?"

"We saw them in the moonlight, Sir, one fish passing well ahead, the other going under the ship. Then just as we gave the alarm the storm broke."

So once again Nature had come to our aid, covering our escape by darkness and the rain.

But at four o'clock in the afternoon came another threat to fidget us. The sky was clear again, and towards the north a tiny speck appeared, growing ever larger, and materialising eventually into a single-engined Japanese aircraft. Single-engined! Could it be carrier-borne? If it were then we could anticipate further callers.

But the aircraft continued to circle round the two small ships, the *Verspeck* being completely defenceless and the corvette equipped with only a pop-gun armament. And this cat-and-mouse game continued for nearly two hours until, evidently deciding that it was high time to go home, the Nip roared into the attack, aimed a couple of bombs at the Australian, both of which missed, and disappeared in the direction of Java. At first we couldn't believe our luck and waited apprehensively for a follow-up, but it did not come. Then, after half an hour, darkness descended, and we felt free to relax.

Next day the sky was cloudless and, as the sun rose higher, life on the boat deck became extremely uncomfortable. It was bad enough for patients such as myself but for those more seriously wounded it was almost intolerable and though they themselves did not complain Doc was vociferous on their behalf, demanding that they be placed in the cabins.

Although, to give them their due, the vast majority of the passengers were willing enough to surrender their bunks, there were a few, a handful of wealthy businessmen, who actually protested against the move. "We are entitled to our comfort," argued one of them. "It's what we've paid for and we've a right to it."

He was quickly disillusioned, and so were his supporters.

*   *   *

Farquharson regarded them incuriously, these gentlemen passengers whom he had "fell in" like a row of defaulting matelots. He thought of Singapore, and he thought of the oil tanks burning over the East Indies; he thought of the Java Sea and the fleet that had not returned, and he thought of the conditions in which the naval survivors were working—in the boiler rooms, in the engine room, and the bunkers of the ship. And then, having thought, and having kept his audience waiting while he thought, he spoke.

"I am a naval officer," he said, "and responsible for the safety of this ship. I have all the power in the world to tell you what to do and how to do it, and to clap any of you in irons if you raise a voice against me, or disobey me in the smallest way. We are not far from Java, gentlemen, but we are a long way from Australia."

There was a respectful silence.

"If you want to go to Australia," he said, "you will not only get out of your cabins and make way for my poor devils, and the poor devils of Dutchmen too, but you will also, each and every one of you, take your turn in the stokehold and the bunkers at shovelling coal."

Faces paled.

"So get your shirts off now," he roared, "and for God's sake try and behave like men!"

There was no further argument.

*   *   *

I looked at the calendar—the tenth of March. Nineteen days had passed since *Electra*'s ending; nineteen days that might have been as many years. And at last we had reached safety, safety in Australia.

The tenth of March. It should have been a special sort of day, such a very special day—a day to remember. For we had arrived at Fremantle to a warm Australian welcome; and our relief should have been undiluted, and yet, of course, it was not.

Electra had sailed from Tanjong Priok with a total complement of 178. Now, here in Australia, there were only forty-two survivors—eleven of them wounded. Behind us, 2,000 miles behind us, left in a different world, were another ten, and two Dutch doctors as devoted and uncomplaining as they. Ten men . . . but when I thought of those ten I found the memory almost unbearable. And what of the rest? Some we had seen killed, and some we had guessed were killed—when the rafts had been shelled by the Japanese; when the shrapnel had rained upon the swimmers in the water. But what of the others? Save for Lieutenant Cruden and four ratings, enduring together on a broken raft the tortures of the damned before being taken by the Nips, we were the sole survivors. But we did not know it.

In the meanwhile we were glad—desperately glad—to be

alive, to be more or less intact, to know that with a bit of luck we would again be able to see the ones we loved. Yet even now our hearts played traitor to our heads, and sent our thoughts a-wandering. For this date, this 10th of March, was a dividing line in our lives . . . a dividing line just as that rainy day in Greenock once had been. For nearly two years we had worked and fought together, but from now on what little remained of our company would no longer function as a single team; it would divide, it would be scattered, and its parts would serve in many ships—ships of all shapes and uses, and employed in every theatre of war. And whereas each of us would carry in his mind some fragment of *Electra* that, come what may, would never be abandoned, not one of us could ever again be *solely* *Electra*'s; for *that* was the privilege of the dead. New sphere of duty—even Duty itself—would serve to divorce us still further from our erstwhile comradeship. Nor with the final battle fought could all of us, even we forty-two, rely on effecting a reunion. Some would doubtless perish on other ships; their escape after *Electra*'s passing being but a temporary reprieve; their names withheld from her list of casualties only to grace another's death-roll. And the rest? We'd be different, have fresh loyalties and new headaches. Some would be pre-occupied with their lawns, the need to pay the electricity bill, the rush for the 8.15. And others would go back to the Navy— to the Navy which we'd swear had changed, and yet would never change.

The tenth of March. A glad day, and a sad day, mixed inextricably, each with each. Hitherto the need for self-preservation had kept us fully occupied, forced us to exert ourselves and exclude, save in nightmares, the memory of what was past. But now there was time to think and to realise that the past was living, was but a part of our today.

The tide was low, and the gangway steep. But, just as I was to be carried ashore on the stretcher, a heated argument broke out between our lads and the Aussies as to who was to take me. The Australians claimed the right, as skilled medical orderlies. *Electra*'s men claimed the right, as I belonged to them. And this extraordinary dispute continued until, to settle matters decently, I left the stretcher and, very gently helped, made my own way to the ambulance, the others following.

"Well, we've had quite a time together," I asserted somewhat breathlessly. "And *Electra* will take a lot of beating."

"She'll *never* be beaten," they replied.

At which we felt suddenly embarrassed . . . I looking up at them from the shade, they looking down on me as they crowded round in the sunshine.

"See you in England, lads."

"*England*! Ah, that'll be the day, Sir."

And then the door of the ambulance was closed, and I, realising how much those chaps had meant to me, and to each other—and to the others, the chaps now dead—was immensely saddened.

I was weak, I was lonely. I felt that it would never be the same again.

Shadows from the Sea

"*Electra* attacked through the smoke . . . and was seen no more . . ."

It was a brief epitaph to a fine ship and a real band of brothers; an epitaph tucked away beneath more famous names, the names of *Exeter* and *Perth*, our companions in battle.

I read it while I was in hospital, in that wonderful place in Perth that they called the hospital of St. John of God; and, having read it I lay in my bed on the verandah, looking out over the trim lawns as the evening came and the white-robed nuns moved quietly to and fro; looking out and thinking of all those faces, the faces I would never see again . . .

So the Battle of the Java Sea had at last been announced to the world, and the allied losses admitted to Parliament, although many of the details were still vague. And our ship had achieved, for the first time in her life, a "mention" in the national press, however brief. "One of our destroyers" had materialised into a name.

I thought of how in happier times we would have enjoyed seeing her "in print", although pretending of course that we couldn't have cared less. And I thought of how few of us were left—fifty-three out of one hundred and seventy-three. And, as I thought, I closed my eyes and could see once more, as though on a screen, the smoke, and the sun beyond the smoke, and *Electra* plunging to the depths with her battle ensign still defiant.

I had written in my battle report: "I am proud to have served in such a fine ship, and with such a splendid body of men . . ." Yet somehow, in the cool of the Australian evening, the words seemed completely inadequate. How often had I heard similar sentiments, expressed about other ships by other people; and how trite they had seemed, those sentiments, when I was not affected.

But then I thought of my friends, and dwelt upon my thoughts—not morbidly, but gaining comfort from them.

I thought of Commander May, with his deep insight into the hearts of those he led—May with his tranquillity of spirit, his seaman's instinct. And I thought of Jenner-Fust, with the surface polish of Eton and the inner core of steel, with the common touch and the tactical flair combined, with the qualities which could have brought him to the top of our naval administration. I thought of Harry—Harry of the razor-keen mind, the bubbling good spirits; a serious thinker, yet one who knew how to laugh at himself, a young man who, had he survived would have helped shape the destiny of our country. And I thought of Eric Coale; of Eric sacrificing his precious chocolate ration and giving it to my children; of Eric who was, like myself, a Londoner . . . and yet had died so very far from home.

A faint wind rustled as the night came down. The newspaper slid from my bed and on to the verandah floor; the lights began to twinkle in the ward behind me—but still my mind was crowded with memories.

Roger Price, now an undying part of the tradition that had once so irked him, and yet had exacted his very finest service . . . Frank McLeod, with his dry Scots humour, the engineer who made difficulties seem easy . . . Tiger Mash, my reliable, uncompromising Torpedo Gunner's Mate . . . all these, and many more, passed before my eyes—as clear as if I were seeing them in the flesh.

"Sacrifice is Necessary for the Defence of Java . . ."

That's how the order had begun. But Java had fallen, despite the sacrifice.

"Fight to the last gun, the last shell . . ."

That's how the order had continued. And we had obeyed it, obeyed it literally. But *why* we had done so was still a bit obscure. Maybe we had bought time, and maybe we hadn't. Maybe we had inflicted heavy losses on the Nips, and maybe we hadn't. We had fought and we had dared, and we had lost. So what did it all add up to? That we had done what we had been told to do? Well that, after all, was important . . .

Chief Petty Officer Gould, that kindest of coxswains, Tingle, that sterling Yeoman, Petty Officer Allen, alert and keen, and poor Fred Castle, dying without complaint. They had done their duty, the Goulds, the Tingles, the Allens, and the Castles, . . . they had done their duty, and had paid the price. But their kind was not unique to our own ship, nor was it confined to the destroyer service only. Every ship and every branch of the Andrew had them, and would continue to have them for as long as Britain lasted.

The rating from *Hood* who'd quipped when we picked him up, "Blimey, a *Chatham* ship!" . . . the dentist from *Repulse*, moving among the wounded . . . the trawler skipper, wise-cracking on the Russian run, "I'll sweep out the bunkers, no need to worry about me" . . . every ship had them, I slowly realised . . . men ordinary enough to look at, or to listen to, but men who rose to the occasion, persevering until the end. Not expecting much save the bitter final wage, they were true to themselves by being faithful to each other.

Electra had been a happy ship, happy in her company. For a ship is, after all, something more than a structure of steel; it is the collective sum of the individual contributions made by the men who serve in her. Sammy Buss—soon to give his life in the Mediterranean—had hewn our comradeship into shape; and May had perfected the process, instilling into our unity a breath of his own brave spirit. But there would be many more Sammies, there would be many more Commander Mays:

and there would be many more *Electras*—she was not dead for ever. Tradition is a living thing and the human spirit draws on itself only to renew itself. No sacrifice—made for duty—is barren of fruit. Nothing that is worthwhile 'is ever lost irrevocably.

"H.M.S. *Electra* attacked through the smoke, and was seen no more."

I was not to know, on that hushed Australian evening, that the memory of *Electra*—although so cherished then—was to become doubly precious in a few weeks' time. Or that it would be treasured, for three hard years to come, as one of the few things left to me to treasure . . . consoling, sustaining, keeping me alive and sane.

For Fate is not only unpredictable; it is also inescapable. One may travel far; yet never can one avoid it. Thus, in my delusive security in that hospital at Perth I had thought that I had looked my last on the Java Sea, save through the windows of memory. And had imagined that—but for a few poor wounds —I was at last divorced from the consequences of the battle in which our ship had died. But I was never more mistaken . . .

When, having nursed me back to health, the good nuns bade me farewell, and I was placed on the small liner *Nankin*, bound for Ceylon, my old friends chivvied me about my luck —*Electra* Luck! A lazy, relaxed journey through "safe" waters, a comfortable passenger berth, and a cushy appointment . . . what more could I require? A pleasure cruise, they said. That's what it was, a pleasure cruise. It did not stay so for long.

For Australia was fifteen hundred miles away when— roused from sleep—I heard the old familiar "music" . . . the clamour of the alarm bells, the slam of enemy guns, the wail of the shells, passing overhead. We had been attacked by a disguised German raider, later identified as the *Thor*.

Crowded with passengers, and with only one small gun to

protect her, the *Nankin*'s end was inevitable. The "pleasure cruise" had ended in disaster.

As we were brought on board the enemy ship a German officer, glancing at my naval rig, said sympathetically: "Hard luck, to be taken like that . . . But for you the war is over."

To which I rejoined, angry as hell: "Don't you believe it! I'd still give a lot more for my chances than for yours."

But later the retort seemed over-optimistic.

For came the day when—seven weeks a captive on the raider's supply ship, *Regensburg*—I saw, as in a nightmare, the lush green shores of Java once again. And lying alongside the German was a destroyer, a sharp-prowed, black-hulled, oddly oriental-looking destroyer; the sort of destroyer that we'd opposed and fought against in *Electra*'s final battle. I was a prisoner, a prisoner no longer of Germany but of Japan. And by a strange irony, I was being given to Nippon's custody when only a few miles from my old ship's ocean grave.

I do not think that any useful purpose will be served by my recalling, at this stage, the events of the grim years that followed. Except to repeat that it was the memory of *Electra*, and of the people of *Electra*—the realisation that, outside the barbarous world in which I found myself, there were other *Electras*, and men similar to hers—that enabled me to pull through. Nothing, nothing worthwhile, is ever lost irrevocably. The good example of the strong of soul lives on, to sustain the weak.

*　　　*　　　*

"H.M.S. *Electra* attacked through the smoke, and was seen no more . . ."

The words were engraved upon my mind by the time I came home . . . hollow-cheeked and shaven-headed, a comical figure. I was wearing, as was proper, a naval cap, jacket and trousers. And I was also wearing, most improperly, a brown tie, a G.I.'s shirt, a khaki overcoat, and a pair of dark brown boots.

Belles met me at the station—Belles who had twice been informed of my assumed "death", and each time had steadfastly refused to believe such information. And with her were the boys, our sons who could scarcely remember me.

It was the most wonderful moment we had ever known, a moment longed for, often without hope, throughout four bitter years. Yet although, in the privacy of our hearts, we had so often rehearsed our meeting, we stumbled into near wordlessness when it actually came about. For we had been lucky, almost unfairly lucky: so lucky, in comparison with others, that our luck half shamed us.

*   *   *

"H.M.S. *Electra* attacked through the smoke, and was seen no more . . ."

On March 29th, 1947, a large congregation gathered in the Church of St. George at the Royal Naval Barracks, Chatham, to pay homage to *Electra* and those who died with her.

Some of those present had served in the ship, and knew her from experience shared in common. But there were others who had never seen the ship, and yet "belonged" to her even more than they. For these were the people who, while deprived of the comfort of a visible comradeship, and forced to follow *Electra*'s fortunes from the shore, had been as closely bound to her in their hopes and fears as any of her company, and had felt their life-blood ebb at the news of her violent passing.

Commander May's mother, Secretary and Treasurer of the ship's Memorial Fund . . . Harry's father, the Dean of Worcester, sad but proud, and present to read the lesson—wherever I looked I saw the relatives of the fallen, and drew, from these new friends, fresh reminders of old faces. It was moving, intensely personal, a family affair.

Then suddenly, as the sun stole through the clouds and slanted its rays through the stained glass window, newly dedicated to *Electra*'s Dead, the grey church seemed to glow with warmth and colour; and over bowed heads there fell, though for brief moments only, a strange tranquillity—a peace as embracing as the unseen but eternal sea.

Index of Ships

INDEX